# Conceptions of Culture

# Conceptions of Culture

## What Multicultural Educators Need to Know

Thomas E. Wren

ROWMAN & LITTLEFIELD PUBLISHERS, INC.
Lanham • Boulder • New York • Toronto • Plymouth, UK

KH

Published by Rowman & Littlefield Publishers, Inc.
A wholly owned subsidiary of The Rowman & Littlefield Publishing Group, Inc.
4501 Forbes Boulevard, Suite 200, Lanham, Maryland 20706
www.rowman.com

10 Thornbury Road, Plymouth PL6 7PP, United Kingdom

British Library Cataloguing in Publication Information Available

**Library of Congress Cataloging-in-Publication Data**

Wren, Thomas E.
  Conceptions of culture : what multicultural educators need to know /
Thomas E. Wren.
       p. cm.
  Includes bibliographical references and index.
  ISBN 978-1-4422-1637-2 (cloth : alk. paper) — ISBN 978-1-4422-1638-9
(pbk. : alk. paper) — ISBN 978-1-4422-1639-6 (electronic)
 1.  Multicultural education. 2.  Multiculturalism. I. Title.
  LC1099.W74 2012
  370.117—dc23

                                                                    2012009976

♾™ The paper used in this publication meets the minimum requirements of
American National Standard for Information Sciences—Permanence of Paper
for Printed Library Materials, ANSI/NISO Z39.48-1992.

Printed in the United States of America

6/28/13

# Contents

# Preface

This book is about the remarkable and problematic diversity of the ways in which culture has been represented by the social theorists and educators who have shaped the discipline of what is now call multicultural education. I have designed it for a broad cross-section of present and future educators, with special focus on those graduate students who are or will be higher education faculty or educational leaders (administrators, curriculum specialists, policy makers, etc.) as well as for their own professors. Drawing upon the resources of a variety of academic disciplines I have tried to help readers develop for themselves a systematic, in-depth understanding of how the complex concept of *culture* is deployed in the massive literature of multicultural education. The book is full of theory but is not a theoretical book, at least not in the usual sense of that term. It is more like a road map, accompanied by the related theoretical information and tools one needs to navigate the tangled territory of multicultural education.

Although the goals of multicultural education are many, the specific goals of this book can be counted on one hand. They are:

1. *To enable its readers to navigate the extensive literature of multicultural education so that they can recognize and deal with the inconsistencies and complexities of the many different conceptions of culture running through that literature.* It shows how to identify the relation between various authors' implicit *theories* of culture and their educational agendas, which is to say their recommended *practices*. Although it is commonplace to declare that there is a reciprocal relation between educational theory and practice, the book shows its readers how to examine this relationship in the specific context of multicultural education.

2. *To enable its readers to apply the principles explained in this book to their own future practice.* Here the goal is for them to learn how to pick and choose intelligently among the conflicting theories and agendas presented in the multiculturalism literature and thereby create for themselves coherent frameworks that can guide their professional journeys in university-level or K–12 education. For graduate students pursuing a career in higher education, the book shows how to frame their own research questions and pedagogical agendas within the larger corpus of scholarly literature and textbooks on multicultural education. It also provides them with a foundation for teaching their own multicultural education courses against a backdrop of the often bewildering variety of views about the nature of culture and the basic purpose of multicultural education. For those who focus on K–12 education, the book enables them to lead school reform, guide staff development efforts, and develop their own multicultural education curricula.

3. *To prepare its readers for the social changes and accompanying conceptual changes in our notions of culture that are now taking place as part of the "cultural hybridity" of today's students.* To achieve this third goal the final chapter of the book examines the possibility that the conceptions of culture one encounters in today's multicultural educational literature (as well as in everyday discourse) are quickly becoming obsolete, and that new social constructions are now underway in the culturally diverse environments inside and outside our classrooms.

Writing this book was a multicultural experience in itself. I learned from many people, of all ages and backgrounds. Several friend-scholars have read and commented on portions of this manuscript or one of its earlier versions. I received especially useful critical commentary from Georg Lind, Dennis McGuire, and my own colleagues Paul Moser and David Ingram. I am deeply grateful to Ms. Patti Davis of Rowman & Littlefield who saw the project's potential and helped me improve the book on many educational as well as philosophical fronts. Ms. Alden Perkins and Ms. Jocquan Mooney's careful management and copyediting is especially appreciated, as is the help of all those librarians, graduate assistants, and undergraduate students whose names are too numerous to mention here.

I am especially indebted to the Bogliasco Foundation, not only for the fellowship that enabled me write the first draft of this book at their gracious Centro Studi Ligure per le Arti e le Lettere on the Ligurian coast of Italy, but also for their moral support in all senses of that term. I have also received financial and moral support from my own university, which I acknowledge with great pleasure and gratitude. But my greatest pleasure is in acknowledging the support of my immediate family. My daughter, Kathy, and son, Mike, were still in school when I began the research for this book, and it was largely through their eyes that I came to understand what it is like to be a student in our complex multicultural society. My wife, Carol, herself a prominent author and professor of education, has patiently read and re-read every page of this book and saved me from numerous substantive and stylistic blunders, about which the less said the better. What cannot be said often or loudly enough, though, is my heartfelt thanks to all these wonderful people.

# 1

# Defining Culture and Multicultural Education

## How to Do It, and Why

We start with a little story, fictional but easy to imagine. Mr. Peabody is introducing a unit on citizenship to his 11th grade social studies class. "Citizenship," he begins ceremoniously, "has been defined in many ways. For the ancient Greeks it was the capacity to participate in the governance of the city-state or *polis*, which they did by making and enforcing laws, sitting on juries, declaring war, and so on." He then explains that it was different in imperial Rome. "There the political realm was not a small polis but a huge empire, and citizenship was a special status that gave certain people equal protection under the laws though not any authority to make or enforce them." Warming to his theme, he cites Webster's dictionary, according to which citizenship is "the state of being vested with the rights and duties of a citizen."

At this point Mr. Peabody, who has obviously done his homework and is eager to stimulate interest in the new unit, smiles and reels off still more definitions. "Today people define citizenship in various ways. Some understand it as a set of rights and duties, whereas others define it as full membership in the political community. Some insist that citizenship is participation in the public sphere as distinguished from the private and economic spheres, and still others claim that our usual notion of citizenship is now undergoing a transformation from a national to global status, roughly like the transition from the Greek notion of citizenship to that of the Roman Empire. And so it goes."[1]

At this point Albert, a keen but not particularly docile 16-year-old, interrupts. "All right," he demands, "but which definition are *we* going to use?" Mr. Peabody beams. He was about to tell them just that. "In this class," he announces, "we will understand citizenship as a contract between a state

1

and its recognized members in which those members agree to abide by certain duties and the state agrees to ensure that the members enjoy certain rights." Unimpressed by the legal jargon, Albert punctures his teacher's confidence with the ultimate question: "*Why that one?* I don't see what's wrong with the other definitions." Mr. Peabody is taken aback. He doesn't have a ready answer but feels sure that there is a good reason for his choice even though he knows there is nothing fundamentally "wrong" with the other definitions. Fortunately the bell rings at that moment. Relieved, he smiles wisely and tells Albert and his classmates, "Good question. I'll give you the answer tomorrow."

Here the perspective of the story changes. Now *you* are the teacher. Classes are over and you are in Mr. Peabody's shoes, trying to decide how you will answer Albert tomorrow. Suddenly the sky clears. You realize that you do indeed have a solid reason for choosing the definition that you announced to the class, and it is simply that your lesson plans for this unit are all based on the important concept of a social contract. However, with this new clarity come other questions. Did you consciously design your lesson plans around this concept? If so, why? If not, should you make some last-minute adjustments, either to the objectives you have for this unit or to the definition you will use as your point of departure? Perhaps your lesson plans should also have secondary agendas such as clarifying the notion of a common good or promoting loyalty and other civic virtues, so that you now realize a change of plans is necessary. When you return to Albert's question tomorrow you will have to expand your core concept of citizenship to include other features that together add up to a complex but nonetheless coherent mix of definitions that fit with your multiple agendas. For instance, you may decide to tell Albert and his classmates that the class will also discuss how citizenship is a social construction that has evolved and continues to evolve over the centuries as the conditions of social life change.

On the other hand, perhaps you now realize that you don't actually have a good reason for choosing this definition of citizenship. In fact, you are no longer sure that your unit on citizenship should have started with *any* single definition or have a tightly structured master agenda, even though you're still convinced that what you have to say over the next weeks about civic life and citizenship is important and coherent. In that case, what should you do about Albert's question?

## THEORY AND PRACTICE

This book is about culture and multicultural education, not citizenship and social studies, but its central issue is analogous to Mr. Peabody's examination of the relationship between definitions of citizenship and his teaching agendas or—to put it more broadly—the relationship between theoretical inquiry and educational practice. Following the lead of scholars who discuss this relationship as well as the common sense of front-line teachers, I assume throughout these pages that the relationship is reciprocal: that is, that theory informs practice and practice refines theory (Mullen, Greenlee, & Bruner, 2005; Dilworth, 2007). In the present context, this means that in the professional discourse of multicultural education, theory-laden definitions of culture should influence what is said about the contents and methods of multicultural education, and reciprocally, that the educational agendas promoted through those contents and methods should determine which of the many definitions of culture serve as foundational concepts or premises.

The concept of culture sits, clearly but unsteadily, at the heart of the term "multicultural education" and also at the heart of the goals that those in the field have already set for themselves. They want to have something called "cultural competence" as well as to help their students acquire it. They want their students to respect other cultures, but just what is it they are supposed to respect? How has culture been conceptualized? A quick look at the educational literature would show that many quite diverse conceptions of culture run through the theories and practices of multicultural educators: culture as heritage, as discourse, as worldview, as social position, as cognitive style, as a by-product of race and gender, and so on. To adapt Albert's "ultimate question" (*Why choose that one?*) to the present context, the question before us is: How can we make sense of the fact that there are multiple, sometimes even antithetical, definitions of culture?

## MULTICULTURAL EDUCATION AND CULTURE: TWO KINDS OF CONCEPTS

To deal with this abundance of meanings we must understand the logical difference between the two terms "multicultural education" and "culture," each of which has a wide array of definitions. Comparing these two arrays will sharpen our understanding of the concept of culture and prepare us to deal appropriately with multiple definitions of these two very different terms. Each case includes a set of background assumptions about what counts as a good definition. Most of these assumptions are obvious (a good definition is clear, coherent, etc.) but a few need to be spelled out. In the case of everyday terms like "multicultural education," a good definition should reflect the way the term is actually used by most speakers. In the case of theoretical terms like "culture," though, a good definition should reflect the theory that produced it. Let's start with the first case.

In an often-cited article, Geneva Gay (1994) reviewed over a dozen different definitions of "multicultural education" and then declared that their differences were not problematic since multicultural educators agree on the fundamental issues of the field, such as "ethnic identity, cultural pluralism, unequal distribution of resources and opportunities, and other sociopolitical problems stemming from long histories of oppression."[2] There is no consensus about which of these issues are central to the field and which are peripheral, but this absence is not a problem for Gay, who believes that because multiculturalists value diversity it is only to be expected that they will have significantly different views of their own subject matter (see also Bennett [2010]). This is probably true, but there is another, deeper reason for this lack of concern, one that goes beyond mere tolerance of difference.

Multicultural educators can embrace many different definitions of their field without self-contradiction because those definitions are framed in terms of compatible and often overlapping *practical agendas*. In contrast, definitions of *culture* refer to one or another relatively sharp-edged theoretical construct that both informs and is refined by a practical agenda. Unfortunately, this contrast is absent—or at least very blurred—in most of the literature of multicultural education, where we find very little difference in the ways the two terms are treated. Its authors cite multiple definitions of *culture* with the same cheerful, live-and-let-live acceptance that they have for fundamentally different conceptions of *multicultural education*, with no acknowledgment that competing definitions of a theory-based term such as culture are problematic. Open-mindedness and tolerance are intellectual virtues as well as moral ones, but a lazy-minded openness and tolerance of key theoretical differences could lead to indifference and, in the end, a devaluation of the very important ideas of culture and multicultural education. True, some education theorists have little use for the very idea of culture and seek to replace it with notions of power or class. However, the greatest challenge to the validity of the culture concept is found in the mainstream literature of multicultural education, where it seems that almost any definition of culture will do. It is understandable that in this literature there are ambiguities and differences in the treatment of culture. Unfortunately, they are uncharted and, even worse, unacknowledged. As a result it is unclear how a student or teacher of courses about multicultural education is to determine where the experts stand on questions such as: What is culture? How does the idea of culture differ from, include, or oppose other ideas and practices such as race, heritage, or ideology? Is culture the cause or the by-product of social bonds? And so on. To navigate this conceptual terrain we need a map of the educational literature and a philosophical compass to steer by.

## CULTURE FOR MULTICULTURALISTS

You may be surprised to learn that there is an important difference between how culture is discussed in the literature of multicultural education and the way—or better, *ways*—it has been treated in the disciplines of anthropology, sociology, and other branches of social theory. If so, your surprise would be understandable. After all, one might ask, doesn't the literature of multicultural education simply borrow a concept that has already been debated and refined in the social sciences?

Unfortunately, nothing could be further from the truth. Few multicultural education textbooks or scholarly works acknowledge the complexities and historical evolution of the various conceptions of culture that one finds in the social sciences, where culture has always been a vigorously contested issue. In contrast, when culture is discussed in the educational literature, the discussion is typically brief, superficial, and completely ahistorical. Reference is sometimes made to authors and signature quotations from anthropology, sociology, or (somewhat less often) cultural psychology, but the authors' own orientations are not defended and the quoted passages are usually woefully undertheorized if not irrelevant or even misleading. For instance, a reform-minded multicultural education theorist might propose a structural functionalist definition of culture without noting the essentially conservative character of that sociological model, which treats culture as society's thermostat for minimizing conflict and preserving the status quo. A complaint lodged almost two decades ago by the anthropologist Ronald Waterbury is still valid: "The teaching of multicultural courses," he said, "often proceeds with little or, at best, a common sense understanding of the key concept: culture. Of course, getting our conceptual ducks in a row is critically important for any teaching endeavor, but [in multicultural education] it is doubly so . . ." (1993, p. 63). Such misgivings or demurrals by concerned onlookers such as Waterbury as well as by the growing band of outsider-insiders who call themselves critical theorists are at odds with the practice of mainstream multicultural educators, who tend to be much more tolerant of the inconsistencies and ambiguities in the accounts of culture that one finds in this literature.

This tolerance is questionable for several reasons. What are we to think of the absence of any internal debate over a foundational concept such as culture? Does it signal a tacit agreement among multiculturalists on how culture should be understood? If not, why in their literature is there almost no visible exchange of arguments and counterarguments about the nature of culture? Perhaps the source of this seeming unanimity is the fact that authors of multicultural education literature have a virtually unlimited "tolerance of ambiguity," to borrow a term that some personality theorists use to describe the highest levels of ego development. Or is the reason less praiseworthy: perhaps a simple conflict-avoidance tendency or even worse, a morbid lack of curiosity? Correlatively, what would it mean to *define* a complex term like "culture"? Are there different standards of adequacy for understanding the meaning of different sorts of concepts? Or to push this line of questioning to its outer limits, what does it mean to ask for "the meaning" of *any* concept, not just those of culture and multicultural education?

The rest of this chapter is devoted to these and similarly foundational themes such as the difference between abstract scientific terms and terms that stand for concrete social practices. It also takes up the difference between what some philosophers call "open" and "closed" concepts, the utility of parsing existing descriptions of culture or multicultural education into what I will call "formal" and "informal" definitions, and the importance of subjecting those definitions to systematic qualitative analysis. These philosophical themes are especially relevant for professors and students of multicultural education at the graduate level, who need to understand the logical and philosophical underpinnings of the literature they are using. They rightfully expect the presuppositions of their textbooks and other course materials to be discernible, that ambiguities be clarified, and hidden agendas exposed. If these expectations are not met, then they must turn to other resources to discover how to read between the lines in order to interpret their multicultural education materials. This book is one such resource. Its overarching objective is to enable readers such as yourself to interpret and use the many definitions of culture found in the multicultural literature as well as how to identify connections or disconnections between educational theory and practice. The rest of this chapter deals with the theoretical tools you will need for these tasks.

Sometimes, especially in chapters 3 through 5, the tone is somewhat critical but my aim is never simply to score points on authors of textbooks and other resources if they stumble (after all, as the Roman poet Horace said, even Homer nods). The aim is rather to show fellow educators, especially those in colleges of education, how to engage with a multiculturalist author as an equal, by which I mean how to read an author as though they were swapping ideas and challenges in a university seminar or at their favorite watering hole. In a word, I want to show how to turn passive reading into active, constructive discourse.

## THE DEFINITION GAME

In this section I will draw on philosophy and rhetorical theory in order to support what I have already said about how terms such as culture and multicultural education should be defined. The underlying idea, to which we will return over and over again, is that in spite of its extended uses in the popular media, the concept of culture is a *theoretical* concept whereas the concept of multicultural education is a *practical* concept or, as some philosophers prefer to say, an *everyday* concept. To understand the first sort of concept we must understand the theory that shaped it, whereas to understand the second sort we must understand the uses to which it is put. Once these two aspects of conceptual analysis are clarified we will be in a position to chart the various uses that education theorists and others have made of the category "multicultural education," and the various theoretical schemes or paradigms associated with the polysemantic category "culture."

## The Forensic Trap

The first move in constructing a comprehensive account of the difference between the practice-guiding concept of multicultural education and the theory-laden concept of culture is to recognize the serious limits of what for most people—especially teachers—is the standard model of a good definition. These limits are not at all obvious, since so much of western education is *forensic*, using that term in the literal sense of debate in a public forum. To speak only half metaphorically, most of us have been training for a debate tournament that will last for the rest of our lives. Not surprisingly, this training shapes the way educators—who after all were once students too—discuss professional issues among themselves. The first thing debate coaches tell their teams is: "Define your terms!" They know that debaters who construct sharp and concise definitions will endear themselves to judges, force their opponents into certain channels, and otherwise take charge of the forensic situation. The same message is sent by schoolteachers, college professors, and—for students who join the professoriate—scholarly authority figures such as senior colleagues and editors, as though the principal index of a person's intellectual worth were the ability to open any important discussion with a single, clear and distinct representation of the concepts under consideration. It may come as a surprise, then, to learn that for many concepts this familiar view of what counts as careful intellectual discourse, as well as of what counts as a "good" definition, is based on an outmoded, now very dubious, view of what contemporary philosophers are wont to call "the meaning of 'meaning'" (Putnam, 1975). It goes back to John Locke and other philosophers who thought that knowledge consists in a true one-for-one match between concepts that sit in the mind and things that sit out in the world.[3] Words, be they relatively simple terms like "dog" or more complex phrases and sentences, were thought to have their meanings by virtue of one-to-one matches between mental concepts and external reality.

Locke's view has been challenged by many philosophers, but its underlying assumptions about the meaning of "meaning" were not questioned
until John Dewey (1925) weighed in with his pragmatic theory of truth. As
a result, today we find in the opening pages of most educational literature,
especially that devoted to multiculturalism, definition-like statements that
simultaneously yet not always coherently stipulate and advocate, describe
and evaluate, analyze and illustrate the topics to be discussed. It is as
though education theorists know they are supposed to define their terms,
but are wary of doing so too narrowly, which is to say with too much precision. They tend to speak not of the "meaning" or "reference" or "definition" of their subject matter, but rather of its multiple "conceptualizations,"
"construals," "dimensions," or "approaches." Careful readers may find such
statements exasperating since they do not provide clear and distinct definitions of their subject matter. However, exasperation would be the wrong response. They should be relieved to discover that education literature tends
to avoid stating "the" definitions of complex social concepts and practices
such as multicultural education.[4]

The admonition of the late John Wilson, a philosopher of education
trained in the Oxford tradition of linguistic analysis based on what is usually
called "ordinary language" theory, is worth quoting here at length, since what
he said about words like "work" and "democracy" also applies to the contrast
between "culture" and "multicultural education."

> The best way of looking at this point is to say that in questions of concept we
> are not concerned with *the* meaning of a word. Words do not have only one
> meaning: indeed, in a sense they do not have meaning in their own right at
> all, but only in so far as people use them in different ways. It is better to say
> that we are concerned with *actual and possible uses* of words. . . . Sometimes we
> behave as if all we had to do was to find out the 'real' meaning of a word like
> 'democracy' or 'boat' or 'science', and then the answer to our question would
> be obvious. But unfortunately it is not so simple as that: and a moment's
> thought will show us that words like 'democracy' and 'science'—and even
> words like 'boat'—do not have 'real meanings'. They just have different uses
> and different applications: and our job is to analyse the concepts and map out
> these uses and applications. . . .
>
> Of course there are some words which do have precise definitions: in geom-
> etry and mechanics, for instance, words like 'triangle', 'straight line', 'point',
> and 'force', 'mass' and 'work' are precisely defined. If we are asked 'What is
> work?' in an examination on mechanics, we know that we have to give the
> textbook definition. But that is because mechanics is a highly evolved and rea-
> sonably precise science, and the examination is testing our knowledge of that
> science, not our ability to analyse concepts. If we were asked 'What is work?'
> in a general paper for a university examination, however, our approach would
> be quite different. We should start thinking about the concept of work as it is
> used in everyday life, not just in the science of mechanics. And in everyday life

there is no [single] definition of 'work': we should have to notice various uses of the word, the different meanings it bears in different contexts, and so on. (Wilson, 1969, pp. 10–11)

## Open and Closed Concepts

Wilson's ordinary language account of definition-making, which boils down to the idea that everyday terms should be defined by the way they are *used*, fits nicely with the way education theorists define multicultural education, but not so well with the way social theorists define culture. In the case of culture, a somewhat better fit would be with the forensic or so-called "ideal language" view that a good definition gets at the heart of a concept by stating the necessary and sufficient conditions for applying it. In doing so, one identifies a given concept with a semantic vehicle such as the English word "sphere," and then associates that concept and its vehicle with something in the real world, say a child's ball. Wilson himself recognized that sometimes this can be done, as we see in his example of what he called the scientific (that is, theoretical) concept of work that is part of what he called the science of mechanics. (Promissory note: Such definitions will be the subject of the next chapter, which is a knowledge base of various definitions of culture generated in the social sciences of anthropology and sociology, as well as in the subsequent inventory of definitions of culture drawn from the literature of multicultural education.) More often though, there is *no* set of necessary and sufficient conditions, in which case constructing a rigid, exception-free definition is logically impossible. In other words, in everyday discourse the fit between language and things in the world is coarse and flexible rather than exact or fixed. (Think of the word "art." The *Mona Lisa* is art, but what about a Lamborghini or Duchamp's "readymades"?)

To summarize: The contrast between everyday, open concepts on the one hand and scientific or theoretical, closed concepts on the other is quite straightforward. The meaning of an open concept consists in its *use*, whereas the meaning of a closed concept consists in its *conditions of application*, which is a bit of linguistics jargon denoting the features that a thing must have before it can be counted as a member of whatever category is associated with those features. Thus Aristotle's simple definition of a human being as "a rational animal" purports to list the two necessary and jointly sufficient conditions for calling something "human," and so on.

*The Open Concept of Multicultural Education.* The idea of multicultural education resembles the idea of art more than it resembles the idea of culture. If we actually look and see what it is that people commonly call "multicultural education," we will not find common properties but only strands of similarities. The same point holds for art. Knowing the meaning of either term is not

apprehending some latent essence but rather being able to *use* it in order to
advocate, facilitate, describe, and explain practices that are generally called
by the names "multicultural education" or "art" in virtue of these similarities. (The terms have other uses too, but these are some of the more obvious
ones.) The common characteristic of these terms is their open-endedness.
When I want to illuminate such a concept, I can refer to certain paradigm
cases, ones which nobody in my language community would hesitate to label
as, say, "multicultural education" or "art," but I cannot cite an exhaustive set
of criteria for such cases. The aesthetics philosopher Morris Weitz once made
a similar point, saying, "I can list some cases and some conditions under
which I can apply correctly the concept of art but I cannot list all of them, for
the all-important reason that unforeseeable or novel conditions are always
forthcoming or envisageable" (1956, p. 31).[5]

A related point is that a concept is *open* to the extent that its conditions of
application are easily revised. This is the case with most of the concepts we
use and talk about. New situations require us to decide between the alternatives of, on the one hand, using the old concept in an expanded way to
cover the new situation, or on the other hand, covering the situation with a
completely new concept, perhaps identified as a "term of art." In contrast,
a concept would be completely *closed* if (and only if) it were possible to
state the full set of necessary and sufficient conditions for its application.[6]

*The Closed Concept of Culture.* I said above that a concept is open to the
extent that its conditions of application are easily revised. The opposite also
holds. In principle the application conditions of a completely closed concept
could never be revised, assuming of course that we are not talking about
simple ambiguity or sheer equivocation (as when the word "Banks" denotes
the sides of a river, financial institutions, and the prominent multicultural
educator James A. Banks). Thus within our language system a bachelor is an
unmarried adult human male "by definition," and within the decimal system
there is no way the sum of two plus two can be other than four. However,
these are mere tautologies. Within a scientific paradigm a theoretical term
such as "absolute zero" ordinarily has only one meaning, but its definition
could change if there were a fundamental paradigm shift, just as the theoretical meaning of "culture" has changed several times in anthropology and sociology over the last two centuries. In such cases the concept is only *relatively*
closed.[7] Simply put, the terms "art," "game," and "multicultural education"
are very open, whereas theoretical terms such as "atom," "superego," and
"culture" are very closed, and that is enough of a distinction for our purposes.

## THE ART OF DEFINITION FOR CLOSED AND OPEN TERMS

At this point I want to refine and then apply the foregoing distinction between open and closed terms, or as Wilson put it, the distinction between

the everyday and theoretical meanings of terms like "work." Three small but important qualifications should be added to Wilson's distinction. The first is that the contrast between these two kinds of meaning is not a black-or-white sort of difference but rather the distinction between two points on a continuum. Everyday concepts like multicultural education are simply *more open* than theoretical ones like culture. In other words, some concepts have a narrower range of reference and can be defined more precisely than others, and some are more inclusive than others. The second qualification to Wilson's distinction is that although philosophers differ on whether a completely "closed" concept is not simply rare but rather logically impossible,[8] it is nonetheless convenient here to assume that neither end of the continuum is ever actually reached, except, perhaps, in mathematics. It is enough to say that some concepts are much more open or closed than others. More specifically, a theoretical concept like Wilson's scientific conception of work is almost completely closed because it has, in the absence of any paradigm shift, a single definition that is independent of the social setting or other sorts of context. The third qualification is simple enough. Some words have technical *and* everyday meanings ("culture" is one of them) but this does not mean that when the context makes it clear that one is "speaking technically" the concepts are not really closed.

With these three qualifications in mind, I suggest that not only open and closed concepts but also their respective types of definition are best thought of as *points on a continuum*. We can now chart the different sorts of definition that correspond to the two regions of the continuum, as shown in Table 1.1.

**Table 1.1.   The Continuum of Closed and Open Concepts and Definitions**

| *CLOSED CONCEPTS*.................................................................*OPEN CONCEPTS* | |
| --- | --- |
| Formal Definitions (FDs) provide conditions of application. | Informal Definitions (IDs) provide descriptive features. |
| *Lists of necessary and sufficient conditions, classical categorial format (genus and differentia), etc.* | *Goal statements, examples, ideal types, list of components, etc.* |

The left side of the table, which represents the closed region of the continuum, is the home for theory-based concepts, which as we have seen are best explained by definitions that provide the conditions of application of the term in question. As we also saw, this can be done either by listing all (or virtually all) of the necessary and sufficient conditions that must be satisfied before the term is applied to some entity, event, process, or state of affairs, or else by specifying its generic and specific features (that is, providing its genus and differentia). Throughout the rest of this book I will refer to such explanations as "formal definitions" (FDs), with the background understanding that some of these definitions are more formal than others. In contrast, the definitions appropriate for the open concepts on the right side of the table are more or less informal, depending on how tightly knit their internal resemblances are. Admittedly, calling them "informal definitions" (IDs) stretches the very notion of "definition," since they are often more like descriptions or illustrations than definitions; however, it will simplify matters to do so and the qualifier "informal" should dispel any confusion on that front. Furthermore, to say that these (so-called) definitions are "informal" is not to imply that they are unstructured, since they usually consist in well-formed lists of examples, goal statements, or salient features.

However, when all is said and done what one carries away from an informal definition is only a general idea of how the term in question is being used, not a strict formula for applying it in every circumstance or any sort of insight into some "inner core" of whatever is so defined. The distinction between FDs and IDs will prove useful in the following chapters, but we must not forget that the distinction itself is really only a heuristic device. Each of the two concepts we will be examining in the rest of this chapter, *culture* and *multicultural education,* lie somewhere in the middle of the chart, and so they are best defined by a combination of formal and informal definitions. Both are hybrids.

To summarize, we may say that regardless of how closed the concept in question is, its FD usually looks like a standard dictionary definition, which as we saw above attempts to provide the relevant conditions of application by packaging a complex concept in nested categories of generic and specific features, as in Aristotle's classical definition of "man" as an *animal* (genus) whose distinguishing characteristic (differentia) is *rationality.* Admittedly, the formal definitions that appear in multicultural education publications are not always perfectly well-formed dictionary definitions, but they are nonetheless austere—hard-edged, comprehensive, indifferent to the speaker's intent, and (unless they are simple synonyms) shaped in the format that their authors inherited long ago from their own teachers (perhaps also from their debate coaches). As an added bonus, their austerity reassures the reader that he or she is in the hands of a competent authority.

In contrast, an ID is looser and more varied. In books and articles about multicultural education one finds a general pattern in which formal definitions are succeeded—usually immediately but sometimes only several pages later—by descriptions that elucidate or flesh out the author's understanding of the concept under discussion. They are not nearly as concise as formal definitions, and are more like thumbnail sketches, micro histories, illustrations, or evaluations than taxonomies supplying the necessary and sufficient application conditions of a term. They sometimes stand on their own feet, effectively replacing rather than expanding a formal definition, but they are never meant to provide necessary and sufficient conditions of application.

Even so, there is considerable variation in the way the definition game is played in the literatures of multicultural education and culture. The formal definitions one encounters there are broader and less rigid than the narrower and tighter definitions one finds in the natural sciences, but they are nonetheless formal in one or another of the several senses specified below. In this respect they exemplify the basic principle of ordinary language philosophy, which is simply that there are many ways to define a concept.[9] There are also many ways to informally elucidate or illuminate it, and so throughout this and the following chapters I will use the labels "formal definition" (FD) and "informal definition" (ID) as follows:

> *Formal Definitions (FDs):* The *contents* of formal definitions can be *categorial* (typically having the classic genus-differentia format), *purposive* (goal-oriented), or *genetic* (historical accounts). There may also be other arrangements as well as combinations of those just mentioned, but these are the most common types. As for their *designs,* formal definitions can be either *monistic* (a single concept) or *pluralistic* (a set of concepts, usually coordinate items in a short list that may be unpacked further in an accompanying informal definition). Furthermore, some formal definitions are hybrids, in the sense that embedded within them is a "mini description" such as a brief example, a bit of name-dropping, a quick historical reference, or other sort of content that is actually more illustrative than definitional.

> *Informal Definitions (IDs):* The typical informal description consists of a few sentences that illuminate the concept under investigation by providing an example or string of examples, a paradigm case, or an extended list of features of whatever is being defined. In the latter case, the features listed usually fall under a single general category: for instance an author provides a list of ideal types, one or more goal statements, a breakdown into component parts (that is, ingredients), and so on.

## A FEW FORMAL AND INFORMAL DEFINITIONS OF MULTICULTURAL EDUCATION

To sharpen the contrast between the concepts of culture and multicultural education as well as that between formal and informal definitions, let's take a look at a few prominent formal and informal definitions of *multicultural education.* For convenience I have inserted the markers FD and ID along with numerical tags when citing or referring to the citations. Subsequent chapters will use the same format to analyze the even wider variety of definitions given for *culture.*

At first sight the structures as well as the contents of these and other definitions of multicultural education seem to vary in almost every imaginable way. However, when we track this variance we see that most of these

definitions have both formal and informal components, though a few are
entirely or almost entirely formal or informal—which is to say that some
are completely or almost completely closed and others are completely or
almost completely open. Their contents are similarly varied. Some definitions of multicultural education specify a wide variety of target concerns,
ranging from ethnic pride and cultural competence to social justice and
antiracism, whereas others have a much narrower focus. For instance Mira
and H. Prentice Baptiste (1980) produced for the American Association
of Colleges for Teacher Education a self-standing formal definition that
simply equated multicultural education with the reform movement then
known as cultural pluralism:[10]

❖FD1.1    Conceptually, multicultural education is that which recognizes
          and respects the cultural pluralistic nature of our society in the
          United States. (Ibid., p. 44)

❖ID1.1    (None)

Other early definitions that focused on cultural pluralism include a national policy statement issued in 1977 by the Association for Supervision
and Curriculum Development and similar manifestos in the professional
literature as well as mission statements in local newsletters and school
bulletins. However, cultural diversity or pluralism is just one of several
recurring themes found in definitions of multicultural education, such as
antiracism, social justice, identity formation, and global consciousness.[11]
For instance, whereas the National Council for Accreditation of Teacher
Education had listed racism as *one* of the issues to be confronted in a multicultural classroom, a few years later the chancellor's office of the California
State University system declared in a report to teachers that it was *the* issue.
The report centered on the following informal definition of multicultural
education, which was a simple goal statement unaccompanied by any at-
tempt to define the practice itself:

❖FD1.2    (None)

❖ID1.2    Multicultural education is viewed as a methodology to counter
          racism and prejudice based on ethnic identification and to pro-
          mote positive attitudes about human diversity. (Morey, 1983,
          pp. 85–86)

Four years after this report was issued, it was echoed by a professor in
the same university system, Eugene Kim, for whom the defining feature of

multicultural education was the wholesome effect that an understanding of ethnicity can have on racist attitudes:

❖FD1.3    Multicultural education is a deliberate educational attempt to help students understand facts, generalizations, attitudes, and behaviors derived from their own ethnic roots (origins) as well as others. (Kim, 1987 [cited in Davidman & Davidman, 2001, p. 61] )

Kim went on to unpack his statement by supplying a goal-oriented informal definition that we are told was representative of the thinking of other multicultural educators in the California State University system at that time:

❖ID1.3    In this educational process students will unlearn racism (ethnocentrism) and recognize the interdependent fabric of our human society, giving due acknowledgment for contributions made by various ethnic groups throughout the world. (Ibid.)

Cultural pluralism and antiracism are only two of the many agendas identified in the many definitions of multicultural education. Today they are usually bundled together with other agendas and related themes but this was not always the case. In the first two or three decades of the movement, multicultural education theorists often defined multicultural education in terms of their own specific concerns, in a two-step process that both shaped and reflected the evolution of the field itself. The first themes to appear were, as we just saw, cultural pluralism and then antiracism. In the 1980s and 1990s variations on the general idea of social justice began to appear, including freedom and equal opportunity. For instance in 1983 Donna Gollnick and Philip Chinn weighed in with their still-current formal definition of multicultural education as

❖FD1.4    a field of study and an emerging discipline whose major aim is to increase equal educational opportunities for students from diverse racial, ethnic, social-class, and cultural groups. (Gollnick & Chinn, 1983, p. 5)

They then supplemented their general definition with a short goal statement that makes it more concrete and relevant:

❖ID1.4    One of its important goals is to help all students to acquire the knowledge, attitudes, and skills needed to function effectively in a pluralistic democratic society and to interact, negotiate, and communicate with peoples from diverse groups in order to create a civic and moral community that works for the common good. (Ibid.)

Over the ensuing years the goal of equal educational opportunities for individual students evolved into a more comprehensive goal of large-scale societal transformation through critical pedagogy. However, by then single-theme definitions had gone out of fashion, and so in the first edition of her now classic *Affirming Diversity* (1992) Sonia Nieto proposed a much more complex pair of formal and informal definitions that tied together the themes of cultural pluralism and antiracism under the still more general theme of furthering "the democratic principles of social justice":

❖FD1.5   Multicultural education is the process of comprehensive school reform and basic education for all students. It challenges and rejects racism and other forms of discrimination in schools and society and accepts and affirms [various forms of] pluralism. (Ibid., p. 307)

❖ID1.5   Because it uses critical pedagogy as its underlying philosophy and focuses on knowledge, reflection, and action (praxis) as the basis for social change, multicultural education furthers the democratic principles of social justice. (Ibid.)

What can we learn from this short chronology? The main lesson is that as social and economic conditions change, so do the uses that practice-oriented educational theorists make of their own concepts—and as those uses change, so do their definitions. This is not the place to examine the social and economic matrix within which socially constructed concepts such as multicultural education come into being and subsequently reconstruct themselves (presumably the shift from the civil rights era to the Reagan years would be an important part of that story), but it is worth noting that sometime in the mid-1990s it became obvious that multicultural education is best understood as what Christine Sleeter and Carl Grant (1988) had previously called "an umbrella concept," under which various features—agendas, elements, pedagogical approaches, historical stages, etc.—were gathered.

## FROM MULTICULTURAL EDUCATION TO CULTURE: CHANGING THE FOCUS

In the previous section we focused on a few definitions of multicultural education in order to set the stage for the main topic of this book, which is an in-depth analysis of the role that culture plays in the thoughts and writings of multicultural educators. It is now time to change our focus, but first let's take stock. If you have come this far, you should realize that the concept of *culture* differs in at least four important ways from the concept of *multicultural education:* (1) It is more of a scientific, theory-generated concept than an everyday one; (2) it is the proper object of the social sciences, from which it has been imported into educational practice; (3) it is relatively closed, unlike the open-ended concept of multicultural education; and (4) the reason it has multiple meanings is that it is the product of competing theories, not that it has multiple uses (as does the concept of multicultural education).

With these tools and a bit of hands-on exercise in the conceptual "lab sessions" at the end of chapters 3 through 5, you will be able to recognize and evaluate the subtexts of various books and articles devoted to multicultural education, including introductory textbooks as well as advanced treatises. You already have in your toolkit two of three theoretical resources that will help you read between the lines of multicultural education literature. The first resource is a philosophical understanding of the difference between definitions of everyday, relatively open concepts and definitions of theoretical, relatively closed concepts. The second resource is a philosophical understanding of the distinction between formal and informal definitions. The third resource, which you will possess by the end of the next chapter, is a social scientific understanding of the wide array of theories of culture generated over the last two centuries by anthropologists, sociologists, and cultural studies theorists. These three resources will enable you to sort out the many ways that multicultural educators deploy the culture concept in their books and articles. They will also enable you to read between the lines of this literature when you come to the aforementioned lab sessions.

You will also be able to determine whether those books and articles conform to the well-known adage, "Practice without theory is blind, theory without practice is sterile." You will be able to analyze the professional discourse of multicultural education in order to decide for yourself whether an author's definition of culture influences what he or she says about the contents and methods of multicultural education and vice versa. Finally, you will be able to determine, as our fictional Mr. Peabody tried to do for his unit on citizenship, the extent to which an educational agenda—either declared or implicit—determines which of the many definitions of a key term like culture (or citizenship) are actually in play as foundational concepts or premises. Ideally, a multiculturalist author's agenda will be consistent with and obvious from his or her announced definition of culture, but is it really? Did the author consciously design that agenda around this concept? Or should the author (or perhaps you the reader) make some adjustments, either to the agenda or to the announced definition of culture? Does the author have secondary agendas that require the announced concept of culture to be expanded to include other features, all of which would add up to a complex but nonetheless coherent mix of definitions that fit with those multiple agendas? These are just a few of the questions you may find yourself asking.

The next chapter provides an in-depth review of the major definitions of culture that have been developed in anthropology, sociology, and (to a lesser extent) the interdisciplinary field of cultural studies, since to understand theoretical concepts such as culture one must understand the theories that shaped them. With this knowledge, you will see the social and political implications of the various definitions and appreciate just how controversial the concept of culture has been over the last two decades. You may begin to ask impertinent questions such as why some multicultural education authors do not try to justify whatever definition of culture they have selected. However, before we turn to those theories of culture and their reincarnations in educational literature, one last methodological comment is in order.

## The Art of Content Analysis

By now readers familiar with the research techniques of qualitative analysis—who probably include most who have read this far—may have recognized the analytic methodology we will use.[12] When it is applied to expository texts such as the definitions of culture one finds in the educational literature, the methodology is sometimes called "qualitative content analysis," perhaps in order to distinguish it from literary criticism as well as from a simple review of the literature of some academic or popular genre such as moral development theory or biographies of famous personalities. Using selected quotations and summaries of the contexts within which culture is discussed, chapters 3 through 5 will "interrogate" over two dozen multicultural education authors in order to understand the range this theoretical term has in the professional education literature. Because the term "culture" must be understood in relation to the theory or theories that employ it, the qualitative analysis in those chapters will focus on ways that multiculturalists' conceptions of culture embody a specific anthropological or sociological model of culture (or, as is also common, two or three such models). In other words, we will not only examine the use multicultural educators make of the term "culture" but also—and much more importantly—how their statements about culture align with the definitional categories associated with the classical and contemporary cultural theorists surveyed in chapter 2. In doing so we will focus on the core questions of content analysis, which the political sociologist Harold Lasswell (1948) famously summarized as: "Who says what, to whom, why, to what extent and with what effect?"

Finally, a word about quantity. In the foregoing discussion of the every-day term "multicultural education" I chose only five definitions because that seemed enough to illustrate how the FD/ID distinction works, even though it does not show the wide range of uses that term has. In contrast, the discussion of the theory-based term "culture" in the lab session chapters will be much more robust and will employ a much larger sample of defi-nitions.[13] I will wait until chapter 6 to weigh in with my own views about the nature of culture and how it should figure into educational theory and practice, since the purpose of the content analysis provided in chapters 3 through 5 is not to prove any specific empirical or philosophical thesis about culture but only to give you the experience of reading the multicul-tural literature carefully and with an eye to what lies between the lines of an author's express statements about the nature of culture. As explained at the outset, the point of the present chapter is to provide a philosophical compass for those who want to navigate through this literature. However, even the best compass only points the way. It does not go there itself.

## QUESTIONS FOR REFLECTION

The ideas presented in this opening chapter are unusually abstract, but once they are understood the basic program of this book will seem surprisingly straightforward. To see why, recall the following distinctions made in the previous pages and try to apply them to other areas of human life as well as multicultural education:

- *Formal and informal definitions.* Try to construct formal and informal definitions of some other area of social life besides education, such as art or democracy. Is there always a clear difference between the formal definition of a practice and its informal definition/description? Are some informal definitions, such as those involving the purpose of a practice or institution, more like formal definitions than others such as historical accounts of its origins?
- *Theoretical inquiry and educational practice.* Can you give examples from some other area of human life of how theory and practice can affect each other?
- *Closed and open concepts.* Is there ever a completely closed concept? Would the concept of "bachelor" as an unmarried adult male be com-pletely closed? What about a widower? What are some other examples of closed and open concepts? For instance, can the terms "game" or

"intelligence" be defined in terms of one or more features that all games or all recognized IQ tests have in common? What would be a necessary condition for calling something "beautiful" (or "moral" or even just "funny")?

- *The concept of multicultural education and the concept of culture.* In the educational literature one finds a wide variety of formal and informal definitions for each of these two concepts, but it is not clear that this is always a good thing. Do you see why significantly different formal definitions of culture can create challenges that are not associated with the different definitions of multicultural education?

After you have reviewed these four general distinctions ask yourself some more speculative questions such as the following, in order to articulate your present suppositions about the central issues to be examined in the next five chapters. (Think of this as a pretest. For a posttest, re-read this chapter after you have finished the book.) Assuming that the relatively open concept of multicultural education includes a wide variety of educational agendas such as those listed above, are any of them clearly central to your own understanding of what it means to be an educator? If so, which are they and of course why are they especially important for you? Are you aware of any debates about goals, rationales, or related topics among the major (or not-so-major) authors of books and articles about multicultural education? If not, would you expect to encounter such debates if you had enough time to make an exhaustive review of the literature of multicultural education? How would you proceed if you were asked to construct a definition of culture appropriate to the way you think the practice of multicultural education should proceed? Do any conceptions of culture seem incompatible with your present understanding of multicultural education? If so, why?

Also think of other examples of the general reciprocity between theory and practice. (A few possibilities: successful coaching in the complex and highly unpredictable realm of collegiate sports, the delicacies of international diplomacy, informed but flexible parenting, best practices in trauma center decisions, context-sensitive assessment and management of disabilities, academic administration in times of social crisis.)

## NOTES

1. The dictionary definition is from the *Random House Webster's College Dictionary* (1991). The other definitions are from Stuart Hall and David Held (1989) and Richard Bellamy (2008). Mr. Peabody's opening announcement to his students ("There are many definitions . . . The one we will use is . . .") is adapted from introductions to the culture concept found in several prominent multicultural textbooks.

2. Unfortunately, a closer look at her statement reveals that the agreement she has in mind is really only a consensus on which *topics* should be discussed, which is hardly the same as a shared understanding of the foundational concepts framing those discussions. Even so, the apparent absence of any shared understanding of basic issues did not bother Gay, who dismissed such deeper problems with an almost breathtaking flourish to the effect that since multiculturalists value diversity it is only to be expected that they will have significantly different views of their own subject matter.

3. This view of knowledge actually goes back far beyond Locke. The medieval philosophers understood knowledge as congruence between the mind and things *(adequatio intellectus et rei)* as did Aristotle. But it was Locke who inspired the modern view, even though he also believed that many types of ideas had no worldly correlates. What do correspond, he insisted, were certain relationships that (internal) signs have with each other and certain relationships that (external) things have with each other.

4. Attempts to do so would amount to either mere stipulation or misrepresentation—since in most cases there simply are no such definitions. In the first kind of attempt (stipulation), the solipsistic author achieves precision at the expense of relevance. What looks like a sharply delimited concept is really the product of what T. S. Eliot, in quite another context, called "an artificial distinction, peculiar to the book, which the reader would have difficulty in retaining; and which, after closing the book, he would abandon with a sense of relief" (1948, pp. 85–86). In most important discussions there are "enough inevitable obstacles," he added, "without erecting unnecessary ones." In the second kind of attempt (misinterpretation) an author wrongly presents some characteristic feature or set of features as a term's real or "essential" definition. Such a misrepresentation may not be intentional, but the effect is the same as if it were.

5. Weitz's application of Wittgenstein's idea of family resemblance to aesthetics provides a good illustration of how the meaning of a term (in this case, "art") is a function of its use, but like Wittgenstein he seems to think it is impossible to define art at all. Another philosopher of aesthetics, George Dickey has gone beyond Wittgenstein and Weitz to give what he calls an institutional definition of art, according to which the meaning or use of the term "art" is socially constructed by a specific language community that he calls the Art World (1984, pp. 79–81). I have drawn from both authors to make my own points about multicultural education even though their respective positions are in fact quite different from each other.

6. Unfortunately, this happens rarely, if at all, and only in logic, mathematics, and highly esoteric branches of science. It does not occur with empirically descriptive and normative concepts unless we close them by arbitrarily stipulating the range of their uses, hoping against hope that the next generation of language users will not undo our stipulations.

7. Admittedly, this is a paradox, which only makes sense if we consider the meaning of the term "closed" as itself, well, somewhat open.

8. I share this view, and would add that at the other extreme, a completely open concept would be unintelligible for the same reason that we cannot take seriously Humpty Dumpty's claim in *Through the Looking-Glass* that a word means "just what I use it to mean—neither more nor less."

9. Admittedly, not everyone shares this view of what counts as an adequate definition. I reach toward the bookcase and find my well-worn copy of the venerable *Prentice-Hall Handbook for Writers* (Leggett, Mead & Charvat, 1965). Injunction 37a tells me, in bold face: "Define terms whose exact meaning is essential to clear and logical communication" (p. 278). The reason behind this categorical imperative, I am then told, is: "Clear-cut definition is a key feature of logical thinking and writing. Your reader must know how you define your terms before he can comprehend your meaning. Much senseless argument, in fact, arises because people fail to agree on meanings" (pp. 278–79).

10. The reform movement itself was born in the 1970s but both terms had already been coined. "Cultural pluralism" was introduced by American pragmatist philosophers such as John Dewey and Horace Kallen, and the hyphenated "multiculturalism" was first used in 1957 to describe Switzerland (Marshall, 2009, p. 239).

11. For instance, after defining multicultural education as essentially coextensive with cultural pluralism, the 1977 policy statement of the Association for Supervision and Curriculum Development went on to commend it as "a humanistic concept based on the strength of diversity, human rights, social justice, and alternative life choices for all people." Though not itself a definition of multicultural education, this statement foreshadowed the tendency of later multicultural educators to center on justice issues rather than on cultural ones. Although these alternative themes became increasingly prominent as the next decade progressed, cultural pluralism continues to be an important and contested public issue as well as a major theme for multicultural educators, partly because it exposes social and political divisions in our society and partly because it shows that deep theoretical questions about the linkage between culture and socioeconomic forces remain unanswered.

12. Those not familiar with this sort of analysis might wish to consult Neuendorf (2002).

13. Are these good numbers? There is no simple answer to this question, so I leave it to the reader to decide when to move on to the next category. What Amia Lieblich and her colleagues once said about "the optimal number of categories" in qualitative analysis also applies to the optimal number of specimen texts, which in this case are the formal and material definitions of culture that appear in the professional literature of multicultural education: "What is the optimal number of categories [or texts], and how extensive can they be? Answers to these questions naturally depend on research goals as well as practical considerations between two very different tendencies. One is to define many, subtle categories that retain the richness and variation of the text but require meticulous sorting of the material. The other is to define a few, broad categories of the text" (Lieblich, Tuval-Mashiach, & Zilber, 1998, p. 113).

# 2

## The Concept of Culture
## in the Social Sciences

This chapter provides a knowledge base that distinguishes the many different notions of culture that are in play in the literature of multicultural education. That diversity reflects the diversity of conceptions of culture one finds in the source disciplines of social theory, by which I mean primarily anthropology and sociology but also cultural studies and cultural psychology. For that reason it would be unreasonable to demand that authors of multicultural education materials all use the same notion of culture, and even more unreasonable to expect them to construct a truly original meaning for that term. Their proper subject matter is education, not culture or for that matter any of the other important load-bearing concepts of multiculturalism, such as personal identity, cognitive development, and social justice. Such concepts are imported from other disciplines, where they have long and complex histories. As is the case with those other imports, culture is a highly contested concept, a fact that education theorists seldom clarify when they introduce it in their discussions of multicultural issues.

Ideally, every textbook or scholarly analysis concerning multicultural education would clearly indicate not only the specific academic discipline from which it draws its conception of culture but also the scholars or schools of thought that have been most influential for its author. In this ideal scenario each book or article would also provide its readers with a short but serious explanation of this and other source concepts, so that they could appreciate just where the author is coming from and how he or she fits into the larger scene of multicultural education scholarship. Unfortunately, such acknowledgments and clarifications are rare and seldom go beyond a bit of name dropping, a stylized quotation, and perhaps one or two relatively useless scholarly citations whose main purpose seems to be to reassure readers that the authors have done their homework. We are usually left to ourselves to do the heavy interpretative work needed to appreciate the authors' own standpoints on culture. Furthermore, even when an author produces an informative definition of culture (with or without reference to its sources), it is often unclear just what this definition of culture has to do with the rest of the book or article under discussion. In other words, it is left to us to determine how it relates to the author's main pedagogical or curricular themes, the underlying agenda, and so on.

The next chapters will show how to interpret multicultural education materials in the light of the major conceptions of culture found in the relevant classical and contemporary social theories. However, for those chapters to make sense it is first necessary to appreciate the logical geography of the social theories themselves. To this end I have provided in this chapter a knowledge base that will provide you with a supportive *context* as you move through the succeeding chapters as well as later, when you read about culture in the books and articles of whatever part of multicultural education is your chosen field. For instance, to properly understand authors who cite Ruth Benedict's famous holistic view of culture as "personality writ large" you should understand how her view went beyond E. B. Tylor's earlier view of cultures as stages of civilization as well as how it foreshadowed the structural functionalist paradigm of Talcott Parsons. Also, you should understand just what a "holistic view" of culture is, and how it differs from, say, a "functional" or "cognitive" view, and so on. Since the present chapter comprises a wealth of information, I will move things along by using the device, introduced above, of packing this information in the format of Formal and Informal Definitions (FDs and IDs).

In addition to building adequate historical and thematic contexts for tracking the concept of culture, this knowledge base provides an interpretative key that will help you identify the conception of culture on which a given book or article about multicultural education has been constructed. The remaining chapters do just this for a number of such works, but their larger purpose is to enable you to do this sort of thing for yourself. To adapt the ancient proverb about teaching someone to fish, the point of this knowledge base and the chapters that follow is not to provide an encyclopedic view of the culture literature or to prepare definitive interpretations of various multiculturalist approaches to culture but rather to give you and the other readers the necessary tools to do your own "cultural fishing."

## THE HISTORY OF THE STRANGE CAREER OF CULTURE

To understand the concept of culture one must understand its history, and to understand that history one must identify its separate streams, which are the disciplines of anthropology and sociology and a few mixed disciplines such as cultural studies and cultural psychology. For this reason our story begins with a few background remarks and then a short description of the birth of the disciplines of sociology and anthropology in the 19th century. It then focuses on the first explicit paradigm of culture, that of E. B. Tylor, the universally acknowledged father of anthropology. In the following decades—roughly, the first half of the 20th century—the treatment of culture in anthropology and sociology developed along separate tracks. Ethnographers such as Franz Boas in the United States and A. R. Radcliffe-Brown in England dominated the anthropological scene and the so-called *conflict theory* sociologists such as Robert Park and Ernest Burgess launched the American sociological discussion of culture that was quickly displaced by a new model that cut across disciplinary boundaries, that of *structural functionalism*. During the watershed decade of the 1950s Talcott Parsons's attempt to sharpen the boundary between sociology and anthropology led to a short-lived turf war. However, in the ensuing decades culture theorists cheerfully crossed the ever-changing boundaries between the two disciplines, motivated largely by the new recognition of the importance of symbols in any account of culture. The subsequent *symbolic interactionism* model introduced by the sociologist Herbert Blumer (himself inspired by the philosopher George Herbert Mead) and its anthropological counterpart, Clifford Geertz's interpretive theory of culture, were firmly in place by the late 1970s. Since then analytic studies of culture have become increasingly interdisciplinary, carried out under umbrella titles such as "cultural studies" and "cultural psychology." (See Table 2.1.)

**Table 2.1. A Rough Timeline of the Strange Career of Culture**

| Period | Discipline | Representative Figures Discussed in This Chapter |
|---|---|---|
| Late 1700s, early 1800s | Philosophy | Hamann, Herder |
| Late 1800s, early 1900s | Classical sociology | Marx (and Simmel), Durkheim, Weber |
| | Anthropology | Tylor |
| 1900—1960 (roughly) | Anthropology | Boas, Benedict, Kroeber (structuralists), Malinowski, Radcliffe-Brown (functionalists) |
| | Sociology | Park, Burgess (early conflict theorists), and Parsons (structural functionalist) |
| 1960—present | Anthropology | Goodenough, Shore (cognitive anthropologists), Geertz, Marcus (interpretive anthropologists) |
| | Sociology | Gordon, Glazer (later conflict theorists), Blumer (symbolic interactionist) |
| | Cultural studies | Williams, Gans |

In many respects the history of the concept of culture resembles recent accounts of paradigm shifts in the natural sciences, such as Thomas Kuhn's famous *Structure of Scientific Revolutions* (1962). In both cases the old paradigms are said to linger, sometimes (but only sometimes) in the same way that earlier styles of music and painting simply resurface in later periods, but more often as richer and more refined versions of the earlier conceptual schemes. Nowhere is this lingering more evident than in the history of the concept of culture. There are many ways to tell this story, and the one I will follow is conveniently chronological. However, we must keep in mind that its convenience is offset by the risk of drawing the lines too sharply between the dates (and themes) of these complex conceptual models. That said, let us begin.

## THE SEMINAL THINKERS OF THE 18TH AND 19TH CENTURIES

The use of the term "culture" as a property of human groups[1] began with the German romanticism of Johann Georg Hamann, Johann Gottfried Herder, and other anti-enlightenment philosophers of the late 18th century. It was used by classical sociologists of the 19th and early 20th century such as Karl Marx and Georg Simmel, Max Weber, and Émile Durkheim, as well as the first systematic culture theorists E. B. Tylor and Franz Boas. It has been a recurring theme in western social thought over the last five or six decades, right up to the present day when the very effort to clarify and apply the concept of culture is under challenge. However, for those early thinkers the concept of culture was a relatively undifferentiated, common-sense equivalent to the much more abstract notion of civilization and hence correlative with society as they knew it.[2] This is not to imply that, on the one hand, their views of the relationship between culture and society were clear and precise or, on the other hand, that their views were hopelessly scrambled, but only that there was no clear line between their understanding of the two domains. It was not until the 1920s that American sociologists (though not the anthropologists) began to treat society and culture as separate concepts, even though they did so in quite different ways and often with little or no formal explanation of the distinction between the two terms.[3] Of these seminal figures Tylor is the most relevant for our purposes since his definition of culture is frequently cited in the literature of multicultural education. However, a few preliminary comments about how the others fit into our story will be useful, especially for readers already familiar with the current literatures of these disciplines but not their intellectual roots.

*Central themes.* One of the central themes of 19th century social theory, regardless of whether it bore the label "sociology" or "anthropology," was *social conflict.* Another was *social cohesion,* and a third theme was the way *symbols* (including norms and rituals) enable the members of a society to share common goals and devise strategies for working together. These three themes have recurred, often in profoundly different ways, in the culture theories of modern anthropology and sociology, whose various branches or eras are usually marked by historians according to which of these three themes is central. For instance, from its beginnings in the late 19th and very early 20th centuries, one of sociology's central concerns was the nature of dominant versus nondominant group conflicts, either the specifically economic conflict described by Karl Marx or (a few decades later) more general notions of conflict such as those described by turn-of-the-century theorists such as Georg Simmel and later cultural conflict theorists. In the following pages we will see other ways in which sociological approaches to culture have been shaped by the ideas of these early theorists, such as Durkheim's holistic notion of societies and their cultures or Weber's emphasis on the role of symbols as sources of meaning and the medium of social interaction.

The same general point applies to the history of the concept of culture in anthropology. The boundary maintenance analysis of culture proposed by social anthropologists reflects Simmel's understanding of group conflict. The notion of cultures as holistic structures reflects Durkheim's view of societies as cohesive systems of collective action, in which social relations are stabilized by powerful, generally accepted symbols—ideas, values, beliefs, and norms—that hold the society together. These symbols operate as what Durkheim called the "collective conscience" of society,[4] an idea that foreshadowed a conception of culture that would later appear in the anthropological writings of A. R. Radcliffe-Brown and Talcott Parsons. The intellectual ancestry of the third, somewhat overlapping theme, namely symbols, is a bit more complex, since it can be traced back to both Weber and Durkheim. For Weber, culture was a set of "world-images" that give meaning to our social life.[5] Talcott Parsons combined this theme with Durkheim's view of social equilibrium and later Clifford Geertz developed his "interpretive anthropology" from Weber's early theory of symbolization. Contemporary critical cultural theorists have combined Weber's insights with Marx's critique of ideology, and so on.

A cautionary note for educators: although these three themes run through the sociological and anthropological literature on culture, they are seldom acknowledged in the literature of multicultural education. However, the two disciplines have influenced each other's understanding of culture in many ways, and so their joint effect on educational theory is as profound as it is elusive. The scholarly references cited in the following pages are hardly encyclopedic but they are nevertheless useful signposts for those who would like to pursue these themes at greater length.

# THE 19TH AND EARLY 20TH CENTURY MODELS OF CULTURE

## Anthropology's Founding Father

The birth of the modern academic discipline of anthropology occurred when the British scholar E. B. Tylor concretized the previously vague theoretical notions of civilization and culture by focusing on the basics of social existence, such as language, tools, food, and family. Anthropologists have abandoned Tylor's original scholarly agenda, which was to trace the developmental principles by which societies move in law-like fashion through increasingly sophisticated stages of civilization, but thanks largely to his rich collection of ethnographies the discipline of anthropology is now firmly rooted in the lived world, which is populated by real human beings and furnished with concrete features such as beliefs, customs, and artifacts, all of which are now referred to as "cultural traits." Even now, well over a century later, anthropology texts typically introduce the concept of culture by citing the formal definition with which Tylor opened his monumental *Primitive Culture* (1871):

❖FD2.1    Culture or Civilization, taken in its wide ethnographic sense, is that complex whole which includes knowledge, belief, art, morals, law, custom, and any other capabilities and habits acquired by man as a member of society. (Ibid., p. 1)

Since references to this definition will appear throughout this and the following chapters, it is worth noting here that although Tylor defined culture as a "complex whole" there is nothing truly holistic about FD2.1. His famous definition is really just a simple list of cultural traits that appear in travelers' reports of how people in other parts of the world live. Much more important to Tylor—though not to those who quote him—was the informal definition (ID2.1) that immediately followed, which describes the essentially historical character of these topics but says nothing about how they are related to each other. What it does provide, though, is a truly momentous statement of his desire to provide an evolutionary anthropology that would reveal nothing less than the universal "laws of human thought and action":

❖ID2.1    The condition of culture among the various societies of mankind, in so far as it is capable of being investigated on general principles, is a subject apt for the study of laws of human thought and action. On the one hand, the uniformity which so largely pervades civilization may be ascribed, in great

> measure, to the uniform action of uniform causes; while on the other hand its various grades may be regarded as stages of development or evolution, each the outcome of previous history, and about to do its proper part in shaping the history of the future. (Ibid.)

As this passage shows, Tylor was concerned with the general question of how "the conditions of culture" (note that he does not speak of "cultures") have developed in various societies. Like most social theorists of his time, he adopted a developmental model of change that had its own suppositions and logic.[6] In our present context, this means that Tylor understood the task of anthropology (or as he preferred to say, *ethnography*) as defining a single linear sequence from less to more complexity. As he put it, "By simply placing nations at one end of the social series and savage tribes at the other, arranging the rest of mankind between these limits . . . ethnographers are able to set up a rough scale of civilization—a transition from the savage state to our own" (ibid.).

Tylor was not unique in his use of a developmental scale to compare societies with each other—by that time evolution had become an extremely popular albeit still contested concept in scholarly circles—but he was definitely unique in his rejection of the then-current assumption that *racial* heredity is the motor of cultural change. He called his approach evolutionary anthropology, but it was *cultural* and not biological evolution that he had in mind.[7] Even so, his evolutionary model had the direct and momentous implication that the peoples of the earth could be ranked according to "its various grades" (ibid.). Since for him Civilization with a capital "C" was a univocal concept, it followed that some societies were simply *more* civilized than others. Not surprisingly, this part of Tylor's concept of culture is never mentioned by those who recycle his definition of culture as "that complex whole which includes knowledge, belief, art," etc.

Also unmentioned by those who cite Tylor's definition of culture is his lack of interest in his contemporaries' debates over whether skills such as weaving or using bows and arrows developed from within the group or were "diffused" from one group to the next. Although he introduced the idea of diffusion in his *Primitive Culture* he did not pursue it, since like other 19th century anthropologists he was primarily concerned with internal, evolutionary explanations—though always with the proviso that what evolves is the practical life and organizational structure of the group, not the genetic structure of individual organisms. As we saw in ID2.1, he believed that cultures should be studied in terms of the "general principles" of social development by which stages evolve according to "the laws of thought and action." The form and content of these stages were by no means culture-specific. On the contrary: cultural stages were rungs on a universal ladder. Tylor did not claim that all social groups had passed through every stage or rung, but he did think they were all moving upward more or less quickly on the same ladder. Hence he understood the task of anthropology as the search for the general principles ("the uniform action of uniform causes") according to which societies became increasingly civilized.

## CULTURES AS INTEGRAL WHOLES

### Boas and the Boasians

Looking back from today's multicultural perspective, it is not surprising that after Tylor the next major shift in anthropological theory was, in its first phase, the rejection of the implications of 19th century views concerning ranking and, in its second phase, the winding down of the old debate of cultural diffusion versus evolution and the emergence of new, metatheoretical discussions of the patterns of culture and its social function. The first important reaction to Tylor's developmental scheme came from Franz Boas and his students, which took place in the United States from the late 19th century through the 1940s. (Boas himself died in 1943.) The influence of Boas on anthropology in the United States was profound, which is why he is regarded as the founder of American anthropology and why his general approach is often called "classical anthropology." For our purposes, his most important contribution was the ground-breaking *The Mind of Primitive Man*, first published in 1911 and revisited over the subsequent decades. Boas understood culture not as civilization but rather as local context, within which a specific group's social life was meaningful. It was only late in his career that he got around to defining culture, perhaps because the word *Kultur* in his native German was a familiar nontechnical term of indeterminate reference—much as it is for most English speakers today. However, like Macbeth he eventually screwed his courage to the sticking-place, and in a long encyclopedia article he presented a formal definition that at first glance may not seem very different from Tylor's catalogue of cultural traits:

❖FD2.2    Culture embraces all the manifestations of social habits of a community, the reactions of the individual as affected by the habits of the group in which he lives, and the products of human activities as determined by these habits. (Boas, 1930, p. 79)

However, unlike Tylor's laundry-list definition of culture, FD2.2 represents culture as an integrated system. It offers a structured and presumably complete set of three components of culture, which together constitute an integrated totality. That Boas understood cultures as *holistic structures* is clear from the informal definition that immediately follows:

❄️ID2.2    On account of the heterogeneity of the habits of life it is custom-
           ary to describe culture from a number of distinct viewpoints: the
           adjustment of man to surrounding nature; the mutual relations
           of individual members of a society; and the subjective behavior
           of man. The adjustment to nature includes the use of natural
           products for the purpose of nutrition and of obtaining shelter,
           as well as for less important purposes. The relations between
           individuals include sexual life and the forms of social conduct;
           the subjective behavior is manifested in art, religion, ethics and
           science. These *various aspects of cultural life are interrelated* and
           their complete separation in a systematic description gives a
           warped impression of the character of culture. Nevertheless a
           full description cannot be given without taking up each aspect
           of culture separately. (Ibid., italics added)

It should be noted that when this encyclopedia article appeared Boas was 72 years old. His best and most influential years were behind him and the structuralist definition of culture it contained was more retrospective than prospective, that is, more of a clarification of what he had already done than a road map for his own future fieldwork and ethnographies. Throughout his long career Boas's great strength was in collecting data, not formulating definitions or constructing theoretical models. He crafted the definitions shown above well after he had reshaped the meaning of the term "culture" for himself and his followers by simply using the word with increasing frequency in contexts that left no doubt of his semantic inten- tions—which certainly did not include any Tylorean desire to represent culture as synonymous with civilization. Not only did Boas regularly use the word "culture" in the plural (whereas Tylor never did), but he wrote highly detailed ethnographic studies of individual groups, describing their customs in terms of concrete historical contexts rather than as moments in an abstract evolutionary process.[8] For this reason Boas's concept of culture offered cultural pluralists of the early 1970s a basic template for the social and educational reforms they sought. Their educational agenda, like that of Boas and his wide circle of followers, had such internal diversity that it would be wrong to stereotype those early multiculturalists as latter-day Boasians. However, it is easy to identify what both groups denied: for them culture was *not* a biological (racial) phenomenon, there is *no absolute form* of culture (such as western civilization) that sets a standard for ranking and "improving" the way other people live, and it was *impossible* to understand any component of a culture without understanding its relationship to the

culture as a whole. Positive assertions about just how one goes about identifying these components and tracking these relationships, not to mention
how one apprehends the cultural "whole," are harder to come by. Those
questions have no single answer, as is evident from the internal debates
among Boasians in the early 20th century and among multicultural educators in the late 20th century. Even so, it is important for today's multiculturalists to see what sorts of answers have been proposed, not only in their
own literature but that of cultural anthropology. Let us return, then, to the
story of how Franz Boas transformed the concept of culture.

His critique of cultural evolutionism began in the 1890s with a series of
critical articles, and by 1904 it had developed into the positive—though
still quite general—assertion that "in place of a single line of evolution
there appears a multiplicity of converging and diverging lines which
it is difficult to bring under one system" (Boas, 1904, pp. 522). These
"converging and diverging lines" were what he investigated in his ethnographic studies, and can be categorized here as *geographical* and *historical*
explanatory schemes. They are geographical in that Boas subscribed to
the diffusionist view of cultural change as borrowings from other (usually
neighboring) peoples, and historical in that he regarded cultural practices,
that is, custom, as rooted in a largely forgotten historical past (see Stocking, 1966, pp. 876–877).

In spite of his general dissatisfaction with single-track theories of cultural
evolution, Boas felt that his fieldwork with the Bella Coola Indians of the
Northwest Coast demonstrated the close relation between the geographical
and historical methods of ethnology. He was even more interested, though,
in what it showed about the need to analyze the *whole culture* of a people.
"The growth of the myths of the Bella Coola can be understood only when
we consider the culture of the tribe as a whole," he concluded. "And so it is
with other phenomena. All traits of culture can be fully understood only in
connection with the whole culture of a tribe. When we confine ourselves to
comparing isolated traits of culture, we open the door to misinterpretations
without number" (1898, p. 127).

Boas and most of his students were sometimes criticized by their British
counterparts (especially A. R. Radcliffe-Brown, as we will see momentarily)
for not providing comprehensive frames for the data they discovered. That
criticism was not entirely groundless, since the American research practice
was to collect first and try to explain later. Explanations, when they were
given, were often ad hoc. Cultural traits were seen not as reflections of differences in collective mental development (as Tylor thought) but rather as
by-products of differences in physical environments and other "accidents
of history." Nevertheless, Boas insisted on the importance of reconstructing
the unwritten historical record of the peoples he studied, gathering folk
tales as well as bits of oral history in order to tap into their collective sense

of who they are as a people, what they have borrowed, and what distinguishes them from their neighbors.

## From Diffusion to Pattern: Ruth Benedict and Friends

The question that originally preoccupied Boas, his contemporary Alfred Kroeber, and the younger Boasian structuralists such as Ruth Benedict and Margaret Mead was how beliefs and social practices spread from one culture to the next. They painstakingly investigated cultural distribution mechanisms such as diffusion, trade, and conquest, and yet—perhaps because of Boas's influence, perhaps simply because they discovered so many things during their own fieldwork—at first they blithely assumed that individual cultures were *aggregations*, mere collections of "shreds and patches."[9] They rejected the idea that groups were innately different, and instead hypothesized that the spread of mythologies, taboos, hunting and fishing methods, and other cultural traits was simply a matter of happenstance. When tribes with different practices and living standards came into contact, they simply borrowed from each other. To establish this relatively modest hypothesis that cultural traits are learned through interaction with other people and not biologically inherited, they were content to trace the lineage of cultures and their traditions. They were what philosophers call "methodological individualists," since they did not yet feel a need to provide holistic accounts of *why* any given set of cultural traits came together in the way that they did.[10] However, as their research agenda matured, Boas and his followers came to realize that their nonhereditary hypothesis had an important corollary: that the content of each culture could be thought of as a single reality ("a way of life," said Kroeber) and that this reality was best regarded as a property of the society as a whole rather than of its individual members.

It fell to Kroeber to develop this corollary formally and technically, using the idea of culture as a "superorganic entity." Though he had introduced this idea as early as 1917 its impact was not felt until several other students of Boas, including Benedict and Mead, became dissatisfied with the diffusionist views that assumed each culture was an essentially ad hoc combination of disparate elements. For this and other reasons such as their respect for the dignity and intelligence of their indigenous subjects, they reconsidered the question of just how contingent these configurations of cultural traits really were, coming eventually to regard cultures as integrated structures rather than grab bags of features that just happened to be mutually compatible. With this seemingly slight change in the ethnologists' attitude toward the people they studied, the concept of culture was again transformed. A group's culture was now an organic or aesthetic unity that could not be graded as better or worse than other cultures (though it could be evaluated as more or less well integrated, and so in that sense could be ranked against its own earlier phases).

The classic statement of this view is the formal definition of culture found in Benedict's *Patterns of Culture* (1934):

❖FD2.3     A culture, like an individual, is a more or less consistent pattern of thought and action. (Ibid., p. 53)

Here as with other definitions of culture already cited, it is the informal part that is most revealing. The pattern mentioned in her formal definition is determined, she goes on to tell us, by the group's "characteristic purposes," which were to be inferred from the pattern itself. (Ibid.)

❖ID2.3     Within each culture there come into being characteristic purposes not necessarily shared by other types of society. In obedience to these purposes, each people further and further consolidates its experience, and in proportion to the urgency of these drives the heterogeneous items of behaviour take more and more congruous shape. Taken up by a well-integrated culture, the most ill-assorted acts become characteristic of its peculiar goals, often by the most unlikely metamorphoses. The form that these acts take we can understand only by understanding first the emotional and intellectual mainsprings of that society. (Ibid.)

Benedict's idea of "characteristic purposes" is that certain master values organize a culture by providing a distinctive meaning in terms of which its members understand their relationships to each other and to the group as a whole. This idea runs through her famous descriptions of the cultures of the Plains Indians and the Pueblos. There she brought together her considerable literary and anthropological talents and borrowed Nietzsche's concepts of Dionysian and Apollonian societies to contrast their two ways of life, which were shaped respectively by the ideas of love and knowledge. She used these broad categories as explanatory constructs for cultural analysis in the grand manner that had been prefigured by aesthetic idealizations found in such 19th century accounts of "high culture" as Matthew Arnold's treatment of Hellenistic and Hebraic civilizations and other, sometimes explicitly Hegelian descriptions of classical and modern world cultures.

Benedict's structuralist conception of culture has probably had a greater influence on the general public, including educators concerned with multiculturalism, than have the theories of any other anthropologist, living or dead. (Her *Patterns of Culture* was the first anthropology book to be published in paperback.) However, she was only one of many in her generation of anthropologists to insist on the internal unity of cultures. Other students of Boas also held that cultures had distinct "patterns," even though they differed as to whether the pattern in question was primarily "phenomenal" (regarding observable features of a culture such as its customs, social institutions, and artifacts) or "ideational" (regarding the beliefs, motives, and other attitudes of the people of that culture). And so it came to pass that in spite of Benedict's continued popularity with the general public, among anthropologists, sociologists, and other social theorists the strongest and by mid-century most influential version of the Boasian view was Kroeber's conception of culture as a *superorganic entity.*

Although the term "superorganic" is no longer used, the structuralist idea behind it is still relevant to multicultural education in at least three ways, all indirect. The first is that it hardens the holistic notion of culture propounded by Benedict, whose own theorizing in this area (like that of her friend Margaret Mead) asserted that cultures were more than the sum of their parts even though they did not share Kroeber's view that the very *concept* of a cultural whole is irreducible. Today's multiculturalists[11] do not usually cite Kroeber himself on this point but the literature of multicultural education often reflects this tendency to reify cultures, as though they were things one has, social facts, objects of affection, or causes that act on other things in the world.

The second way in which the strong Boasian notion of culture as a superorganic entity is relevant to multicultural education is that it emphasizes the influence culture has on psychology rather than the other way around. For instance, although Kroeber was not prepared to abandon the notion of personal agency altogether, he believed that one's personality is profoundly shaped by one's culture, a shaping process that is typically discussed by cultural pluralists under the headings of cultural identity and self-esteem.[12] The third way that the superorganic notion of culture is relevant to multicultural education is its emphasis on history. A culture exists before and after individuals are born, grow up, live, and die "in it." Its history is not a chronicle of events ("just one damned thing after another," said the 19th century pundit Elbert Hubbard) but a *story that can be taught,* even to school children from other cultures.

## Back to Britain: The Psychosocial Functionalism of Bronislaw Malinowski

At the same time—roughly the interwar years—that the Boasians were insisting that cultures were real things having the formal unity characteristic of aesthetic patterns, British anthropologists were investigating a much different sort of formal feature of culture, namely its systematic and purposive character, or as they preferred to call it, the "functionality" of culture. There were, in fact, two competing notions of function operating in the anthropological literature of that time. The first was launched in the

early 1920s by Bronislaw Malinowski, a Polish émigré who was as powerful a personality in England as the German-born Boas was in the United
States and who was generally sympathetic to Boas's work. The second
was introduced a few years later by A. R. Radcliffe-Brown, whom we will
consider in the next section.

For Malinowski, the functionality of cultures was the way cultural practices shaped and satisfied basic human needs such as hunger and sex, as
well as more complex ones like the need to deal with death. Thus he defined culture as

❖FD2.4      the vast instrumentality through which man achieves his ends.
            (Malinowski, 1941, p.182)

He then cashed out this highly formal definition by listing the needs of the
"man" in question—who is understood here as a prototypical individual,
not the species itself or the society he lives within. This man has two sets
of needs:

❖ID2.4      both as an animal that must eat, rest, and reproduce; and as the
            spiritual being who desires to extend his mental horizons, pro-
            duce works of art, and develop systems of faith. Thus, culture is
            at the same time the minimum mechanism for the satisfaction
            of the most elementary needs of man's animal nature, and also
            an ever-developing, ever-increasing system of new ends, new
            values, and new creative possibilities. (Ibid.)

In other words, the overall function of culture was understood by Malinowski and his adherents as a set of specific subfunctions of specific institutions (for example, funeral rituals), each of which was to be analyzed in
relation to the psychological and biological properties of individual men
and women. His *Argonauts of the Western Pacific* (1922), *The Sexual Life of
Savages in North-Western Melanesia* (1929), and other ethnographies were
devoted to showing this relationship, which consists in "the dependence
of social organization in a given society upon the ideas, beliefs, and sentiments current there" (ibid., p. 164). Malinowski regarded social organization itself as an objective fact, something to be discovered in fieldwork that,
when carried out with due care, would leave the ethnographer with not only
artifacts, photographs, transcripts of interviews, and descriptions of discrete
behaviors and practices, but also an objective understanding of the social
organization and structures of these phenomena. For Malinowski, once the
anthropologist had done this ethnological spadework it only remained to
establish *which* "ideas, beliefs, and sentiments" are associated with these
social phenomena. Some of these ideas are the so-called savage views (often

"quite unexpected and far-fetched") about natural processes like sex and reproduction, which Malinowski explored in his studies of the matrilineal society of the Trobriand Islanders. Others are the ideas and desires that the people being studied have concerning the social structures themselves.

## MODERN STRUCTURAL FUNCTIONALISM:
## HANDS ACROSS THE SEA

### The British Version

An alternative conception of "function" was developed a few years later by another highly influential British anthropologist, A. R. Radcliffe-Brown, who rejected Malinowski's individualistic approach to the function(s) of culture in favor of a more collectivist and more systematic functionalism (see Radcliffe-Brown, 1935[1952]). However, what was most interesting for him was not culture or cultural traits but rather what he called "social structure." For him this term of art meant not socioeconomic class (its usual meaning in contemporary social theory) but the entire network of observable and orderly relations that connect people to each other. For this reason, he called his approach "social anthropology" in contrast to the "cultural anthropology" practiced in the United States. Whereas the latter approach was focused on the historical development and contents of particular cultural phenomena, Radcliffe-Brown's social anthropology aimed at the law-like generality and scientific rigor characteristic of the hard sciences. This sort of anthropology, he claimed, "deals with man's life in society . . . in exactly the same way that chemistry deals with chemical phenomena" (1930, pp. 3–4). In what he argued was a more scientific theory of society, individual needs were replaced by those of the social structure itself. In a scientific theory, he argued, a structure should be understood generically as a set of externally observable relationships: from this methodological principle it followed that a specific social structure was to be understood as a set of externally observable relationships that help hold a society together. The net effect of these structured relationships was what Durkheim had called social solidarity and his structural functionalist successors would call stability, harmony, or consensus. By reconceptualizing the function of culture as the preservation of social structures rather than as the satisfaction of individuals, Radcliffe-Brown transformed Durkheim's somewhat opaque idea of a collective conscience into a refreshingly clear model of social consensus and equilibration that was embraced by social anthropologists in Britain though not, by and large, by cultural anthropologists in the United States. However, American sociologists were more receptive to his model than their anthropological cousins were, and so from this point on the distinction between society and culture was drawn

quite sharply by sociologists on both sides of the Atlantic, including those
not directly influenced by Radcliffe-Brown.

In short, Radcliffe-Brown was less interested in culture and its contents
than in the way institutions worked together to ensure the continued existence of the social group. Culture was an aspect of society rather than
the other way around (as Boasians and other cultural anthropologists
had thought); or to put the same idea in structural functionalist terms,
Radcliffe-Brown thought culture is best understood as a kind of social glue.
"We do not observe a 'culture,'" he claimed, "since that word denotes, not
any concrete reality, but an abstraction, and as it is commonly used a vague
abstraction" (1940, p. 2). The definition that he did provide for culture was
certainly vague enough, though. Culture, he declared, is simply

❧FD2.5     a mode or process of social integration. (1930, p. 3)

Radcliffe-Brown unpacked this rather cryptic definition in categories
that straddled the two disciplines of anthropology and sociology, explaining that culture should be understood in terms of its socializing potential.
Rules of morality, religious beliefs, rituals, and other so-called "elements of
culture" are important, he declared, only because they transform individuals into members of groups, and groups into interlocking parts of a society.
In his view, the best way to understand culture is not to ask what it is but
rather what it does. His answer to that question amounts to an informal
definition of culture:

❧ID2.5     By any culture . . . human beings are united together into a
           more or less complex system of social groups by which the so-
           cial relations of individuals to one another are determined. . . .
           The function of any element of culture . . . can only be discov-
           ered by considering what part it plays in the social integration
           of the people in whose culture it is found. (1930, pp. 3–4)

Commenting on this passage two decades later, Kroeber and Kluckhohn
complained that Radcliffe-Brown had reduced culture to "a mere derivative
by-product of society," but it would be more accurate to say that what he
reduced was its logical status: for him the *idea* of culture was but a corollary of his more fundamental *idea* of society. Culture itself was regarded
not as a derivative by-product but rather as a mere means toward the all-
important ends of social solidarity and stability. One might also say, in
light of Radcliffe-Brown's many other remarks about methodology, that
he turned the concept of culture into a mere shorthand device for referring to "real" (by which he meant plainly observable) social practices and
institutions. Admittedly, for many sociologists of the 1930s these reductive

tendencies were virtues, not vices. What was missing, though, was a well-developed account of *why* the process of social integration actually worked. In spite of his idealization of society as an ordered system of institutions, Radcliffe-Brown's structural functionalist account of culture was long on structure and woefully short on functionality.

## The American Version

This was not the case for the American version of structural functionalist theory, dominant in the 1940s and 1950s but still influential today. The change was gradual, though. For a while, privileging social structures over cultural patterns continued to be standard practice for sociologists working in the long shadows of Radcliffe-Brown and the young Talcott Parsons—though as we will see it was certainly not standard procedure for cultural anthropologists.[13] When Parsons's influential *Structure of Social Action* appeared in 1937 its primary focus was on structure (the collective relationships among social institutions), not function (the dynamics of the interaction among groups). However, as Parsons's star rose over the next decades the emphasis switched. He and his growing band of structural functionalists became increasingly interested in the ways social interactions constituted society as a smooth-functioning system. He proposed that scholars should accept a clean and well-disciplined division of labor according to which sociologists would study the ways in which social groups and institutions function, psychologists would examine how the human organism (including relevant biological processes) functions, and anthropologists would map the underlying symbol system through which culture holds the entire social system in equilibrium.

To do their job sociologists were to replace the conflict model of society with a thoroughly structural functionalist view of society as inherently self-regulating. To this end Parsons domesticated and modernized Radcliffe-Brown's account of primitive societies, and conceptualized his own social world as a homeostatic system à la Durkheim rather than as a dialectical struggle à la Marx. (This contrast is full of political implications. Parsons himself was keenly interested in social change, especially in the developing societies of Asia and Africa, but for him change consisted in reform, not revolution. As with so many mid-century liberals, Parsons could not have imagined that just a few decades later social theorists would dismiss his structural functionalism as sheer hegemony, which is to say as a smokescreen for vested interests.) Within this grand scheme culture was understood as a congeries of symbols that constituted a well-structured system in its own right. It was self-contained and coordinate with the two other comprehensive systems: the psychologists' realm of *intrapsychic events* (including the nonvoluntary mechanisms of affect, motivation, and other aspects of personality) and the sociologists' realm of *voluntary human action* (the social world). Even so, since Parsons saw culture as the most abstract of the three systems he thought it was best understood not by itself but rather in terms of whatever relationships it might have with the two other, supposedly much more concrete realms.

For this and other reasons Parsons was just as unhappy with Tylor's laundry-list definition of culture as Radcliffe-Brown and other first-wave structural functionalists had been. Cultural systems are pure abstractions, Parsons thought, not empirically observable social phenomena such as the cultural traits itemized in Tylor's definition. As Parsons had famously put it in his *Structure of Social Action*, cultures are "both non-spatial and a-temporal" (1937, p. 763). In spite of or perhaps because of its extraordinary abstractness, Parsons's conception of culture as a functional symbol system quickly gained traction in both sociology and anthropology.[14] By mid-century Tylor's loose enumerative definition had been boiled down to a small, tight set of defining "elements" of culture that were charged with functional significance. There was some variation over the ensuing years in the way Parsons and his co-workers defined culture, but the most frequently cited formal definition is probably the one that appeared in his *Social System* (1951; see also Parsons and Shils, 1951) :

❖FD2.6     Culture, in terms of the conceptual scheme of this work, con-
            sists, as we have seen, in *patterned ordered systems of symbols*
            which are [1] objects of the orientation of action, [2] internal-
            ized components of the personalities of individualized actors
            and [3] institutionalized patterns of social systems. (Parsons,
            1951, p. 327 [italics and numerals added])

This definition is a good example of Parsons's tendency to be perfectly clear and maddeningly obscure in the same sentence. The italicized portion is clear enough. But does the "which" that follows refer to the symbols or their systems? Are these "objects of the orientation of action" anything other than simply goals? Why does he say the actors are "individualized?" And so on. Fortunately for readers unused to the jargon of systems theory, a few lines later he lists for us the three sorts of problems that his tripartite division addresses, and concludes with a set of familiar labels that I will discuss momentarily:

❖ID2.6      The most fundamental starting point for the classification
            of cultural elements is that of the three basic "functional"
            problem-contexts of action-orientation in general, the cogni-
            tive, the cathectic [affective], and the evaluative. . . . These
            considerations provide the basis for the initial classification of

cultural pattern types, namely [1] *belief* systems, [2] systems of *expressive symbols*, and [3] systems of *value-orientation*. (Ibid., italics and numerals added)

This short list, sometimes expanded to include otherwise implicit categories such as "norms" or "patterns of behavior," constitutes what is now the standard sociological definition of culture, even though structural functionalism itself is no longer the prevailing sociological model of either culture or society. The list often appears in contemporary sociology textbooks, few of which spend much time discussing Parsons or structural functionalism as such. Jonathan Turner's opening explanation of culture and social organization is a good example. "Patterns of social organization are possible only through the sharing of cultural symbols among individuals," he writes, adding that these symbols include a language and repertoire of signs whose meaning people agree on, a common body of knowledge, and conceptions of what they are supposed to do and see in certain situations. Turner then ties these ideas together with a pair of very concise formal and informal definitions of culture:

❖FD2.7      These common views are often conceptualized by sociologists as culture. Such systems tell us how to act, shape what we see, and condition the way we experience life. (Turner, 1985, p. 66)

Finally, he expands his formal definition by adding the cognitive contents of culture to the expressive contents (that is, symbols) already mentioned:

❖ID2.7      Typically they are categorized as (1) values, (2) beliefs, and (3) norms. Different sociologists may label each somewhat differently, but the phenomena described are the same. (Ibid.)

At this point it is important to recognize the difference between values and norms. In the sociological literature influenced by Parsons, values are not simple beliefs: they are profoundly personal commitments or, when considered as public symbols rather than as private propositional attitudes, they are choice statements that prioritize and otherwise regulate the behaviors and goals of a person or cultural group. Norms are similar to values except that the behaviors and goals they regulate are more public: norms control interactions across the entire social system. Although it is now commonplace to include norms in the list of cultural elements (as in Turner's ID2.7), an orthodox Parsonian would not consider norms as part of the cultural system per se. Norms are *social* institutions even though they normally reflect the personal, "bred in the bone" values that are part of one's *cultural* heritage. However, this seemingly purely verbal distinction raises substantive questions about causation across Parsons's three action systems. In his voluminous writings he often suggested that norms produce values, that is, stable and deeply felt commitments to certain goods, as well as the other way around. It remains unclear whether what we have here is a case of reciprocal influence or an infinite chicken-and-egg regress.

# CULTURE THEORY IN THE
# SECOND HALF OF THE 20TH CENTURY

## The End of the Turf War

Parsons's grand scheme drew a mixed reaction from anthropologists. On the one hand its exclusive focus on "action" eliminated or at least marginalized such traditional interest areas of anthropology as archeology, the cultural evolution vs. cultural diffusion debate, and indeed the general subject of historical anthropology (see Kroeber & Kluckhohn, 1952, p. 269). On the other hand, the disciplined methodology and narrow range of inquiry he proposed meant anthropologists could at last call themselves "scientists" and secure autonomy for their discipline.[15]

After a flurry of demurrals and qualifications, most cultural anthropologists eventually accepted some variation of this trade-off. It was, after all, but an extension of their long-standing belief, rooted in the German romanticism underlying Boas's own thinking, that culture was a comprehensive system of ideas and values, expressed in specific belief systems (especially religion) and material products (especially art). These ideas and values were more than abstract objects on a theoretical chessboard, since by internalizing them individual men and women find a purpose in life and a sense of self.

In 1952, just a year after Parsons's *The Social System* appeared, Kroeber and Clyde Kluckhohn—by then two of the decade's most prominent American anthropologists—objected to his proposed partition between culture and society: "In particular," they wrote, "we are resistant to [Parsons's] absorbing into 'social systems' abstracted elements which we think are better viewed as part of the totality of culture" (ibid.). However, their resistance was short-lived. Kroeber and Kluckhohn, as well as most of their fellow anthropologists, eventually accepted the culture vs. society distinction, and distilled from the literature of classical anthropology a formal definition of culture the essence of which continues even today to inform much of the literature of both anthropology and multicultural education. Because it is fundamentally semiotic—that is, concerned with symbols—it was completely congruent with Parsons's now-defunct grand project and is still cited in the literatures of anthropology, sociology, and multicultural education.

❖FD2.8    Culture consists of patterns, explicit and implicit, of and for behavior acquired and transmitted by symbols, constituting the distinctive achievement of human groups, including their embodiments in artifacts. (Kroeber & Kluckhohn, 1952, p. 357)

However, they went on to explain, the relationship between culture and society is bi-directional, in that the two domains influence each other over the passage of time:

✸ID2.8    [T]he essential core of culture consists of traditional (i.e., historically derived and selected) ideas and especially their attached values; culture systems may, on the one hand, be considered as products of actions, on the other as conditioning elements of further actions. (Ibid.)

In this new, symbol-oriented approach, the set of cultural traits showcased in the ethnographies of Tylor, Boas, Malinowski, and other classical figures was not culture but only its external manifestation. Culture itself was a formal system of ideas that were observed and communicated indirectly, by means of symbolic expressions or embodiments, and at the heart of each idea system were the "attached values" that gave the rest of the system its relevance and uniqueness. Even the most primitive culture was a complex system, with multiple dimensions, patterns, and expressions. It was therefore not a radical conversion when six years later Kroeber joined with Parsons to issue a joint manifesto spelling out the relationship between the two disciplines of anthropology and sociology. In a nutshell, their declaration was that culture is a symbol system, consisting mainly of ideas and values, whereas society is a network of formal relationships among groups and institutions (Kroeber & Parsons, 1958).[16] The turf war was over, at least for a while. The next generation of anthropologists wholeheartedly embraced the basic concept of culture as symbol system and generally resisted the temptation to poach on the adjoining territories of sociology and psychology. When the poaching did resume a few years later, system-building was out of vogue, Parsons was no longer the dominant figure in social science, and interdisciplinarity was once again respectable. Since then anthropologists, sociologists, and psychologists have cheerfully drawn from each other's work, and multicultural education theorists have incorporated ideas from the social sciences with little thought about which discipline begot them.

## The Revival of the Conflict Model

While anthropologists were busy observing and interacting with relatively primitive peoples in exotic locales, sociologists were working closer to home, using quantitative methods to study a group's observable patterns of behavior rather than its shared beliefs or other sorts of cultural traits. Of particular relevance here are the "assimilation studies" first produced in the 1920s (Park & Burgess, 1924) and revisited in the 1960s and 1970s by Milton Gordon, Nathan Glazer, and Daniel Moynihan.[17] Although sociologists had long been using the in-group vs. out-group framework to study social conflict, Gordon renovated it in his *Assimilation in American Life* (1964), a classic that framed the central issues and terminology for virtually every sociological discussion of race and ethnicity that would be published in the United States over the next two or three decades.[18] It provided them with a clear target as well as a useful set of categories for their various critiques of mainstream educational practices, even though it did not provide a radically new conception of culture. The most important difference between the two models was that whereas the early conflict theorists Park and Burgess had thought of assimilation as a long, virtually unending single-stage process, Gordon portrayed it as having several stages and substages through which minority ethnic groups quickly passed on their way to full membership in the social whole (ibid., pp. 69–71).

He called the first of these stages "cultural assimilation" or sometimes simply "acculturation" to indicate that the first changes made by newly arrived immigrants are in their cultural patterns, a general category that includes religious beliefs and practices. In what seems in retrospect to be an astonishingly naïve understanding of cultural bonds, he regarded this change as rapid and relatively unproblematic. Obviously, this confidence in the acculturating magnetism of the mainstream was misplaced. Gordon failed to take into account the possibility that immigrants might adopt mainstream behavior patterns without ceasing to think of themselves as members of importantly unique groups having certain entitlements, by which I mean among other things that as they became stronger and more politically savvy they would form what are now called special interest groups in order to engage in "identity politics," demanding legal recognition and resource allocations to preserve their cultural distinctiveness. This miscalculation was probably less a matter of naïveté on Gordon's part than an ideological stance common to liberals of his day, namely the view that everyone, including the most heavily accented and darkest skinned immigrants, wanted to be "100% American." In spite of earlier writings by educators and philosophers such as John Dewey and Horace Kallen, for most sociologists of Gordon's scholarly generation as well as most of the earlier conflict theorists, cultural diversity was not a goal to be pursued but rather an obstacle to be overcome in the name of liberal ideals such as fairness and equality. In short, cultural assimilation was the only reasonable and morally acceptable game in town.

The same liberal supposition marked Gordon's other stages, each of which was a movement through various strata of society, conceived in terms of Max Weber's (1946) famous three dimensions of wealth, prestige, and power. None of these strata was conceived in terms of its *cultural* contents, such as religious beliefs or moral norms, since stratification was a sociological conception, not an anthropological one. As he explained early in his book, Gordon understood social life as having two dimensions, *social structure* and *cultural heritage*. The first of these two concepts was a distillation of the prevailing functionalist idea that society is a more or less equilibrated system of impersonal rules and relationships within and between institutional domains such as education, economics, and politics, each of which contributes in its own way to the smooth functioning of the society as a whole. As Gordon put it, the social structure of a society is "the set of crystallized relationships which its members have with each other which places them in groups" (1964, pp. 30–31).[19]

His concept of cultural heritage is more elusive. He introduced this concept by citing Tylor's "classic definition of culture" as a complex whole, etc. (ibid., p. 32). However, on the very next page Gordon served up his own formal definition of culture, in which he interpreted Tylor much more narrowly, boiling the latter's famous definition down to the idea that culture is essentially the historical residue of a group's *social life*, not its worldview or symbol system:

❖FD2.9    The term culture is used specifically to refer to the social heritage or way of life of a particular society at a particular time. (Ibid., p. 33)

He followed up with an informal definition that cashes out FD2.9 in terms of general normative categories that during the 1950s were the standard elements of the structural functionalist notion of culture:

❖ID2.9    It is obvious, then, that the term may be applied to human groupings of various dimensions, whenever these groupings involve shared behavioral norms and patterns that differ somewhat from those of other groups. . . . [The] groups within a national society may differ somewhat in their cultural values since in a large, modern, complex, multigroup nation, cultural uniformity of the type approximated in a primitive society is impossible of attainment. Thus we may speak of the culture of a group smaller than that of the national society. (Ibid., p. 34)

Having defined social structure and social heritage (that is, culture) to his satisfaction, Gordon went on to develop his central thesis about ethnicity, which is that because of their social heritages, ethnic groups have a much different relationship to the dominant social group than the relationships which nonethnic minorities such as the impoverished or the disabled have. Unfortunately, he never expanded his concept of culture as social heritage even though he spent many more pages developing his notion of social structure. But fortunately, this glaring omission on his part was quickly noted by others, who proceeded to reexamine his premise that ethnicity is grounded in a common heritage.

Not all of Gordon's contemporaries shared his blithe confidence that complete cultural assimilation was only a matter of time, but in the 1960s and early 1970s few mainstream sociologists expected that later generations of ethnic groups would retain their ethnicity in any deep, identity-constitutive sense. For instance, Glazer and Moynihan, whose first edition of *Beyond the Melting Pot* (1963; substantially revised in 1970) appeared a year before Gordon's book was published, thought that although a later generation might continue to retain a relatively distinct ethnic identity it would be substantially different from the identity its families had left behind in the old country. What endures, Glazer and Moynihan argued, is not a set of specific cultural traits but a general process of self-categorization:

> [A]s the groups were transformed by influences in American society, stripped of their original attributes, they were recreated as something new, but still identifiable as groups. Consequently persons think of themselves as members of that group, with that name; they are thought by others as members of that group, with that name; and most significantly, they are linked to other members of that group by *new attributes that the original immigrants would never have recognized as identifying their group,* but which nevertheless serve to mark them off, by more than simply name and association in the third generation and even beyond. (1970, p.13, italics added)

Commenting on this passage two decades later, the social psychologist Nimmi Hutnik (1991, p. 36) suggested that "an emergent culture" is produced by the confluence of the original immigrant culture and the local mainstream culture. However, a more austere (and in my view much more persuasive) account of self-categorization had been proposed several years earlier by Fredrik Barth, a social anthropologist whose study of ethnic groups was informed by a sociological perspective. As he explained in an influential essay entitled "Ethnic Groups and Boundaries" (1969), although ethnicity is indeed much more long-lasting than Gordon thought, what is critical in the maintenance of an ethnic identity is not the "cultural stuff" of a given group's heritage but rather the various ways in which the group's *boundaries* are maintained. One of these ways is reactive: the group simply internalizes the image it has in the eyes of the mainstream and other groups. Other ways are more active, and can be more or less self-conscious, as when founding myths are invented or embroidered. However the general dynamic remains the same: regardless of whether it is actively or passively constructed, ethnicity is produced not by common living nor, as Gordon thought, by having a heritage of "shared behavioral norms and patterns" mentioned in ID2.9, but by the awareness on the part of a group's members that they belong to a particular group that is distinctly different from other groups. The group's basic *ethnic* identity is constituted by this self-awareness, which is itself sustained by social interactions with other groups even though, paradoxically, the group's specifically *cultural* features change in the course of various internal and external power struggles with other groups. For this reason Barth later suggested that ethnic studies should stop focusing on cultural contents such as art and religion and instead examine the social, group-on-group relations that are involved in "the continuous dichotomization between members and outsiders" (1994, pp. 14–15). Or more simply: in studies of ethnicity the focus should be on boundary maintenance.

Much more could be said about the different ways that sociologists and crossover social anthropologists like Barth have approached ethnicity and other group-on-group issues. However, our concern in this chapter is not the history of sociology as a discipline but rather its approaches to culture that have significantly influenced some of the theories and practices of multicultural education. In that respect the influence of sociological theory was greatest in the 1970s, when the relatively moderate academic agendas of ethnic studies programs were overtaken by the stridently activist agendas of cultural pluralism. In the aftermath of the civil rights movement, minority groups—especially African-Americans—redefined their situations and in doing so transformed the conflict model once again. The struggle for liberal values of equality and civil liberties that had been so important in the 1960s shifted so that in the 1970s those values became the agenda of white reformers, in contrast to the minority groups' newly articulated communitarian agenda of cultural pluralism.[20]

## THE COGNITIVE TURN

Parsons's conceptual influence on the disciplines of anthropology and sociology was much greater than it was on psychology, which had already partitioned itself off from the social sciences by the time he carved out the three domains of action theory. Although by mid-century the hybrid subdiscipline now known as social psychology had come into its own (Kurt Lewin's field theory comes to mind here), its early representatives had little to say about the personal subjectivity of their subjects and virtually nothing to say about their culture. Their interest in anthropological research was minimal.

Mainstream anthropologists reciprocated. The subject matter of psychology was of little or no interest to them because they too regarded basic

psychological processes as universal, that is, as culture-neutral, utterly un-
affected by time, place, or social context. However, on the anthropological
fringe was a small group of linguistically keen culture theorists—in the early
1950s they called themselves "ethnoscientists" but are now considered the
original "cognitive anthropologists"—who suspected that some psychological processes are truly culture specific, especially those processes concerned
with language. Over the next decades their numbers grew, the theories
broadened, and by the end of the century what had begun as a narrow and
quite technical research interest of a few psycholinguistically knowledge-
able anthropologists had become one of the most important conceptions
of culture in play in anthropology as well as in the literature of multicultural education. Of course all of this happened gradually. Like the cultural
and cross-cultural psychologists[21] on the other side of the aisle, these early
cognitive anthropologists bleached the otherness out of their subject matter by assuming that cross-cultural variations in psychological phenomena,
though real, could be systematically represented and explained in the investigator's own idiom without loss or distortion. However, over the next
two or three decades views changed in both subdisciplines, and cultural
differences began to play a more important role in cultural psychology and
in cognitive anthropology. Conversely, psychological processes and structures came to be seen as shaped by culture—that is, by a society's shared
meanings and practices—and it was eventually recognized on all sides that
these meanings and practices differed strikingly and profoundly from one
cultural group to another. Today the dominant view in both cognitive anthropology and cultural psychology is that cultural and cognitive phenomena are mutually constitutive.[22]

*The early stage.* At the beginning of the turn cognitive anthropologists and
psychologists ignored the external features of culture and turned their attention to the ways people in different cultural groups *think.* Their new object
of study was "cultural knowledge," a quasi-technical term used to denote
the way members of a culture actually understand the world. (This is also
how the term is used today by multicultural educators.) Borrowing heavily
from the flourishing science of linguistics, the early cognitive anthropologists went beyond the familiar but unanalyzed western categories of concrete "beliefs" and "values" that had been described so vividly by classical
ethnographers such as Benedict and Mead. Instead they drilled down to the
deep linguistic structures that correspond to these and other sorts of mental
states and constitute the rules of thinking, talking, and acting that one must
observe in order to fit into a society.

These rules are so fundamental that cognitive anthropologists have regarded them as emblematic of culture itself. Or better, they have treated the
individual person's *knowledge* of these behavior-shaping rules as the center
of the cognitive repertoire that constitutes his or her cultural knowledge.

As in the case of linguistic knowledge (that is, knowing how to talk to others, in itself an important form of cultural knowledge), what was under investigation was never a simple behavior or behavior pattern but rather an essentially cognitive *competence*, which like all competences is known only indirectly, that is, by observing various overt performances. This idea that cultural knowledge is a competence was the premise for the standard cognitive conception of culture, formulated by Ward Goodenough in 1957 as "what people have to learn" and reformulated several times over his long career. Multiculturalists and others influenced by Goodenough usually cite the following formal definition, which Geertz would later call the *locus classicus* of the entire cognitive anthropology movement:

❖FD2.10    A society's culture consists of whatever it is one has to know or believe in order to operate in a manner acceptable to its members. (Goodenough, 1957, p. 167)

He then draws a sharp line between the cognitive and classical conceptions, explaining that

❖ID2.10    [Culture] does not consist of things, people, behavior or emotions. It is rather an organization of these things. It is the forms of things that people have in mind, their models for perceiving, relating, and otherwise interpreting them. (Ibid.)

Goodenough's formal definition, usually unaccompanied by ID2.10, is sometimes cited in the literature of multicultural education, although it is not always clear whether those who cite it recognize the radical character of his cognitivist model of the mind. Nor is it clear that the many other social theorists who deploy Goodenough's definition are also on board with his cognitive theory, even though he repeated it verbatim or with only slight variations many times over the years.

*The middle stage.* By the early 1960s Goodenough and his colleagues had created a whole new agenda for anthropology. The classical search for familiar cognitive traits or objects like religious values and beliefs, supposedly implicit in the language and practices of other cultures as well as our own, had been abandoned by an increasing number of cognitive anthropologists who looked instead for ways to represent both familiar ("our") and unfamiliar ("other") cognitive structures in terms of transcultural principles of communication. The first wave of cognitive anthropologists and like-minded psychologists had constructed elaborate lists of highly formal linguistic universals. However, in the decades that followed (roughly 1960–1980), cognitivists—including Goodenough and others who had led the first wave—came to see that cultural knowledge is much more complex, much more loosely organized, and much less easily translated into the categories of the investigator's own cultural knowledge. More importantly, they recognized the significance of a third kind of linguistic structure, namely *performative structures*, in which speakers *interact* with their interlocutors by persuading, querying, exclaiming, challenging, etc.

It was against the work done during this middle period by Goodenough and others that Geertz launched his famous objection that from their mentalistic view of the nature of culture "follows a view, equally assured, of what describing it is—the writing out of systematic rules, an ethnographic algorithm, which, if followed, would make it possible so to operate, to pass (physical appearance aside) for a native. In such a way, extreme subjectivism is married to extreme formalism, with the expected result: an explosion of debate as to whether particular analyses (which come in the form of taxonomies, paradigms, tables, trees, and other ingenuities) reflect what the natives 'really' think or are merely clever simulations, logically equivalent but substantively different, of what they think" (Geertz, 1973, p. 11). Over the next decades the debate between these two thinkers continued, each the unofficial envoy of the kind of anthropology he represented. However, for many anthropologists then and now this was not a serious debate but only a question of emphasis. Looking back twenty years later, Goodenough himself admitted, "As Geertz has stressed, a culture arises and is maintained in the course of human action." Even so, he argued, "A theory of culture gets into trouble if it sees a culture as having an existence apart from the individual people whose interactions give rise to it. It is natural for people to see their culture as having such a separate existence. They feel constrained by the expectations of others. It is not surprising, therefore, that we anthropologists have done what comes naturally to us as humans and have thought of cultures that way, too." Then, perhaps feeling he had given too much away to the other side, Goodenough dug in his heels and insisted on the necessity of taking a cognitive approach: "But theory requires the contrary view, namely that a culture (and language) exists as an aggregate of the somewhat different individual understandings that each participant attributes to the group" (Goodenough, 1994, p. 267; see also Strauss & Quinn, 1994).

*The third stage: The present situation.* In the first two stages, cognitive anthropologists focused first on simple and then on complex symbols that they regarded as the units of meaning in a person's or group's cultural knowledge. However, in the 1980s they took over the concept of *schemas*, which had already gained currency in cognitive psychology, linguistics, and neural science. Schemas—also called "schemata," "models," "scenarios," "frames," "scenes," and "scripts"—are higher-order or supervenient representations that link and organize otherwise disparate units of meaning to form a coherent model of real things and events in the world or of concrete actions to be performed. As the cognitive psychologist George Mandler has explained, a cognitive schema is a "bounded, distinct, and unitary representation" that is formed as we interact with our environment. Once in place, schemas enable us to understand the various processes that go into factual judgments and practical decisions, for example, selecting evidence or constructing plausible hypotheses (Mandler, 1984, pp. 55–56).

What moved cognitive anthropology to this new level of abstraction was the fact that the relatively self-contained symbolic representations that were featured during the second stage turned out to be too simple to explain the workings of real-life discourse, where a speaker's schematic representation of the world ("the scene") is picked up, modified, and thrown back to the speaker by the interlocutor. Roy D'Andrade explains this point with a clever word choice: in such discourse, he says, the scenes that are tossed back and forth are "highly schematic," by which he means that they have a specified number of slots that are to be filled in by the other speaker (D'Andrade, 1995, p. 123).

It was upon this background that Bradd Shore, one of today's most prominent cognitive anthropologists, defined culture in thoroughly cognitive terms as simply

❖FD2.11    a very large and heterogeneous collection of *models* or what psychologists call *schemas*. (1996, p. 44)

Using this new conception of culture, the third wave of cognitive anthropologists have been able to formulate and explore new questions, such as how schemas are shared and modified, to what extent the larger social environment or culture shapes the interactions between individuals, and whether these interactions significantly shape the culture itself. D'Andrade's own view is that such issues have moved the discussion of schemas out of anthropology's mainstream over to psychology but this does not seem to be the view of Shore and other important cognitive anthropologists (such as Strauss and Quinn). For instance, Shore declares that his definition of culture has "much to recommend it for anthropology" since it provides an answer to Geertz's above-mentioned objection that that there is something so public about culture that to say it "consists of mental phenomena" constitutes a *cognitive fallacy* (1973, p. 12). On the contrary, replies Shore: Geertz's objection can be circumvented simply by unpacking his (Shore's) definition FD2.11, which does not deny that cultural models are out in the world as well as in the mind. Shore's explanation of this point provides us with a useful informal definition that explicates the term "models" that appears in FD2.11 and, he believes, refutes Geertz's charge of a cognitive fallacy:

❖ID2.11    To the extent that they are public artifacts, cultural models are out in the world, to be observed by outsiders as well as

> experienced by locals. In this sense, cultural models are em-
> pirical analogues of culture understood as knowledge. . . .
> [T]hey are not analogues in any simple sense, since public
> models are not exactly the same thing as mental models. But
> approaching culture as a collection of models has the advan-
> tage of showing that making sense of culture as an aspect of
> mind requires that we both distinguish and relate these two
> notions of model. (Ibid.)

In the grand scheme of things Shore's question of whether contemporary schema theory is truly "anthropological" rather than, say, a subdomain of cultural psychology may not be worth asking. But because of Geertz's objections it continues to be asked, and it leads to a larger question, namely whether we are really forced to choose between, on the one hand, the way cognitivist anthropologists—including those who have adopted some form of schema theory—use symbols and, on the other hand, the semiotics employed by Geertz and his fellow interpretive anthropologists. Regardless of what one thinks of Geertz's claim that the cognitivist account of culture is a cognitive fallacy, it is now clear that the mainstream has definitely shifted or at least divided on this issue, not only in anthropology but also in the field of multicultural education where, as we will see later, schema theory and other cognitive conceptions of culture regularly appear in books and articles written over the last decade or two (one example is Joel Spring's *Intersection of Cultures*, which first appeared in 1995 and is now in its 4th edition [2008]). However, in spite of questions about how it fits with today's mainstream, Geertz's emphasis on the public character of culture is important, not only in what D'Andrade called the ontological debate about the locus of culture but also in its long-term effect on the career prospects of the very concept of culture.

## Symbols and Interpretations

In the 1950s most of the prominent studies of cultural symbols and symbol systems were carried out by Parsonian structural functionalists, but in the following decades symbolization was a leitmotiv in many different kinds of social theory, ranging from the cognitive anthropology and cultural psychology discussed above to the symbolic interaction and cultural studies approaches discussed below, which tried to preserve Parsons's own retrieval of Weber's insight that cultures—and hence the congeries of symbols that constitute cultures—are best thought of as semiotic systems or "webs" of meaning. The best-known of these was the erudite interpretative anthropologist Clifford Geertz.

*Interpretation in search of meaning.* During the 1960s Geertz, who was trained at Parsons's Department of Social Relations at Harvard, produced two sorts of writing: relatively concrete problem-oriented monographs and philosophical or semi-philosophical essays about the nature of culture. The monographs dealt with issues in the development debates of that period of decolonization (see Kuper, 1999, p. 96ff.), the general point of which was that culture—especially its religious dimension—"inflected" the social, political, and economic developments taking place in Indonesia, Morocco, and points in between. In contrast, Geertz's essays—the most important of which were gathered in his famous 1973 publication *The Interpretation of Cultures*—took up questions about symbolization, narrative, interpretation, and as just said, the nature of culture. His ideas are summed up in a definition that is probably cited as widely as Tylor's initial definition of culture (FD2.1) as "that complex whole . . ."

❖FD2.12    The concept of culture I espouse, and whose utility the essays below attempt to demonstrate, is essentially a semiotic one. Believing, with Max Weber, that man is an animal suspended in webs of significance he himself has spun, I take culture to be those webs . . . (Geertz, 1973, p. 5)

To operationalize this very abstract concept he then asked just what it is that anthropologists do when they study a culture. His answer was that the study of culture proceeds by ethnography (so far no surprises) and that the proper subject matter of ethnography is the vast array of symbols or symbolic forms that constitute everyday life, ranging from language and sacred rituals to artifacts and etiquette. These symbols must be understood from the actor's own perspective, which is an active, purposive point of view full of desires, hopes, needs, and other sorts of intentionality that are, not coincidentally, the stuff out of which great literature is made. Hence Geertz insisted that ethnography, like literary criticism, must be thought of as *interpretation*, which, borrowing from the philosopher Gilbert Ryle, he also called "thick description." Geertz fleshed out his definition of culture by saying that he takes

❖ID2.12    the analysis of it to be therefore not an experimental science in search of law but an interpretive one in search of meaning. It is explication I am after, construing social expressions on their surface enigmatical. (Ibid.)

From this understanding of ethnography as interpretation we can see that Geertz was committed to a much more robustly semiotic conception of culture than anyone else had proposed as of that time except, perhaps, a few sociologists and cultural studies theorists working in the emerging symbolic interactionist tradition (see below). Cultures were seen as similar to literary works—in fact he identified cultures as texts—and as such must be understood not by decoding them one symbol at a time but rather by seeing the interplay among the symbols and between the subtexts that constitute what might be called the culture's intertextuality. As with the interpretation of a literary text, the interpretation of a culture is the recognition of a set of interrelated meanings, intentions, and communications that are shared by a community of interlocutors. For Geertz cultural symbols are *models* in roughly the same two senses of that word that appear in the cognitive anthropology literature: they are models *of* reality (or of what the symbol claims is reality) and models *for* acting upon reality. It is because of the latter function that Geertz and others followed Weber and Parsons in regarding a culture's symbols as guides and motives for social action, and it is because of the former function that they regard them as constituting a worldview that endows life itself with meaning since it rescues it from chaos and uselessness. To paraphrase a line from Adam Kuper's (1999, p. 99) own paraphrase of Geertz, culture has its aesthetic dimension, but it is more than mere ornamentation. Each culture is a shared and more or less adequate struggle with the "big issues" of life, death, freedom, and chance, and in so doing it addresses the human condition itself.

At this point one might well ask why Geertz drew such a sharp line between his interpretive approach and that of cognitive anthropologists such as Goodenough. On the face of things the two approaches had much in common, if not in their intellectual genesis (Straussian linguistics vs. Parsonian functionalism) then in the approaches they took to their subject matter. My own view is that the difference between the cognitive approach and the interpretative approach is important even though it is easily blurred. Both approaches are described by their proponents as based on semiotic considerations—"symbol systems" is the preferred phrase of cognitive anthropologists whereas interpretativists favor Geertz's more picturesque expression "webs of meaning." Cognitivists and interpretativists both tend to play down the importance of a cultural group's history in the course of representing its culture. Both attend to present-day behavioral patterns. However, the important differences between them emerge when we ask what symbols *really do* for us.

The cognitivists understand symbols functionally in a way that is reminiscent of Malinowski's psychological functionalism. They regard a group's shared cognitive infrastructure of beliefs, values, and expressions as a culture-specific recipe for satisfying the universal needs for fitting in, for being accepted as a member of the group, for successfully coping or at least better co-coping with various problems. In short, for them cognitive structures are basically physical and social survival strategies. In contrast, the interpretavists insist that the fundamental motivation for creating and using symbols is not the desire to fit in or survive, but the need to create meaning. Their preoccupation with "meaning," or better "meaning-making" understood as an ongoing collective activity rather than as a people's cultural heritage, is reminiscent of Parsons's functionalism but they have a much greater tolerance—indeed, enthusiasm—for internal diversity and ambiguity than Parsons himself ever had.

A second, equally important difference between cognitive and interpretive anthropologists is in how they construe the public character of symbols. The cognitivists, at least more recent ones such as Shore, recognize and allow that symbols are public but believe their publicness is a by-product of more fundamental, private processes in which individuals represent to themselves other individuals who, like themselves, manipulate symbols—and, in fact, for the most part manipulate the very same symbols, especially those representing some aspect of "appropriate behavior." For Geertz the order is reversed: the symbols are first public and then become private, since symbols are learned and used in what Geertz calls cultural acts that are "as public as marriage and as observable as agriculture" (1973, p. 91). That symbols such as those associated with marriages and farming (and talking and reading and writing) signify, among other things, shared understandings is hardly mysterious. It simply follows from the fact that for the people who use the symbols they are already public and self-evident. Or in one of those commonsense exclamations with which Geertz loves to interrupt himself: "How else would you spell hippopotamus?"

These differences between the two anthropological conceptions of cultures as symbol systems are reflected in their respective ethnographical practices. As just noted, the cognitivist idea of ethnography was to uncover the knowledge people need in order to act in culturally appropriate ways, and its methodology consisted in formulating the right questions and then asking them in interview situations. The interpretivists' idea of ethnography was much different but equally novel. For them it was neither the classical anthropologists' descriptive inventory of a people's way of life nor the cognitivists' decoding and mapping of a basically static formulary of rules that determine socially appropriate behavior. For the interpretive anthropologists, ethnography was to be a narrative that reveals meanings that *taken together* (recall Geertz's web metaphor) define life and give it its purpose. Even the desperately poor and most heavily oppressed are always trying to make sense of their lives. For them, as for everyone, the alternative is what Sherry Ortner, commenting on Geertz, has called rage, dissociation, and madness (1999, p. 9).

*The aftermath.* Geertz's concept of culture as webs of meaning and his corresponding conception of ethnography as textual interpretation were quickly absorbed not only by anthropologists of the 1970s and 1980s but also by historians, literary theorists, political economists, and sociologists, especially those who identified themselves with the cultural studies movement. Those working outside the narrow world of professional anthropology who were charmed by Geertz's semiotic approach to culture took it as a model for their own research and writing even though they tended to ignore its structural functionalist origins and Weberian underpinnings. The new interpretative anthropologists also began to take a closer look at their own discipline, especially its principles of ethnography. These reconsiderations were already under way in the 1970s but it was in the next decade that anthropologists who had originally welcomed Geertz's semiotic approach began to write books and articles criticizing him for not having carried his own ideas far enough. In particular, they called for a greater awareness of just what was going on when ethnographers went into the field and what they were really doing afterwards when they wrote up their accounts. In a word, these not unfriendly critics of Geertz insisted that interpretivist descriptions of cultures should also include self-referential descriptions of how they were fashioned. For instance, the so-called "native point of view" that was reported in most ethnographies (including Geertz's) was really the view of a *particular* local informant, and this inevitably perspectival report was itself repackaged by the ethnographer at least twice, once while hearing it during the interview session and again in the construction of the written account that reflected the ethnographer's own understanding of the "native's" personal understandings of the culture. The epistemology of anthropological research had changed. Fieldwork was no longer observer-neutral observation—or better, it was now clear that it had never been neutral—and ethnography was now seen as including not only the author's interpretation but also the interpretations made by the informants themselves, who often disagreed with each other on the meaning of certain aspects of their own culture. These subjective aspects were thematized with great fanfare in ethnographies produced by post-Geertzian researchers such as Paul Rabinow & Sullivan (1987) and George Marcus (1999), who wrote extensively about the conversations they had had with their informant-collaborators and in doing so placed on center stage the latters' own voices, preoccupations, and personal histories. The informants were to be understood not only as representatives of their culture but also as "complicit" (Marcus, 1999) with the ethnographer.[23] Conversely, the ethnographer's own culture was objectified or, as George Marcus (ibid., p. 103) once put it, "exoticized" in the process of creating complicity and reducing differences.

## The Microsociology of Symbolic Interactionism

We turn now to what might be called the sociologists' micro version of Geertz's interpretative anthropology, namely *symbolic interactionism*. For non-sociologists this term may seem like empty jargon, but to insiders it is very descriptive. It was coined in 1937 by Herbert Blumer,[24] who turned the pragmatist philosophy of his mentor George Herbert Mead into a new sociological theory, one that reaffirmed Weber's much-neglected focus on human meaning (Mead, 1934). For Mead the interpersonal behaviors of individuals were cognitively and highly adaptive responses to their social environments. Blumer adapted Mead's general philosophical approach for what he considered its fully scientific but utterly unique goal of understanding social processes in terms of the subjective meanings they have for individual human beings in their everyday lives. There are other representatives of this view—in addition to Mead one thinks here of the influential German philosopher and social theorist Jürgen Habermas (1984, 1987) as well as Erving Goffman (1958), Harold Garfinkel (1967), and their successors[25]—but Blumer's sociological application of Mead's philosophy of human interaction is still the most prominent version of the theory within the discipline of sociology. As we will see in the final chapter, it is also the theoretical scaffolding for the "post-critical" approach to cultural diversity that seems to be the next stage of multicultural education.

This approach is called "interactionism" because it begins with easily observable exchanges between concrete individuals such as you and me, that is, our face-to-face interactions, rather than with impersonal structural relationships supposed to exist within or between social institutions such as the legal system, schools, family lineages, voting practices, or property. Although these exchanges are between real people, they are not idiosyncratic, mysterious, or otherwise unanalyzable, but rather are organized, patterned, and recognizably purposeful. What makes our personal interactions interesting for sociological theory is, first of all, that they cannot be understood apart from the understandings that we have of our own social situations and, in consequence, our interpretation of the actions and events we produce (or will produce) in the course of dealing with others. However, they are even more interesting for a second reason. In symbolic interaction theory the face-to-face interactions that scholarly investigators observe are understood by them in the same way that the real-life participants understand them, namely in terms of the participants' own definitions of their respective situations. Consequently, interactionist theorists place far less importance than functionalists do on cross-situational norms, beliefs, and values; they look instead at the way real-life participants are constantly readjusting their responses to each other as well as to their new understandings of their continually changing situations.

In other words, symbolic interactionism sees members of society as creative *agents* who construct, or better co-construct, shared meanings that convert their common environment into a social world. This approach is, therefore, quite different from the top-down view of cultural symbols held by Durkheim and the structural functionalists who followed him, according to which culture supplies ready-made symbols designating the objective meanings needed for holding society together. For Mead conventional meanings were only "first drafts" that individuals revise as needed in order to make sense of their own experiences and actions as well as to interpret the communicative behaviors of the other persons with whom they are interacting.

Writing and teaching for over four decades after Mead's death in 1931, Blumer drove this point home even more clearly than his teacher ever did. He rejected the declining but still influential Parsonian paradigm and also the conflict view of culture that had made a comeback in the 1950s and 1960s. Those schemes, he complained, understood human society as "an established order of living, with that order resolvable to adherence to sets of rules, norms, values, and sanctions that specify to people how they are to act in their different situations" (1969, p. 18). It cannot be true, he insisted, that society is simply the expression of prefabricated cultural norms and other forms of joint action, since new situations constantly arise for which the established symbols are inadequate. Even in cases of what he called repetitive joint action—that is, when new interpersonal situations arise that are not particularly novel or problematic—each instance is formed anew. "The participants still have to build up their lines of action and fit them to one another through the dual process of designation and interpretation," he wrote. "Repetitive and stable joint action is just as much a result of an interpretative process as is a new form of joint action that is being developed for the first time" (ibid.). In short, interpretation is always involved since even the most familiar symbols are inherently ambiguous.

As far as I can tell, neither Mead nor Blumer ever published a formal definition of culture as such. However, from these and similar comments that they made over the years concerning the interpretive process through which signs become meaningful symbols and not just official icons or slogans, one can distill a symbolic interactionist definition of culture that revolves around what Blumer called the "root image" of the nature of human society. He insisted (as always, taking his cue from Mead) that human groups are made up of concrete human beings engaged in action, and so the starting and ending points of any empirical social theory (anthropological, sociological, or whatever) must be a picture of humans in action. The genius of Mead and Blumer was to recognize that this picture, like all pictures, is constructed by human beings. From this recognition it followed that an important part of any theory of human action is its analysis of the various ways to draw such a picture. It followed in turn that culture was a regressive concept that should be understood as both a cause and also a product of human interaction. From these conclusions Blumer arrived at a meta-level conception of culture as

❖FD2.13  a second-order conception that brings together various first-
order conceptions of the social world such as customs, traditional beliefs, norms, values, and rules, all of which are vehicles of meaning (symbols) generated by concrete individuals
in the course of living their group life. (Adapted from Blumer,
1969, pp. 6–7, 18)

In other words, the concept of culture is itself a symbol and hence suscep-
tible to multiple interpretations, negations, and reconstructions. However,
Blumer did not think that all of the first-order conceptions mentioned in
FD2.13 are equally adequate ways of understanding culture. He had deep
reservations about the long-term theoretical utility of all the "customary
sociological concepts of culture, structure, values, norms, status positions,
social roles, or institutions" (Blumer, 1981, p. 903). He felt that none of
these concepts caught what was essential in group life, namely its ongoing
activity. This point, emblematic of Mead's own pragmatic theory of knowledge, shaped the research designs of the classical interactionist sociologists.
It was developed in the same chapter of Blumer's *Symbolic Interactionism*
that is the source of FD2.13, where we also find this short but useful informal definition that clarifies his view that culture is a second-order concept:

❖ID2.13  Culture . . . is clearly derived from what people do. . . . A cardi-
nal principle of symbolic interactionism is that any empirically
oriented scheme of human society, however derived, must respect the fact that in the first and last instances human society
consists of people engaging in action. (Ibid., pp. 6–7)

Unfortunately, as he went on to say, this neglect of personal agency is
typical of the sociological theories of his time, which ascribe behavior to
external factors such as social status and cultural norms. Social interaction,
he complained, is reduced to "a mere forum through which sociological
or psychological determinants move to bring about given forms of human
behavior" (ibid., p. 7).

*The Cultural Studies Approach to Social Interaction.* Blumer's influence on
American sociology was considerable even though his was not the only
sociological reconstruction of Mead's philosophical pragmatism (role
theory was another; see Collins, 1994). However, about the same time
that Blumer wrote the passages just cited, another interactionist account of
culture was emerging, first in Britain and later in the United States under
the title "cultural studies." In its early, exclusively British phase sociologists
and humanities scholars associated with the Birmingham Centre for Contemporary Cultural Studies (and influenced by the left-leaning literary critic
Raymond Williams as well as the emerging postmodern literature) jointly

revisited the relationship between culture and social interaction. Working independently of American symbolic interactionists they arrived at many of the same conclusions regarding symbol production, but they took very different roads to get there.

What is interactive, both groups argued, are not personal exchanges but socioeconomic structures and culture. More precisely: social contexts are incorporated into cultural objects and practices, and these objects and practices have their impact on society precisely because people understand them as *texts*. To be meaningful, they argued, a text must have an internal structure or "inner logic," the most basic level of which is simply the function of a symbol to point at something beyond itself, which is to say its *referentiality*. Beginning with this basic principle, namely that texts are inherently referential (and hence symbolic), they concluded that sociologists have much to learn from literary theorists. What they said by way of developing this point went beyond the neo-Marxist and postmodernist views associated with the Birmingham Centre, and applied equally well to the more centrist views of American cultural studies theorists such as Herbert Gans (1988, 1999[1974]) who understood culture in terms of taste rather than ideology. Commenting on their approach the American sociologist Robert Wuthnow conceded that "[a] sociological theory of culture must . . . demonstrate greater awareness of textual construction itself: of genre, methods of objectification, voice, dialogue, interpolation and interpellation, textual authority, redundancy, embedding, parallels, and contrasts" (1992, p. 168).

By the middle or late 1980s the British cultural studies theorists (and later their American counterparts) had completely given up the view of culture as a code—analogous to a professional code of conduct, a genetic code, or even a translation code—that rules the social lives of individuals or the structures of society as a whole. They believed instead that their new conception of culture as an assemblage of texts called for a new methodology. Unlike cognitive anthropologists such as Goodenough or semiotic anthropologists such as Geertz these scholars did not try to discern a cultural code by means of field observation and ethnographic analysis, and unlike positivist sociologists they did not try to "read off" any such code from statistical data about behavioral patterns, values, attitudes, preferences, religious beliefs, or political engagements. Instead they examined the ways in which cultural symbols, objects and practices are *produced* by group activities—typically, the social interactions of middle-sized groups such as members of a given profession but sometimes those of larger groups such as the members of a socioeconomic class or the audiences reached by the mass media.

The cultural studies approach had a profoundly political dimension as well as the sociological one just described, thanks mainly to its overlap with the increasingly prominent literature of critical theory. Although it is difficult to track these and other currents of social thought in the 1980s, by the end of that decade cultural studies and critical theory had merged with the postmodernist philosophy of Jean-François Lyotard (1984) and other critics of the rationalist character of modern thought in order to challenge basic concepts in all fields of inquiry, including the concept of culture. The post-Geertzian anthropologists and symbolic interactionist sociologists mentioned above re-examined their own presuppositions, including those about the very legitimacy of their attempts to refine existing models of culture. As a result, for many cultural theorists of the late 1980s and 1990s the old debates such as those between Geertz and Goodenough or between Boasians and Parsonians were of purely historical interest, and the spotlight was on "writing against culture."[26] We will return to this literature later within the context of critical multiculturalist education, but it is worth noting here that the demise of culture is still on hold. It is easier to let go of specific conceptions of culture than it is to ignore the underlying need for an explanatory scheme that accounts for our seemingly natural experiences of communicative action, shared values, and other sorts of symbolic interaction. The flood of books and articles by anthropologists and others who claimed to be "writing against culture" seems to have crested but as we will see in the final chapter the culture concept itself is still at issue among educators as well as social theorists.

## SUMMARY

The strange career of culture is hardly over, but its so-called classical period came to an end a few years before the word "multiculturalism" was born. In the later decades of the 20th century, cultural anthropologists and sociologists broke away from the holism that flourished under Boas and his American successors, was challenged by the functionalism of Radcliffe-Brown and other British social anthropologists, and then was rehabilitated by Parsons and brought into a temporary alliance with other social sciences in his grand theory of action.

Subsequent developments produced more nuanced conceptions, and few would argue today that we should return to the old ways of thinking about culture. It is now generally agreed that culture is transmitted from one generation to the next neither biologically nor by simple diffusion or evolution, but rather semantically. That is, culture is a web of public meanings that are learned in roughly the same inherently social and interactive way that languages are learned, although the debate continues as to whether culture is best thought of as something between people or inside their heads. Whatever one thinks about that issue, the analogy between culturation and language acquisition is revealing, not only because language is itself a vehicle for transmitting cultural meanings (as well as being the product of other cultural influences) but also because it shows the intimate connection between one's (first) language and one's sense of self. Both are "internalized" in ways that go far beyond the simple acquisition of information or behavior patterns. Both shape the way one presents oneself to others. Perhaps most important of all, both culture and language are necessary and sometimes sufficient conditions for giving meaning and importance to life itself and for exposing the fault lines in the societies where we live our lives. For better or worse the literature of multicultural education has been deeply influenced by the classical anthropological and sociological conceptions of culture, and so anyone who wishes to understand the former literature should also understand something of the latter as well as something about the cognitive, interpretive, interactionist, and postmodern conceptions that are now common parlance among cultural anthropologists and sociologists.

As we have seen throughout this chapter and especially in the last few pages, over the last decades anthropology and sociology have taken on the job of moral critique, including critiques of the Eurocentric perspective from which social theory as we usually know it was invented. However, anthropology and sociology have been "moral sciences" from the outset, when Tylor resisted the racist paradigm of culture that had been in place since the discovery of the New World and Marx decried the alienation of humans from their labors. The next generation of social theorists was also motivated by moral concerns: Boasians asserted the equal dignity of otherwise incommensurable cultures and felt it their duty to preserve them in the face of the modern era's looming threats of extinction. Conflict theorists drew attention to power differentials, functionalists believed their analyses of cultures as structures would secure the moral values and beliefs that hold society together, and cultural psychologists looked for commonalities across national and racial lines. Cultural studies theorists, postmodernists, and critical theorists, all taking cues from the new humanistic approach associated with the interpretativists but also implicit in much of cognitive anthropology, re-valorized culture as an exercise of human creativity—a collective exercise but one with deeply personal implications for individual dignity and self-efficacy.

To these positive moral dimensions of culture theory I would add a negative one that maps onto what many consider the central agenda of multicultural education, namely the claim that no culture has the right to oppress another, either intellectually, politically, or economically. For this reason culture theorists such as Terence Turner (1993) or Shohat and Stam (1994) see a convergence of the critical wings of anthropology, sociology, and multiculturalism—a convergence in which culture is understood as capacity and empowerment. For instance Turner has singled out two features of the anthropological concept of culture that he thinks are particularly relevant to the relationship between anthropology and multiculturalism: the inherently *social character* of culture and its virtually infinite *plasticity*. "The capacity for culture," he writes, "is not inherent in individuals as such but arises as an aspect of collective social life with its concomitants of cooperative human and social reproduction. Its almost infinite malleability, however, means that there are virtually no limits to the kinds of social groups, networks, or relations that can generate a cultural identity of their own. . . . The point here is that multiculturalism in this larger theoretical and historical context implicitly becomes a program not merely for the equalization of relations among existing cultural groups and identities but for the liberation and encouragement of the process of creating new ones" (ibid., pp. 422–23).

## QUESTIONS FOR REFLECTION

Early in this chapter you read that to understand Ruth Benedict's holistic view of cultures one must know how her view went beyond E. B. Tylor's earlier view of cultures as stages of civilization. Now that you have finished this long chapter, recall the difference between Benedict's and Tylor's views of culture. Using Franz Boas as a transition figure, ask yourself how over two professorial generations Tylor's conception of culture as a stage-developmental process of civilization was replaced by Benedict's view that culture is "personality writ large." Be sure that you understand how her comparison of cultural wholes and psychological patterns differed from the cognitive accounts of culture developed in the wake of Talcott Parsons's structuralist functionalist paradigm of action.

Also, be sure that you understand just what a "holistic view" is, how it differs from "functional" and "cognitive" views, and why postmodern culture theorists find it so objectionable.

By the 1960s the "classical anthropology" of Boas and his followers was considered obsolete by professional anthropologists, but was taken very seriously by social activists during the civil rights era that ran into the mid-1970s. In your opinion, was this obsolescence primarily the result of heightened sensitivity to racial injustice or to new developments in culture theory such as Goodenough's cognitive anthropology in the 1960s and the appearance in 1973 of Geertz's hugely popular *Interpretation of Cultures*? Do you agree with Geertz's critique of Goodenough's cognitivism, which like Geertz's own view went far beyond the old idea of culture as a set of objectively observable traits?

As its title shows, Herbert Blumer's "symbolic interactionist" sociology emphasized symbols as much as Geertz's interpretive anthropology did. Ask yourself what are some of the differences between these two accounts of symbols and the semiotic dimension of culture. How relevant do you think this question is to the fact that Blumer was a sociologist and Geertz an anthropologist?

Be sure you understand why the many anthropologists who welcomed Geertz's interpretative anthropology in the 1970s severely criticized him in the 1980s. Was there a political edge to their critiques? Would it surprise you to learn that Geertz later accepted their criticisms as far as ethnographical practices were concerned but never considered himself a postmodernist or critical anthropologist?

Unlike earlier culture theorists, the American critical anthropologists of the 1980s and 1990s considered themselves a political force, for roughly the same reasons that animated the cultural studies theorists from the Birmingham Centre in England. What were those reasons? Do you consider it ironic that both national groups were deeply influenced by French postmodernist philosophy?

## NOTES

1. As its etymology shows, the term "culture" originally evoked the notion of *cultivation*, which itself evokes inherently developmental notions such as growth, maturation, and progress. It was therefore a short step from the original, biological idea of cultivating crops and other sorts of organisms (including the human body, the subject of what used to be called "physical culture") to the educational idea of developing or "cultivating" a person's mind or character. The supposedly universal methods and criteria for successful human development were rooted in Europe's ancient classics and the subsequent Judeo-Christian tradition. However, the term "culture" has its own complex developmental history, or as Michele Moody-Adams (1997) has put it, its own "strange career."

2. Max Weber is the exception here. As we will see, his definition of culture is much more philosophically nuanced than Tylor's, which is not surprising considering Weber's belief that our social life is shaped by morally charged and explicitly metaphysical worldviews such as the Protestant work ethic.

3. The brief survey of sociologists' use of the term "culture" around the 1920s provided by Kroeber and Kluckhohn in *Culture: A Critical Review of Concepts and Definitions* (1952, pp. 292 ff.) remains the best short historical account of this period.

4. Since the French word *conscience* can be translated as either "conscience" or "consciousness," Durkheim's term *la conscience collective* is often translated "collective consciousness" as well as "collective conscience." In any event, the reference

here is not to a specifically moral conscience but rather a general awareness of normative issues.

5. Although Simmel understood society in terms of intergroup conflict, his view of symbols is closer to that of his contemporary and personal friend Weber than to Marx's earlier notion of ideology.

6. On the general logic of development, see van Haaften, Korthals, and Wren, 1997.

7. Tylor's notion of cultural evolution, never entirely dead, was reincarnated a century later by Richard Dawkins (1976) and E. O. Wilson (Lumsden & Wilson, 1981) as a quasi-mathematical model analogous to contemporary genetic theory, with "memes"—analogues of genes—as the unit of analysis. The most effective opponent of this view is the well-known geneticist R. C. Lewontin (1991), who claims that science and society inevitably influence each other. It seems unlikely that this still-continuing debate will affect the literature and practices of multicultural education, owing to its highly technical nature as well as its apparent irrelevance to curricular and instructional issues. However, one never knows in advance how intellectual currents will affect each other or how they will enter into public discourse about society and education.

8. However, since Boas was a transition figure one can find (especially in his early writings) instances in which he reverts to the "evolutionary" or "humanist" concept of culture as civilization. The view of Boas as a transition figure is presented quite persuasively in Stocking (1966). Even at the end of his career Boas was willing to allow the possibility that cultural evolution theories contained some small kernel of truth (see Cook, 1999, ch. 6).

9. This famous characterization of the way diffusionists viewed cultures was suggested to Benedict by another student of Boas, Robert Lowie. It is also worth noting that Benedict's own dissertation, written under Boas a decade before her *Patterns of Culture* appeared, was firmly in the diffusionist tradition. On the transformation of her view of culture between 1923 and 1934, see Handler, 1990.

10. To illustrate this point in simple terms, we may consider three well-dressed gentlemen—Tom, Dick, and Harry—standing on a street corner. The methodological individualist believes this situation is fully accounted for if we trace the chain of events and motives that led each man to this corner: Tom is window shopping for his wife's birthday, Dick is looking for a taxi because he has an important appointment, Harry is a professional pickpocket looking for victims. A holistic account, in contrast, would go on to explain that this street corner is located in a high-end shopping district and hence attracts affluent shoppers, cruising taxis, and thieves who know how to blend in with their surroundings. In the latter account it is no coincidence that Tom, Dick, and Harry are all standing on the same corner. Each of their stories is part of a more comprehensive narrative.

11. An important exception who will be discussed in chapter 3 is the Australian theorist Brian Bullivant (1984; see pp. 2, 116).

12. Kroeber himself never quite sorted out the difference between psychological and cultural processes, or the relationship between them. As he grew less convinced by diffusionist accounts of how cultures spread, he became more critical of the psychologism that accompanied those accounts. For instance, he felt his mentor Boas

tended to explain the movement of cultural traits in terms of how people *thought* about them, as though a tribe adopted the long bow or some other weapon because it satisfied a felt need on the part of its members for aggressive activity, or a myth took hold because it corresponded to the awe people felt toward their natural environment or their emotional attachment to ideas they already had about how to live. Kroeber allied himself with Benedict when she described cultures as patterns, but he could not accept her view that culture was simply personality writ large.

13. Kroeber and Kluckhohn admitted that some mid-century cultural anthropologists shared the tendency of sociologists and social anthropologists to regard cultures as by-products or epiphenomena rather than as a source of human action, but in such views culture was supposedly derived "from the interaction of personalities as opposed to society as such" (1952, p. 179).

14. The influence of European structuralists such as Claude Lévi-Strauss and before him Ferdinand de Saussure, though considerable, is omitted here.

15. "Only by some such definition of its scope can anthropology become an analytical empirical science which is independent of both sociology and of psychology" (Parsons, 1951, p. 554).

16. For a more detailed account of these events and the relationship between Parsons and Kroeber, see Adam Kuper's several historical studies of anthropology, especially Kuper, 1999.

17. There was a middle period of conflict theory in the 1950s, but it had little to do with cultural differences (see Collins, 1994).

18. It was also the most influential work on these issues for multicultural educators of the 1970s such as Banks, Grant, and other prominent figures in what was then called the cultural pluralism movement (see Banks, 1974; Grant, 1977).

19. The full text is worth citing: "By the social structure of a society I mean the set of crystallized relationships which its members have with each other which places them in groups, large or small, permanent or temporary, formally organized or unorganized, and which relate them to the major institutional activities of the society, such as economic and occupational life, religion, marriage and the family, education, government, and recreation" (Gordon, 1964, pp. 30–31).

20. One of the earliest milestone markers was the resounding success of a conference that took place in Chicago in 1971 under the somewhat nervous auspices of the U.S. Office of Education (for details see Bigelow, 1971, and Rivlin & Fraser, 1973, pp. 4–7). The conference papers, most of which were later published in a book entitled *Cultural Pluralism in Education: A Mandate for Change* (Stent, Hazard, & Rivlin, 1973), made no attempt to provide a logical analysis or technical definition of the concept of cultural pluralism. The authors assumed, no doubt correctly, that because most of those attending were members of minority groups (mainly blacks, with some Chicanos) they and their primary audience already had a shared understanding of the meaning and practical urgency of this idea. The conference was supposed to lead to action, not theory, and that is what it did. On the last day, the "National Coalition for Cultural Pluralism" was formed spontaneously, in order to provide a broad base for future action, with representation from many ethnic groups and from many occupations. At the same time a "Temporary Steering Committee on Community Participation in Education" was also established to help the coalition define its structures and implement the hundred-plus recommenda-

tions that had been formulated during the Chicago conference. The starter's pistol had been fired for the multicultural education movement whose leaders had, so to speak, been waiting at the opening gate wearing the colors of cultural pluralism.

21. The distinction between cultural and cross-cultural psychology is much sharper now than it was sixty years ago, when universalism was the default assumption for all psychologists. Today cross-cultural psychology, also called comparative psychology, typically tries to determine similarities and differences in psychological functioning within two or three specific cultures, while cultural psychology, sometimes called indigenous psychology, aims to understand the general interdependence of mind and culture. Although exceptions abound, the rule of thumb is that cross-cultural psychologists begin with the assumption that basic cognitive processes are universal and then look for counterinstances, whereas cultural psychologists take a relativist position from the outset.

22. As the cultural psychologist Joan Miller has reported, in the literature of her discipline "it is assumed that culture and individual behavior cannot be understood in isolation yet are also not reducible to each other. Such a stance contrasts with the tendency particularly in early work in cross-cultural psychology, for culture and psychology to be understood as discrete phenomena, with culture conceptualized as an independent variable that impacts on the dependent variable of individual behavior" (Miller, 1997, p. 88).

23. There is an irony here, a type of performative contradiction. As Lila Abu-Lughod (1999a; 1999b) has noted, for many ethnic groups having a culture of their own is now politically crucial for their efforts to resist the homogenizing forces of globalization, even though these same groups, at the grassroots level as well as in the writings of contemporary postcolonial intellectuals, resist being studied as "specimens" of otherness.

24. "The term 'symbolic interactionism' is a somewhat barbaric neologism that I coined in an offhand way in an article written in *Man and Society* [1937]. . . . The term somehow caught on and is now in general use" (Blumer, 1969, p. 1n).

25. Later sociologists working with what might be called the classic symbolic interactionist model include Howard Becker, John Kitsuse, Malcolm Spector, and Randall Collins, to name just a few.

26. The reference is to the title of a well-known article by Abu-Lughod (1991, p. 138), who declared that "the notion of culture (especially as it functions to distinguish 'cultures'), despite a long usefulness, may now have become something anthropologists would want to work against in their theories, their ethnographic practice, and their ethnographic writing." Her remarks were directed to the post-Geertzian ethnographers who contributed to a volume entitled *Writing Culture* (Clifford & Marcus, 1986).

# 3

# Topical, Structural, and Functional Conceptions of Culture in the Professional Literature of Multicultural Education

The preceding review of paradigm shifts in anthropological and sociological conceptions of culture provides a knowledge base, or better, a roadmap, for the journey we will take in this and the next two chapters. That review as well as what we saw in the first chapter about formal and informal definitions will enable us to identify the various conceptions of culture used in the extensive literature of multicultural education. In other words, the themes and distinctions developed in the previous chapters can now be deployed in a content analysis that will reveal what might be called the intellectual topology of that literature. To this end I will use a template that divides the major anthropological and sociological conceptions of culture into nine ideal types, the first three of which will be discussed in this chapter and the others in chapters 4 and 5. Before getting into any of this, though, let us recall what was said in the opening chapter about the differences between the concept "culture" and the even broader concept "multicultural education."

We saw there that the everyday term "multicultural education" has many uses and meanings. We also saw why it would be a mistake to rank any one of these uses or meanings over the others as though it were some sort of transcendent standard in terms of which various curricula and pedagogies could be counted as more or less "authentic" instances of multicultural education. In the present chapter we will see how the same general points apply to the technical uses of the term "culture," which has its own complex history. Here the matter of meaning is much more problematic since, unlike multicultural education, culture is a theoretical construct, not a pedagogy or reform movement. Although there is no self-standing ideal of "Pure Culture" or "Culture As Such," and although the meaning of culture has changed over the years, anthropologists and other culture theorists are right to insist on the importance of having a clear and distinct idea of what it is they are investigating. In short, although multicultural education is an umbrella concept that includes anti-racist education, global studies, critical reconstruction, and other important agendas, its component concepts are not. Its umbrella stretches over a relatively small set of key concepts such as *race, gender,* and *culture* that are themselves technical terms borrowed from other disciplines for use in the various approaches to multicultural education. For the discourse that educators carry out within or about those approaches to be productive, the meanings of these terms must be as clear and stable as possible. This is not to say that there is (or should be) no variety in the way those terms are used, but only that variations should always be identifiable and coherent. Thus race theorists are careful to distinguish between the concepts of race and ethnicity, and gender theorists are equally careful to distinguish between gender and sex. In each case the underlying methodological assumption is that the use of key terms should be internally consistent and meaningfully distinct from other ways in which these key terms are used in everyday discourse. But is this a realistic expectation in the case of *culture?*

I think it is. Over the last two decades new, fine-grained conceptual models of culture have been constructed by social theorists talking to other social theorists. In contrast, the multicultural education literature, especially its teacher preparation materials, continues to treat culture in quite general and often ambiguous language. For this reason, this and the following chapters present an in-depth examination of the ways in which culture has been and continues to be portrayed in that literature. Using the basic principles of content analysis laid out in chapter 1, we will examine a number of definitions of culture featured in education textbooks and other preservice and inservice materials published since the beginning of the multicultural education movement. The hope is that sorting out the important but unacknowledged differences and implications running through these resources will help those who use them come to appreciate important distinctions and nuances that are not readily apparent.

## THE DEFINITIONAL MODES: FROM TYLOR TO THE PRESENT

The typology of what I call the "definitional modes" of the culture concept has its own modest history, which is worth a few comments before we actually apply them. As the early cultural pluralist educators moved beyond ethnic studies programs focused on single-groups to more inclusive multicultural agendas, their conceptions of culture multiplied, as did their debts—usually unacknowledged—to the social sciences. Considering that

E. B. Tylor's famous definition of culture as "that complex whole" continues to appear in virtually every introductory anthropology textbook, it is not surprising that it has also surfaced in many articles, textbooks, and monographs on multicultural education. What *is* a little surprising, though, is the absence in most of that literature (but see Gollnick and Chinn, 1994, p. 3) of any criticism of Tylor's hierarchical, undeniably ethnocentric view of culture as a linear progress to a final stage suspiciously similar to his own late Victorian England, in terms of which the various grades of culture "may be regarded as stages of development or evolution" (Tylor, 1873/1958, p. 1). Also surprising—though perhaps less so, considering the eclectic styles of most authors who write about education—is the fact that one seldom if ever finds a multicultural education text complaining about the unwieldy, laundry list character of Tylor's first, most famous sentence, which as we saw in chapter 2 was:

> Culture or Civilization, taken in its wide ethnographic sense, is that complex whole which includes knowledge, belief, art, morals, law, custom, and any other capabilities and habits acquired by man as a member of society.

Tylor's panorama of cultural traits includes ideational, behavioral, institutional, and material or artifactual features, as well as "any other" human capabilities except those inherited biologically. Though breathtakingly wide it offers no suggestion of any structure or hierarchy among these features, even though he did not hesitate just a few lines later to rank entire ways of life against each other. However, as we saw in the previous chapter subsequent generations of anthropologists and sociologists on both sides of the Atlantic strove to develop more systematic lists of cultural features. Although the complex whole that Tylor had in mind was the totality of human culture (generically, "civilization"), 20th-century social theorists localized the notion of culture such that each people was seen to have its own complexity and unity. With this shift, cultural complexity became a theme in its own right. Although it had different nuances from one theorist to the next depending on how they understood the dynamics of cultural evolution and diffusion, by mid-century there was universal agreement among anthropologists and sociologists that to the ingredients of culture such as those listed by Tylor there should be added meta-level features such as the patterning, integration, purpose, and functioning of those ingredients.

Of course none of these revisions took place formally, as though on some afternoon in the 1920s or 1930s a resolution were passed at an international congress of social scientists declaring that culture would no longer be understood as a thing of "shreds and patches"[1] but henceforth as a set of features that were somehow clustered and patterned, purposive and rank ordered. Even so, it is correct to say that when Kroeber and Kluckhohn's famous inventory of definitions of culture appeared in 1952 it was well received and immediately became the standard source for scholars probing the supposed "essential core" (ibid., p. 357) of the concept of culture. They reduced 164 definitions to a common denominator, which they proposed to their scholarly colleagues and the world at large as the definitive descriptive and prescriptive definition of culture on which future anthropological research should be based:

> Culture consists of *patterns*, explicit and implicit, of and for *behavior* acquired and transmitted by *symbols*, constituting the distinctive achievement of human groups, including their embodiments in *artifacts*; the essential core of culture consists of *traditional* (i.e., historically derived and selected) *ideas* and especially their attached *values*; culture systems may, on the one hand, be considered as products of action, on the other as conditioning elements of further action. (Ibid., italics added)

In this definition artifacts are mentioned, but only incidentally as embodiments of "the essential core of culture," which turns out to be a set of ideas and values that bear the pedigree of historical tradition. In fact the entire phenomenal side of culture—its products, symbols, and of course observable behaviors—is subordinated to the ideational side, which includes not only ideas and values but also the patterns and purposes discernable among these features. Most importantly, culture is understood as something real, capable of being a cause as well as an effect of human action.

Kroeber and Kluckhohn found patterns not only in culture but also among its many definitions, and assembled an extensive, complicated list of ways that scholars since Tylor had defined culture. Their list was later streamlined by John Bodley (1994) and revised slightly to include later developments in anthropology and sociology. I have revised it further (Table 3.1) in order to provide a template or framework for sorting out the various ways of defining culture that one finds in the literature of multicultural education. In this and the following chapters I will call these ways "definitional modes" and show how they shape formal and informal components of a few representative definitions culled from the theoretical and applied literature of multicultural education.

This table is, of course, only a brief snapshot of how scholars have understood culture since Tylor, and there is no reason to believe these nine ways of defining culture are the only possible definitional modes. Much of the recent work on culture also fits into these categories, but in the late 20th century many anthropologists and other social scientists proposed critiques of the uses to which the concept of culture is put by those in power, after which they moved on to a more radical questioning of the notion of culture altogether, as we saw at the end of chapter 2. Like postmodern critics from cultural studies and other academic disciplines, they have found it

**Table 3.1.   Nine Ways of Defining Culture (Definitional Modes)**

| | |
|---|---|
| 1. Topical | Culture consists of everything specified on a list of topics or general categories such as "ingredients," "cultural traits," or "attributes." (E. B. Tylor) |
| 2. Structural | Culture is an integrated pattern of ideas or behaviors. (F. Boas) |
| 3. Functional | Culture is the way individuals or societies solve problems of adapting to the environment or living together. (A. R. Radcliffe-Brown, T. Parsons) |
| 4. Historical | Culture is a group's shared heritage. (A. Kroeber and C. Kluckhohn) |
| 5. Normative | Culture is a group's ideals, values, or rules for living. (T. Parsons) |
| 6. Behavioral | Culture is shared, learned human behavior, a publicly observable way of life. (W. Goldschmidt) |
| 7. Cognitive | Culture is a complex of ideas and attitudes that inhibit impulses, establish shared meanings and goals, and enable people to live in a social system. (W. Goodenough) |
| 8. Symbolic | Culture is a set of shared, socially constructed representations and meanings. (C. Geertz) |
| 9. Critical | Culture consists in those symbols and symbol-making activities that typically reflect and promote a society's current power relationships. (R. Rosaldo) |

difficult to make their case without using the very concepts they mean to expose. Their "writing against culture" is often paradoxical and larded with elusive tropes and jargon (such as the word "trope"). To put it mildly, most postmodernist studies of culture, including those written by hardheaded anthropologists and sociologists, are not exactly straightforward or immediately useful to classroom teachers or other school personnel. For this and other reasons, the tendency of many social scientists to critique or deconstruct the very idea of culture has not had much influence on the theory or practice of multicultural education, except in the case of critical multiculturalists, whose own influence in educational circles is now considerable. Accordingly, I have included the "critical mode" in the list of definitional modes, and will go on to show in the final chapter that its perspective ought to be taken very seriously by multicultural educators.

## SOME (FOR THE MOST PART) TEXTBOOK CASES

Thematic content analysis is important for many reasons. One is that it is based on a conviction that readers of a second-order study like this one have a right to see the textual evidence for its claims, especially when the subject matter is as extensive and varied as the literature of multicultural education. I also believe that analyzing a few examples of each definitional mode will help those others who read that literature navigate through what might otherwise seem to be either a wasteland or a jungle. The match

between the nine definitional modes listed in Table 3.1 and the texts examined in the following pages is sometimes imperfect, since the authors of
those texts did not design their definitions to fit into one or another box on
that table. It is my hope, nonetheless, that examining even these imperfect
matches will reveal the logical geography of contemporary multicultural
scholarship, especially its uses and abuses of the concept of culture.

As in all geographies, the mappings that follow are sharper and simpler
on paper than in real life. As explained in chapter 1, the contrast between
formal and informal definitions is only a heuristic device designed to help
the reader, not a prescription that authors are expected to follow. Furthermore, the formal/informal contrast can be more or less complex, as we will
see in the pages that follow. Each analysis begins by citing the formal and
informal components of a prominent multiculturalist's definition of culture and then identifying their respective definitional modes. For example,
the mode of its formal component may be topical and the mode of its informal component may be structural or even, say, structural and behavioral.
Bimodal or multimodal combinations like these are not uncommon, and
they are usually easy to identify once one learns what to look for.

Two more general comments are in order before we set out on our journey through the sometimes confusing literature of multicultural education.
The first is that the definitions I have selected as exemplars of the various
conceptions of culture come from every decade of the multicultural movement (including the early 1970s when it was usually called "cultural pluralism"). Many of the older definitions are still cited in the current editions
of multicultural education textbooks as though the concept of culture had
never been modified or challenged by anthropologists or cultural sociologists. The contrast between treatments of culture in that literature and
scholarly discussions in, say, the American Anthropological Association's
*Anthropology and Education Quarterly* is, to my mind at least, often striking.

The second comment is that the expression "way of defining X" has two
meanings, one substantive and the other procedural. In the first case, the
way one defines X simply *is* the definition of X (that is, it is the meaning or
content of the definition). In the second case, it is the *definitional mode itself*
(that is, it is the method or approach that one uses to define X). The subject
of our inquiry is the second of these two senses.

1. Topical Definitions *(Culture consists of everything specified on a
list of topics or general categories such as "ingredients," "cultural traits,"
or "attributes.")*

The first way to define culture that we will consider is the topical list,
which deploys the idea of cultural traits introduced in chapter 2. Each of
the three examples I have selected are bimodal or multimodal in the sense

explained above, and can be charted as follows. (I will begin each of the following sections with this sort of chart.)

| Authors | Mode of Formal Component | Mode of Informal Component |
|---|---|---|
| Banks (3.1) | Topical | Structural |
| Nieto (3.2) | Topical | Topical and Structural |
| Spring (3.3) | Topical | Cognitive |

Our first example of a primarily topical approach to culture is an often-cited formal definition proposed by James Banks in a short but influential paper that he presented at several multicultural education conferences in the late 1970s and later published as the lead article of a special issue of *The Journal of Negro Education* devoted to "Multicultural Education in the International Year of the Child" (Banks, 1979a).[2]

❖FD3.1   Culture consists of the behavior patterns, symbols, institutions, values and other human-made components of society. (Ibid., p. 238)

Unlike Kroeber and Kluckhohn's otherwise very similar list, the wording of Banks's 1979 definition implies that his list is complete rather than merely illustrative. However, except for this probably unintended difference, FD3.1 simply repackages Kroeber and Kluckhohn's earlier conception of culture. A more significant difference appears in the accompanying informal definition (ID3.1), where Banks redescribes his conception of culture in holistic, structural terms, according to which it is a Chinese box of assorted "micro cultures":

ID3.1   It [culture] is the unique achievement of a human group which distinguishes it from other human groups. While cultures are in many ways similar, a particular culture constitutes a unique whole. Thus culture is a generic concept with wide boundaries. Consequently, we can describe the United States [as having a] macro culture as well as the micro cultures within it. . . . These cultures may be social class cultures, regional cultures, religious cultures, and national cultures. (Ibid., pp. 238–39)

We saw in the opening chapter that the multicultural education movement has room for many different agendas, ranging from the relatively apolitical goals of mosaic or salad bowl multiculturalism to the stridently reformist or quasi-revolutionary goals of what is now called critical multiculturalism. Within this complex literature, formal definitions of key concepts such as culture sometimes reflect an author's specific educational agenda but not always, especially when culture is understood in the open-ended way characteristic of purely topical definitions such as Banks's FD3.1. Such definitions are so general that they often seem compatible with virtually any multicultural education program. However, this is not always the case, especially when a topical definition such as Banks's FD3.1 is supplemented by an informal definition such as his ID3.1. In this instance the structuralist character of Banks's informal definition offsets the otherwise loose, topical character of his formal definition by insisting that cultures have their own internal complexity and corresponding inequities.[3]

Another frequently cited topical definition of culture comes from Sonia Nieto's *Affirming Diversity*, which first appeared in 1992 and as of now has gone through multiple editions. Her definition, which also appears in her other writings such as *The Light in Their Eyes* (2010), declares that

❖FD3.2     Culture can be understood as the ever-changing values, tradi-
            tions, social and political relationships, and worldview created,
            shared, and transformed by a group of people bound together
            by a combination of factors that can include a common his-
            tory, geographic location, language, social class, and religion.
            (Nieto, 1992, p. 129)

Nieto immediately unpacks this definition in a short commentary that is itself a model of what I am calling informal definitions:

ID3.2     As is clear from this definition [that is, FD3.2], culture is com-
            plex and intricate; it includes content or product (the what
            of culture), process (how it is created and transformed), and
            the agents of culture (who [are] responsible for creating and
            changing it). Culture cannot be reduced to holidays, foods,
            or dances, although these are, of course, elements of culture.
            This definition also makes it clear that everyone has a culture,
            because all people participate in the world through social and
            political relationships informed by history as well as by race,
            ethnicity, language, social class, gender, sexual orientation, and
            other circumstances related to identity and experience. (Ibid.)

Like her topical formal definition, ID3.2 is a list of cultural traits but Nieto goes on to tell us how they are ordered and why. For this reason her informal definition is no mere laundry list since it also explains how the items mentioned (the "what," "how," and "who" of culture) are so-cially mediated and, for that reason, constitute one's personal identity and interpersonal relations. For this reason the informal component of her definition of culture is probably best thought of as a hybrid of the topical and structural modes. Its most important point is probably that although cultural traits such as holidays, foods, and dances are indeed "elements" of culture (and hence not mere by-products), culture cannot be reduced to these or (presumably) any other such traits.

Some might complain that Nieto's distinction between the contents, processes, and agents of a culture is a bit too quick, since it fails to add that culture is itself the process that produces our cultural contents and channels our personal agency. To this complaint others (I am one of them) might reply that a closer reading of this and her other books would show that she does indeed see culture as primarily a process and only secondarily a set of products and agents. However, this is not the place for such a debate, since our concern in these pages is the much more modest one of identifying the different ways in which culture is actually defined in the existing educational literature.

A very different sort of topical list appears in another widely used teacher preparation text, Joel Spring's *The Intersection of Cultures* (2008). Here the news is not so good. On the very first page Spring serves up a virtually useless pro forma definition of culture, reeling off a quick list of cultural traits that constitutes his official definition of the term:

❖FD3.3 "Culture" here refers to socially transmitted behavior patterns, ways of thinking and perceiving the world, arts, beliefs, institutions, and all other products of human work and thought. (Ibid., p. 3)

It is hard to tell what led Spring to include these but not other equally prominent ingredients of culture such as language and ritual, and even harder to see just what constraints if any this loose list puts on his subsequent analysis of and prescriptions for multicultural education.[4] What we can learn from this example, though, is that in the literature of multicultural education, especially its preservice textbooks, not all definitions of culture are equal, and that some are simply irrelevant window dressing. In other words, what purports to be a definition of culture is not always a useful introduction to an author's substantive views about culture and the cultural issues involved in multicultural education. However, in fairness to Spring we should note that later in his book he does get down to brass tacks, drawing from cognitive anthropology and cultural psychology the important psychological concept of *cultural frames*,[5] which turns out to be the unifying theme for his book. He never returns to the formal definition of culture with which his book opened, and apparently feels no need to do so in order to flesh out his cultural frame theory. However, the second item listed in FD3.3, which was "ways of thinking and perceiving the world," provides a tenuous link between his definition of culture and his idea of cultural frames.

Even so, it seems odd to collapse the distinction between cultures and cultural frames since it is *through* such frames (also described as filters or lenses) that cultures are understood. The difference is never clearly spelled out, though, and Spring sometimes eliminates the distinction altogether, suggesting that culture is itself a frame or series of frames. Under the latter interpretation the following passage could be interpreted somewhat generously (it appears more than a hundred pages later) as his informal definition of the concept of culture. He says that it is through cultural frames that one sees the world, and then adds the important but often neglected point that a person can employ more than one cultural frame:

⋯❀⋯ID3.3    Cultural frames of reference [include] ways of seeing, knowing, and interrelating with the world. . . . In a multicultural society such as the United States, there can be frequent switching of cultural frames, creating the phenomenon of biculturalism or the multicultural mind. A person growing up in a multicultural society might learn to live in two different cultures. However, some people in multicultural societies are socialized for a single culture, and they filter their information through the lens of that single culture. This is referred to as *monoculturalism*. To a certain extent, all people learn to function in different cultural contexts. (Ibid., pp. 119–120)

Here Spring uses a simplified version of the cognitive schema theory described in chapter 2 to develop his important insight that a single person can embody several cultures. He argues that in our contemporary society thoroughly monocultural individuals are increasingly rare. Given that a cultural perspective is an individual's unique combination of lenses that selectively reveal the social world, one person could interpret the world through a cultural frame whose filters are female, upper-class, bicultural, and shaped by a particular understanding of history. Another person with different filters might be mainly monocultural but having a different understanding of history, and so on. "The sharing of perspectives," Spring concludes, "can give a person a group identity. On the other hand, the unique combination of lenses can create an individual identity" (pp. 138–139). The possibilities seem endless.

*Discussion:* The topical definition approach to culture is common in the multicultural education literature but its usefulness varies. Books and articles that define culture in the everything-but-the-kitchen-sink fashion do not offer their readers much if any information about their authors' own conceptions of culture beyond the insight, striking in Tylor's day but not in ours, that culture is not biologically inherited. It is only when authors of topical definitions go beyond open-ended lists to offer more informative informal definitions or side comments that their discussions of culture are useful for aspiring or practicing multicultural educators. For instance, after Banks offers his structuralist informal definition (ID3.1) he draws the conclusion that because "culture" is the root of "multicultural," the agenda of multicultural education is related to a range of cultural groups, such that a "major aim" of multicultural education is to enable students to function competently in diverse culture environments, as well as to reform the school environment so that students from those environments are equally accommodated. Unfortunately, how this important goal is related to his conception of culture is never explained, nor is the relation between school reform and societal reform.

In other words, authors who construct formal definitions of culture in the topical mode do not seem to favor any particular educational approach to multicultural issues, which is hardly surprising since there are no limits on which cultural traits can be cited in a topical list. The examples just cited originally appeared in textbooks that proposed three quite different educational agendas. (1) In 1979, when Banks proposed FD3.1, he was still using a culture-with-subcultures model of American culture within which the point of multicultural education was to enable children to function successfully on both the macro and micro levels of civic life; to this end he argued that American schools should promote cultural literacy and respect for the cultural integrity of other micro cultures. (2) Nieto's agenda is expressed in her well-known title *Affirming Diversity*, since her announced goal is to correct assimilationist-based inequities in our educational system through culturally responsive teaching and culturally democratic learning environments. (3) Spring's general educational agenda is directed toward cultural identity and social critique and has little or no connection with the largely irrelevant topical list that he provides at the beginning of his book.

Finally, two general points can be made about the educational implications of this first definitional mode. One is pedagogical and the other is metatheoretical, but each applies to all of the many topical definitions of culture I have found in the educational literature. The first point is that multicultural agendas for which a topical definition of culture is an author's true point of departure and not mere window dressing presuppose that cultures are interesting for their own sake, that cultural knowledge is a proper object for multicultural pedagogy, and that cultural pluralism is quite literally a respect for other *cultures* as well as for the individuals who participate in them. However—and this is my second point—what is most striking about these and most of the other topical definitions of culture one finds in the literature of multicultural education is not what they include but what they omit, namely any suggestion that the various cultural traits which they mention are related to each other by some overarching theory of culture.[6] The topical definitions of culture that I have found in the literature of multicultural education are far more eclectic than the anthropological definitions catalogued by Kroeber and Kluckhohn. Here again we see the difference between multicultural education and social theory as such—by which I mean primarily anthropology but also sociology and cultural studies when they step back to thematize culture. The former is a reform movement whereas the latter is a family of scholarly disciplines. Social theorists' definitions of culture are designed to delimit and organize their subject matter and thereby streamline future research, whereas multiculturalists' definitions, especially those that take the form of topical lists, often seem designed to include as much as possible in hopes that everyone will find something in them that sounds familiar and pedagogically useful. Fortunately, this is not always the case.[7]

## 2. Structural Definitions *(Culture is an integrated pattern of ideas or behaviors.)*

Many definitions of culture that include lists of cultural traits also show how those traits fit together as a more or less holistic "way of life," in which case it may be hard to determine whether the definitional mode is primarily topical or structural.[8] To put it gently, the structural definitions of culture found in the literature of multicultural education have varying levels of organization and determinateness. Some structuralist formulations stress organizational features such as pattern, coherence, and interdependence of the parts more than others do, but there is no sharp dividing line between topical and structural definitions of culture. As I see it, the most we can say is that since structural definitions of culture *emphasize* structure and pattern, they are likely to list multiple cultural traits or "topics" in their general mode of presentation, even though the line between structural and topical definitions is not always easy to draw (as when Banks characterized cultures as "unique wholes" in ID3.1). In short, holism admits of degrees.

What Kroeber and Kluckhohn said six decades ago about anthropologists of their day also applies to contemporary mainstream multicultural educators: "There are probably few contemporary anthropologists who would reject completely the proposition 'A culture is the distinct way of life of a people,' though many would regard it as incomplete" (1952, pp. 98–99). When Tylor called culture "that complex whole" he meant only that culture is complicated, not that its components are integrated into an organic structure or system. In contrast, the later Boas and his followers argued that cultures are distinct, internally coherent and incommensurable unities, each having its own pattern, design, organization, and so on. (Recall the contrast Benedict (1934) drew in her aptly titled *Patterns of Culture* between the Apollonian culture of the Zuni Pueblos and the Dionysian culture of the surrounding Plains Indians, as well as Herskovits's [1958] various accounts of organizing themes in African cultures.) Although by 1970 anthropology had gone well beyond the Boasians' strong incommensurability view of cultural difference, their influence on the early cultural pluralists was profound, especially though by no means exclusively their influence on black and Native American educators of the 1970s and 1980s. From the premise that cultures could not be ranked against each other, cultural pluralists concluded that all cultures are equally deserving of respect and, most important of all, that every group of people who share a culture—and by extension, every person in those groups—is equally worthy of respect and equally entitled to an adequate education and other public goods.

As in the previous section, the definitions I have selected exhibit a variety of definitional modes. At the risk of gross oversimplification I have charted them as follows, though I have no idea of how their authors would feel about this scheme:

| Authors | Mode of Formal Component | Mode of Informal Component |
| --- | --- | --- |
| Adler (3.4) | Structural | Structural |
| Shade et al. (3.5) | Structural | Cognitive |
| Cartledge & Feng (3.6) | Structural and Topical | Structural |

During the 1970s the idea of specifically *cultural* equality also began to circulate among educators who had no personal stake in the black struggle for equity and who did not identify themselves as cultural pluralists. Becoming what Peter Adler (2007) once called "a multicultural man"—later revised as "a multicultural person"—came to be seen as a matter of personal growth as well as a social justice issue. In a frequently reprinted essay originally written for communication scholars as well as professional educators, Adler combines the classical Boasian idea of culture as structure with an account of psychosocial development (Singer, 1971) in order to explain just what is involved in becoming a multicultural person. His essay includes a formal definition of culture that runs as follows:

❖FD3.4    Culture, the mass of life patterns that human beings in a given society learn from their elders and pass on to the younger generation, is imprinted in the individual as a pattern of perceptions that is accepted and expected by others in a society. (Adler, 2007, p. 230)

After a short discussion of cultural identity as the ongoing experience of incorporating the worldview and other elements of a given culture, Adler makes it clear that the "mass of life patterns" mentioned in FD3.4 has its own logic and structure. In a short but revealing informal definition of culture (ID3.4), he summarizes the logical, moral, and psychological implications of his conception of culture in three basic postulates that follow from his view that culture is a socially constructed pattern of perceptions as well from his understanding of psychosocial development:

❖ID3.4    1. Every culture has its own internal coherence, integrity, and logic.
2. No one culture is inherently better or worse than another.
3. All persons are, to some extent, culturally bound. (Ibid., p. 236)

That each culture has its own unique structure and worth is of course the classical structuralist view of Boas and his followers, according to which each culture has a unique pattern. What Adler adds to that view is the claim that his three postulates are "fundamental to success in cross-cultural adaptation" and should be internalized and reflected in the thinking and behavior of any "multicultural person," including any student whose cross-cultural experience includes a properly delivered multicultural education.

A more extensive example of the structuralist approach is provided by Barbara Shade and her co-authors Cynthia Kelly and Mary Oberg (1997), who answer their own question "What is culture?" with a freewheeling survey that conflates not only the usually distinct ideas of culture and social system but also the structural and cognitive modes. Echoing Benedict's remark that culture is "personality writ large," they conclude their survey with an image of culture as a systematized pattern of thought that serves as a collective selection mechanism or filter.[9]

❖FD3.5    Culture is a *social system* that represents an accumulation of beliefs, attitudes, habits, values, and practices that serve as a filter through which a group of people view and respond to the world in which they live. (Ibid, p. 18, italics added)

As the authors immediately explain, they have based their definition on the work of post-Boasian cognitive sociologists for whom culture is a set of invisible patterns that have become normal ways of acting, feeling, and being (Maehr, 1974), or as one of their sources puts it, "a group's preferred way of perceiving, judging, and organizing the things they encounter in their daily lives" (Hall, 1989).[10] Following this path Shade and her colleagues proceed to amplify their structuralist formal definition (FD3.5) of culture as a social system with an informal definition in the cognitive mode (ID3.5). There they introduce a set of cognitive categories that they will eventually deploy in an extensive comparison of culture-specific types of student-school communication and other forms social interaction:

❖ID3.5     Thus, culture represents a collective consciousness or a group state of mind. If people in a group share situations and problems . . . they develop a common way of speaking, acting, thinking, and believing. As the behavior is institutionalized through intergenerational transmission, it becomes culture. (Shade, Kelly, & Oberg, p. 18)

It is worth noting that their structuralist conception of culture involves no suggestion of any sort of primordial reality or group essence. For Shade, Kelly, and Oberg, what binds a group together is the simple fact that its members "share situations and problems." Although some multicultural educators who understand cultures as holistic structures represent culture in unapologetically essentialist terms, we must not forget that structure and essence are independent concepts. Culture can be understood as a structure that is not an essence (that is, as a socially constructed system) or vice versa as an essence that is not a structure (that is, as a primordial but indeterminate quality).[11] However, this is not the place to lament such naïveté. What is important in the present context is the fact that even though most contemporary multicultural educators are probably too sophisticated to fall into the trap of thinking that cultural differences are due to some mysterious X-ness, many understand culture as in some sense a single thing that is greater than the sum of its parts, the proper understanding of which requires a knowledge of how its component features are related to each other as well as what they are in themselves. We have already considered Adler's neo-Boasian claim that each culture has its own internal coherence, integrity, and logic. Gwendolyn Cartledge and Hua Feng have a similar view, which as they explain was derived from structuralist anthropologists who

❖FD3.6     define culture as the way of life of a particular group of people, including such dimensions as their traditions, language, religion, marital and family life, values, and organization of the economic system. (Cartledge & Feng, 1996, pp. 13–14)

The anthropologists whom Cartledge and Feng have in mind include Peoples and Bailey (1991), whose structuralist conception of culture as a "webbed system" they borrow in the course of filling out the way-of-life conception of culture proposed in FD3.6. As they go on to explain,

❖ID3.6     Culture is integrated. It is like a webbed system, in which various aspects of life are interconnected. The various components of culture are not discrete but interactive. Kinship, economic, and religious subsystems, for example, all affect one another and cannot be understood in isolation. (Cartledge & Feng, 1996, p. 14).

*Discussion:* At this point one might ask just how the structuralist definitions reviewed here correlate with educational agendas. For the authors of the structuralist definitions just cited, the main answer to this question is roughly the same: they want to develop general cultural knowledge across the student population and thereby increase the self-esteem of minority students. This is the agenda Adler proposed under the rubric of the "multicultural personality." A related agenda popular in the 1970s and 1980s was to promote social justice by simply increasing children's cross-cultural competence, but it was later criticized for its lack of any serious critique of existing social structures. Obviously it is difficult—sometimes even misleading—to completely disentangle these very interdependent goals. Cartledge and Feng's book is a case in point. Their discussion of culture constitutes the first part of a chapter entitled "The Relationship of Culture and Social Behavior," the central idea of which is that as a society becomes more diverse, cultural background becomes increasingly important as a means for interpreting and addressing behavioral differences among students. However, the rest of their book deals with the quite different issue of the link between cultural identity and self-perception. The hidden curriculum of our schools, they insist, "affects the way students view themselves, relate to peers, and deal with academic learning" (p. 40). By the end of the chapter the authors have come a long way from their introductory, relatively abstract and idealized conception of culture as an integrated, webbed system. They finish with concrete proposals for assessing culturally specific social skills among fifth-graders and corresponding intervention strategies. Even so, they have remained squarely within the structuralist paradigm of classical anthropology according to which, as Boas argued so vigorously, each culture has its own unity and hence its own criteria for social competence and moral excellence.

   In the abstract, none of these educational goals is objectionable, though of course educators have significantly different views on how they should be prioritized, combined, or pursued. However, two unfortunately common epistemological assumptions should be identified. The first is the assumption that cultures are inherently stable, either because cultures are by definition static ("This is our way!") or because when cultural change does occur it comes from within. In the latter case, change is regarded as merely a matter of retrieval ("Going back to our roots") or a new social or physical environment (the emergence of the "new American" in the melting pot account), or else a set of minor adjustments (culture as a self-correcting, homeostatic system). This is not so much a criticism of those authors as a caution about any strong structuralist model of culture, which has little room for novelty and even less room for hybridity in any serious sense of that term. In the eyes of structuralists, changes caused by external events, such as population shifts, technological advances, or economic pressures, are ruptures, not progress. (For the moment it is enough to identify this assumption, but I will challenge it in the final chapter.)

The second unfortunate assumption in strong structuralist discussions of culture is that cultures can be equated with an ethnic or any other type of human group, for example Hispanic culture with Hispanics. This is a category mistake, not a factual error. Its danger is that well-meaning educators might forget that *cultures are not people or groups of people,* but rather constructions made by theorists (including ordinary lay observers as well as professional scholars, teachers, and fieldworkers) in order to account in a tidy and interesting way for differences between more or less (usually less) easily circumscribed groups. To say otherwise would be to commit what philosophers sometimes call the fallacy of misplaced concreteness. Although the term "culture" can be used in many ways, it is extremely misleading and counterproductive to identify culture with real people or with groups of people who share a culture or even a subset of cultural traits. Nor should culture be thought of as a free-standing reality analogous to the so-called cultural objects that anthropologists love to study, namely pots, rituals, sacred texts, and so on. So put, my point may seem boringly straightforward, but multicultural educators who use the term "culture" in their work as scholars or teachers face an enduring temptation to reify it. The temptation is especially strong when culture is understood as an integrated structure, as is the case in many books and articles that focus on the education of ethnic minority children.[12] Clearly, the different needs (and strengths) of minority children are always matters of great complexity and delicacy, but especially when cultures are represented as closed structures rather than as, say, open-textured symbol systems.

3. Functional Definitions *(Culture is the way individuals or societies solve problems of adapting to the environment or living together.)*

The concept of structure is closely allied to the concept of *function.* We saw this in the last section as well as in the discussions in chapter 2 of the anthropological theories of Malinowski and Radcliffe-Brown and the structural functionalism of mid-century sociologists such as Parsons. In all these cases culture was understood functionally, though with different understandings of just *which* function a culture is supposed to fill. Malinowski understood culture as the *members-functional* way in which practices and institutions shape and satisfy the basic human needs of individuals, but he did not attend to the structural relationships that exist among those needs or among the cultural elements that satisfy them. For Radcliffe-Brown and Parsons, on the other hand, culture was the *group-functional* way in which social systems preserve themselves, and each component or subsystem—religion, marriage, kinship system, etc.—was itself an institutional structure that holds the society in equilibrium. However, the distinction between the two sorts of functionalism is not so sharp in the definitions of culture provided by multicultural educators.

Here again we begin with a chart of the mix of definitional modes used in three representative definitions:

| Authors | Mode of Formal Component | Mode of Informal Component |
|---|---|---|
| Bullivant/Banks (3.7) | Functional | Functional |
| Hoopes & Pusch (3.8) | Structural | Topical and Functional |
| Mitchell & Salsbury (3.9) | Structural | Functional |

In the literature of multicultural education the most prominent functional definition of culture is probably still the one proposed by the influential Australian educator and anthropologist Brian Bullivant (1993).[13] Like Radcliffe-Brown and other social anthropologists, he regards culture as an abstract "design" rather than a group of flesh and blood human beings or their day-to-day practices. "We cannot emphasize the correct usage enough," he cautions his readers. "People belong to, live in, or are members of social groups; they are not members of cultures" (1993, p. 30).[14] On the first page of his influential essay, he offers a concise formal definition that is unambiguously functional since it specifies what cultures *do* for us. Culture, he tells us, is simply

❖FD3.7    a social group's design for surviving in and adapting to its environment. (Ibid., p. 29)

The rest of Bullivant's essay is an extended informal definition in which he explains the three environment types he has in mind and the relationship of culture to its "expressions," namely knowledge, ideas, behaviors, and artifacts. It can be summarized as follows:

❖ID3.7    Culture is a shared survival plan whereby a group adapts to (1) the geographical environment, or physical habitat; (2) the social environment, which includes the customs and rules that enable various scales of human interaction to be carried on smoothly; and (3) the metaphysical environment, which is dealt with by religious beliefs and institutions. Since culture is a "shared survival plan," it should not be identified with either the group or its behaviors and artifacts, which for all their importance are nevertheless only the *expressions* of culture. This is not to minimize the importance of behaviors and artifacts for the ethnologist, for whom they along with the more abstract survival plan or "cultural form" are the material out of which the "thick descriptions" examined by Geertz are to be constructed. (Compare ibid., pp. 30–35)

Bullivant is not the only multicultural educator who conceives culture as an environment-response system. About the same time that educators in the English-speaking world began reading his work, a similar theme was sounded by the education and communication theorists David Hoopes and Margaret Pusch (1979). At first sight their conception of culture seems confused: an almost vacuous formal definition cast in the structural mode is followed by an informal definition that is simultaneously topical and functional. However, this is one of those places in educational theory where the authors' ideas are better than their prose styles. Closer inspection shows that Hoopes and Pusch's conception of culture is actually quite coherent, though not as well-written as it could have been. They open their discussion with a very general formal definition to the effect that a culture is a set of "ways"—that is, patterns or structures—within which people live their lives:

❖FD3.8     *Culture* is the sum total of ways of living. (Ibid., p. 3)

Here the vague little word "way" is used in the plural, but as the word itself indicates, each of the constituent ways has its own integrity, as does the totality which they constitute. Admittedly, if we read FD3.8 by itself then the "sum total"—that is, culture—could be understood as either an unstructured aggregate or as a structured whole. However, the authors immediately clarify their formal definition by an informal definition (ID3.8) that describes these culture-constituting "ways" in both structural and functional terms. The so-called "ways of living" turn out to be coordinated parts of a complex whole that is itself a collective and purposive response to the environment. The response consists in

❖ID3.8     values, beliefs, esthetic standards, linguistic expression, patterns of thinking, behavioral norms, and styles of communication *which a group of people has developed to assure its survival in a particular physical and human environment.* . . . Culture is the response of a group of human beings to the valid and particular needs of its members. It, therefore, has an inherent knowledge and an essential balance between positive and negative dimensions. (Ibid., italics added)

There is an important complexity hidden in Hoopes and Pusch's environment-response account of culture. In the first part of their informal definition, the "ways of living" assure the survival of the group, but in the second part they respond to the needs of the individual members of the group. In other words, culture is defined first vaguely as some sort of totalized structure (FD3.8), then described in terms of its group-functionality (the italicized clause in ID3.8), and finally in terms of what it does for the group's members. Two pages later the authors try to reconcile these two sorts of functionality with another pair of brief considerations that are respectively members-functional and system-structural. The first is that although the principal function of culture is to ensure the survival of the group, it exercises that function in terms of the needs of its individual members. The second consideration, which illustrates the general tendency of functionalists to incorporate structural categories into their explanations, is that culture possesses "an inherent logic and an essential balance between positive and negative dimensions" (p. 5). Unfortunately, we are never told what that logic is or how it holds the group or its culture in equilibrium.

Other functional conceptions of culture that also include structural categories such as "pattern" are easy to find in the educational literature. For instance, Bruce Mitchell and Robert Salsbury begin the entry for "culture" in their *Encyclopedia of Multicultural Education* (1999) with a formal definition that is purely structural:

❖FD3.9    Culture refers to the patterns acquired and transmitted by groups of human beings. (Ibid., p. 55)

Then, in an abrupt change in auctorial voice as well as of definitional modes, the authors go on to identify their view with the functionalist approach. They report approvingly that

❖ID3.9    [m]any social scientists define "culture" as a pattern for survival that is created when groups of people attempt *to satisfy their survival needs.* Social scientists also view artifacts and material objects as a part of culture. These values and mores distinguish one group of people from another. (Ibid., italics added)

Unfortunately, it is not clear in this account just whose survival is at stake, since the word "their" in the first sentence of ID3.9 is grammatically ambiguous. Does it refer to the *groups* mentioned in the formal definition, or does it refer to the *individual human beings* who are members of those groups? This question is more important than it might first seem. Radcliffe-Brown and Parsons would have said the former, since they focused on the need of the collective to preserve itself by preserving its social structure, whereas Malinowski would have said the latter, since he focused on individual human needs such as the need for food, shelter, sex, and above all, personal survival. Mitchell and Salsbury seem unaware of the difference between these two classical forms of anthropological functionalism, as well as the fact that by the time their encyclopedia was published many if not most anthropologists and sociologists had gone well beyond classical functional models of society, especially in the United States.

*Discussion:* To my knowledge none of the shared-survival-plan or environment-response definitions of culture proposed by multicultural educators develop the distinction between the two sorts of functionalism, which as we saw in previous chapters was so important to anthropologists and sociologists as their respective disciplines matured over the last century. I see three reasons—there may well be more—for this neglect. The first is that although the two sorts of functionalism are quite different, there is a logical continuity between them, as Durkheim pointed out long ago. However, he always insisted that individual needs do not by themselves determine the nature of social institutions. On the contrary, he claimed, "most of our ideas and our tendencies are not developed by ourselves but come to us from without," that is, from society (Durkheim, 1915/1964, p. 4).

The second reason is that in each type of functional explanation the focus is on the maintenance role that culture plays at the present time, rather than on historical conditions that would explain how it came to play that role. One might expect that multicultural education materials that employ either sort of functional definition of culture would take a sociological approach to its subject matter, focusing on social institutions (as Banks did) rather than on the cultural traits that are so important to anthropologists. However, there is no reason in principle that a functional definition cannot be combined with an anthropological approach focused on rituals, beliefs, and other sorts of expressive symbols.

My final reason is a little more tenuous but should be considered. When the "design for living" conception of culture is understood in terms of group-functionality, it is a short logical step to the inherently conservative model of Parsons and other social theorists who understand culture as a set of symbols, norms, and values that hold a society in equilibrium. Few multicultural educators would want to identify their agendas with that inherently conservative view since most if not all see themselves as part of a reform movement. However, their reformist agenda has been challenged by critical multiculturalists such as Solis and Jackson (1995, p. 2), who argue that educators must go beyond the "comfort zones" where multicultural theories and practices are promoted from "essentially additive, procedural, and technical perspectives" that preserve the status quo. We will return to this line of argument in later chapters, but it seems fair to say that multiculturalists who base their views and practices on a functionalist conception of culture need to be aware of the system-maintaining role it assigns to cultural practices and structures, including even those of multicultural education. For instance, we will see in the next chapter that functional and historical conceptions of culture have much in common, since it is only to be expected that a group's survival practices will endure from one generation to the next, encased in time-honored stories and symbols that constitute the group's cultural heritage. Because lessons from the past are inherently conservative, there is an inevitable but seldom articulated tension between functional conceptions of culture and the reformist agendas proposed by most multicultural educators.

## QUESTIONS FOR REFLECTION

The three approaches we have examined in this chapter (topical, structural, and functional) are still current even though they were first taken in the 1970s by educators who understood multiculturalism as synonymous with cultural pluralism. In the next two chapters we will consider six other approaches (historical, normative, behavioral, cognitive, semantic, critical) that were taken over the next decades. Before turning to them, though, we should acknowledge that many substantive questions remain about the three approaches discussed in this chapter. Perhaps the most telling question is whether it really matters how an author defines culture. What is (or should be) the correlation between the way an author defines culture and what he or she takes as the basic point or central agenda of multicultural education itself? How important is it that an author consistently employs the same conception of culture, especially in the follow-up comments that I have characterized as informal definitions? Is it unreasonable to demand precise formal definitions of culture in the literature of multicultural education? Or to put the question broadly and more bluntly, would it have been useful for their readers if the definitions of culture discussed above (especially the topical definitions) had been more consistent and more carefully drawn? If so, why?

An equally broad question is whether the definitions of culture presented in this chapter are truly representative of the literature of multicultural education. I think they are, but readers are encouraged to do their own sampling, with the understanding that the three approaches illustrated above are certainly not the only or perhaps even the most common ones taken in textbooks, articles, and books devoted to multicultural issues. Further questions remain, such as: Within the small group of sample definitions presented above, which ones seem most useful as guides to either the general practice of multicultural education or to the authors' own agendas? Would their authors agree that the descriptions of the agendas provided in this chapter are supported by a close reading of the texts in question? Are some of these agendas, for instance that of promoting cross-cultural competence so that students develop "multicultural personalities," more important than others, and if so, why? As far as the definitions themselves are concerned, do some seem more relevant than others to the increasingly multicultural environments—inside or outside the school itself—within which most students live and learn? If so, which ones and why? For instance, has the conceptually satisfying structuralist approach actually outlived its usefulness in a society in which cultural hybridity is increasingly common? Is a functionalist definition of culture inherently protective of existing social structures, and if so is this protection necessarily a bad thing? Multicultural education is a reform movement, but where is the line between reform and revolution, or between constructive and destructive revolution? Do authors who employ functionalist definitions try to draw this line, and if not, should they? And of course, just *who* are they?

These are only a few of the many substantive questions that arise from the formal content analysis provided in this chapter. It would be easy to think of others, although not so easy to answer them.

*Analysis:* Once again I should remind the reader that the purpose of this content analysis of definitions of culture is not to score points on authors of books and articles about multicultural education but rather to show how the rest of us can "decode" what they have said about the term *culture* and—somewhat more tentatively—how well their theories of culture fit with their practice, especially their educational agendas. In other words, by now you the reader should be ready to do your own content analysis of similar multiculturalist materials. For this reason, the chapter concludes with a brief extract from a recent text that resembles one or more of the definitions discussed above. To see if you can discover the "face in the bushes" for this text, use the nine-item template (Table 3.1) introduced at the beginning of this chapter to answer the following questions. (Suggestions: Photocopy the extract and mark it up. Pay close attention to the author's language and mentally try to rephrase key sentences in your own words.)

1. What is the author's Formal Definition?
2. What is the author's Informal Definition?
3. Can you identify the mode(s) of the Formal Definition?
4. Can you identify the mode(s) of the Informal Definition?
5. Given the importance of coherence between any multicultural education author's *theory* of culture and his or her educational *practice* (curriculum, learning goals, reform program, etc.), what do you think a teacher who shares this author's conception of culture would want his or her students to know and be able to do?

---

### DEFINING CULTURE

The term *culture* refers to an integrated pattern of human behavior that includes thought, language, action, and artifacts and depends on man's capacity for learning and transmitting knowledge to succeeding generations (*Webster's New Collegiate Dictionary*, 1980). Qualities subsumed by the term *culture* generally refer to shared personal qualities that can be categorized in a three-tier hierarchical model. Level I consists of shared biological and physical qualities (for example, height and weight, skin color, inherited propensity for illnesses and physical problems, and other qualities that have a decided biological basis). Level II qualities consist of shared values, goals, beliefs, and attitudes. These qualities are likely to be influenced by traditions within one's ancestral cultures (and thus transmitted through genetic and family patterns) together with one's current environment and personal decisions. Level III qualities consist of preferences for foods and eating habits, dress, and language as well as methods for disciplining, educating, communicating, working, dating, marriage, and playing. Compared to Levels I and II qualities, those associated with Level III are impacted more strongly by personal choice, are more modifiable, often more superficial, yet often seen as an expression of one's culture.

Cultural awareness and understanding require one to understand similarities and differences between one's own culture and other cultures. Thus, this process begins by understanding critical elements of one's own culture. Although considerable differences exist in the American culture, Americans generally respects rules and laws, strive to correct injustice, communicate explicitly and directly, embrace egalitarianism, value time as linear and exact, believe they control their destiny, and value work. Knowledge and display of common beliefs, goals, and values provides social cohesion and reduces tension.

Cultural awareness and understanding also require understanding other cultures. This requirement assumes reliable and valid information on a culture that is stable, generally homogeneous, and with degrees of variance known. This information is not available for the largest immigrant groups entering the United States or for most of the subgroups that have lived in the U.S. for generations.

From Thomas Oakland, "What Is Multicultural School Psychology?" (2005, pp. 3–13, passim)

---

## NOTES

1. This rather dismissive phrase, often quoted by cultural anthropologists, was introduced by Robert H. Lowie, who borrowed it from either *Hamlet* or Gilbert and Sullivan's *Mikado*. See chapter 2 n. 9.

2. The page references here are to this article. For its previous history, see Banks, 1979b.

3. Banks has consistently argued that multicultural education is a "reform movement." See his early article "Shaping the Future of Multicultural Education" (1979a, p. 237), where he introduced the reformist agenda that runs through all of his later work: "Since culture is the root of 'multicultural,' multicultural education suggests

a type of education that is related in some way to a range of cultural groups. The concept ['multicultural education'] itself implies little more than education related to many cultures. A major aim of multicultural education should be to educate students so that they will acquire knowledge about a range of cultural groups and develop the attitudes, skills, and abilities needed to function at some level of competency within many different cultural environments" (ibid., p. 239).

4. In the first edition of this book Spring provided an even more generous omnibus definition: "In this book, within the term *culture* I am including literature, music, religion, and modes of social interaction such as family organization, child rearing practices, social status, gender roles, and manners. In addition, I am including attitudes about property, morality, work, crime, leisure, government, and authority" (1997, p. 4). One can only guess as to why he later shortened his list in the way he did.

5. See Hong, Morris, Chiu, and Benet-Martínez (2000) and Kim (2001), who are cited by Spring in his discussion of cultural frames. See also the discussion of D'Andrade (1995) and Shore (1996) in the previous chapter.

6. Banks is an exception in that although his concept of a macro culture in FD3.1 does not suggest a structuralist perspective, his claim in ID3.1 that each micro culture is a "unique whole" does.

7. I say "fortunately" because a topical list of cultural traits such as behavior patterns, values, and symbols unaccompanied by any hint of how they are related to each other could easily lead one to conclude that in any given society whatever relationships might exist among its cultural traits are purely arbitrary. Such a conclusion would not only be highly questionable in itself but also leave the prospective teacher with the still more unfortunate impression that it is not necessary to explore these relationships in order to give one's students a reasonably comprehensive understanding of cultural diversity.

8. It may also be hard to see why an overworked on-the-line teacher would ever need to make such a fine-grained determination, but that is a different point. Here the task at hand is learning to cope with the professional literature of multicultural education, not its classroom challenges.

9. The systematizing role of Shade's notion of culture as filter is more explicit in an earlier essay, where she declares, "Culture is, in part, an aggregation of beliefs, attitudes, habits, values, and practices that form a view of reality. *This systemized pattern of thought serves as a filter* through which a group of individuals view and respond to the demands of the environment . . ." (Shade and New, 1993, p. 317, italics added).

10. In this connection they acknowledge M. L. Maehr (1974), E. T. Hall (1989), and R. A. LeVine (1991, as well as—in a later section—several others who have worked in specific areas of cross-cultural psychology.

11. A cautionary note: Although holistic definitions are not *necessarily* essentialist in the pejorative sense of that term, there is a tendency among multiculturalists who define culture holistically to posit a primordial, vaguely metaphysical reality that causes cultures to have the shapes that they do. For multicultural educators the best-known example of this tendency is probably the *Portland Readers* project, especially the Afrocentric materials prepared under the direction of Asa Hilliard, where discussions of ethnicity and race blithely refer to primordial qualities such as "Blackness."

Lawrence Hirschfeld (1998) provides an excellent psychological analysis of this tendency to posit primordial properties.

12. Even Margaret Gibson's claim that "the members of any given ethnic group will represent a range of cultures" (1984, p. 108) seems to assume that cultures are really "out there," notwithstanding her acknowledgment that cultures are distributed in a much more complex way than the early cultural pluralists thought.

13. Most of Bullivant's books and articles are about multiculturalism in his own country, but in 1989 he published an essay on the meaning of culture that appeared in the United States in the highly regarded anthology *Multicultural Education: Issues and Perspectives* (Banks and Banks, 1989/1993; page numbers are to the later edition). His definition, which James Banks adopted in his own contribution to the same volume (Banks and Banks, 1993, p. 8) and which is repeated elsewhere (for example, in Shapiro, Sewell, and DuCette, 1995, p. 29), is an interesting blend of British and American anthropological traditions.

14. Bullivant takes this claim very seriously. At this point in his exposition he further underscores the abstract nature of culture by quoting the anthropologist Louis Schneider's remark that "Putting people into culture is a sad maneuver into which social scientists slip time and time again" (Schneider & Bonjean, 1973, p. 119).

# 4

# Historical, Normative, and Behavioral Conceptions of Culture in the Professional Literature of Multicultural Education

In this chapter we will consider three ways of defining culture that focus directly on its contents rather than (as in the last chapter) on ways in which these contents are organized. Here many readers will feel they are on familiar ground. Instead of abstract and woolly categories like "aggregation," "structure," and "function," the key terms in these definitions are "history," "behaviors," and "norms," all of which are old friends—easy to identify, catalogue, and illustrate.

However, this greater familiarity comes with a certain loss of complexity and dynamism. As illustrated by the definitions discussed in the following pages, the components of culture are usually treated as *givens* in the literal sense of that term, by which I mean that in the multicultural education literature cultural traits are usually accepted with no questions asked. The processes that shape and reshape a cultural group's histories, behaviors, and norms are seldom discussed, with the result that the nature of *cultural change* is usually unexamined. In other words, definitions of culture that focus on cultural traits tend to freeze and to essentialize them.

Also unexamined is the relation of a multicultural educator's way of *defining culture* and his or her *educational agenda*. (The relation between an announced agenda and actual pedagogy is often problematic too, but that problem is not under discussion here.) Admittedly, there is no reason to think there is or should be a rigid one-to-one correspondence between ways of defining culture and educational objectives. However it is reasonable to expect that a multicultural education author's conception of culture should have *some* relevance to educational practice.

It is also reasonable to expect that some ways of defining culture will be more relevant than others to specific educational settings, such as Afrocentric charter schools, schools on Native American reservations, small elementary schools, large comprehensive high schools, lower-track classrooms, inner-city schools serving mainly nonwhite communities, college preparatory academies with predominately upper-class white populations, and so on. As in the previous chapter I will offer a few suggestions about how conceptions of culture can map onto educational agendas, but here again readers must decide for themselves just which agendas fit best with the types of definition discussed in each section.

### 4. Historical Definitions *(Culture is a group's shared heritage.)*

Design-for-survival definitions of culture, including those discussed in the previous chapter, often carry an unannounced assumption that a group's "shared survival plan" constitutes its cultural heritage. However, "cultural heritage" is a broader notion than "shared survival plan." It is also more than a simple chronicle of events that have led up to a group's present sense of its own identity. For many it is the residue of a carefully filtered, heavily value-laden narrative that enables a group of people to think of themselves as "special" in some invariably positive sense. That these and other assumptions about the importance of a group's history are implicit in many multicultural education books and articles is hardly surprising. Although multicultural education authors approach culture from many angles and with many definitional modes, most would agree that for a culture to endure, the story of this sharing must be told and retold across generations. As the Irish writer and politician Conor Cruise O'Brien (1952, p. 87) once wrote, "There is for all of us a twilit zone of time, stretching back . . . before we were born, which never quite belongs to the rest of history."[1] His observation applies to cultural and national groups as well as to individuals, and is thematized in different ways throughout the multicultural education literature, varying according to the authors' views of the role of the school as well as to their own social and educational goals. Some authors, such as R. Webb and R. Sherman (1989), offer definitions of culture that explicitly reference the history and heritage of a people. More commonly, though, the essentially historical character of a given author's notion of culture is a subtext rather than an announced theme or self-standing definition.

In what follows we will consider three historical conceptions of culture, beginning with two diametrically opposing political models: Dinesh D'Souza's conservative paradigm of multicultural education and Stanley Aronowitz and Henry Giroux's critical multiculturalist view of culture as a subtle but powerful type of power struggle. These statements along with Webb and Sherman's more complex functional-historical-structural conception illustrate in three different ways how a group's history informs its various cultural traits, as the following chart shows:

| Authors | Mode of Formal Component | Mode of Informal Component |
|---|---|---|
| D'Souza (4.1) | Historical | Normative |
| Aronowitz & Giroux (4.2) | Historical | Historical and Critical |
| Webb & Sherman (4.3) | Functional | Historical and Structural |

It is because a people's twilit time "never quite belongs to the rest of history" that many multiculturalist discussions directly or indirectly link culture to a specific set of historical traditions. One example of a direct linkage is provided by D'Souza in an essay entitled "Multiculturalism 101: Great Books of the Non-Western World" (1991a). Although this essay was published at the height of the so-called culture wars and in the same year that his scathing *Illiberal Education* (1991b) appeared, its treatment of multi-cultural education is not at all negative. On the contrary, D'Souza proposes a positive, plausible idea of what a historically oriented and multiculturally designed course might be like at the college level as well as, mutatis mutandis, at earlier levels. In an attempt to identify the positive political and cultural implications that his model has for the multiculturalist movement, he argues that a true respect for a cultural group centers on its high culture, which is to say on the intellectual core of its history, namely sacred and classical texts such as the *Koran, Bhagavad-Gita,* and *Analects of Confucius.* Although D'Souza's essay contains no concise definition of culture, his basic conception is clear: culture is inherently transgenerational and for that reason also inherently normative. His several remarks to that effect can be consolidated into the following formal definition:

EFD4.1    A culture is the constellation of sacred texts and historical narratives that have been articulated by a people's greatest thinkers, writers, and leaders, and are embraced by members of the group as their distinctive heritage and as their authoritative guides for daily life. (Compare D'Souza, 1991a, passim)

D'Souza's treatment of culture is normative as well as historical. Since he believes that cultures tell people how to live, he describes cultures as practical guides as well as objects of nostalgia and aesthetic regard. The normative character of what might be called his intellectual history approach to culture comes through loudly and clearly in his list of three "Principles of True Multiculturalism" that supplements and operationalizes the central idea of FD4.1 and in that way suggests the following informal definition of culture:

AID4.1    *Principle 1:* Non-Western ideas and institutions should be studied in relation to the great works of Western thought.

>*Principle 2:* A multicultural curriculum should teach the "best
>that has been thought and said" in non-Western as well as
>Western cultures.
>*Principle 3:* The curriculum should be politically and cultur-
>ally relevant to American students. (Compare ibid., p. 25)

Readers familiar with the culture wars of the 1980s and 1990s will remember that the bitterest polemics were over political issues such as affirmative
action and college admission rules, not over the nature of culture as such. For
this reason they should not be surprised to see that in spite of his undeniably
elitist approach to culture, D'Souza's conception of what he calls "true multiculturalism" goes beyond the rigid Eurocentrism that was the standard target
of multiculturalists from the earliest days of cultural pluralism and replaces
it with a separate-but-equal pluralism of canons. He views long-standing
historical traditions as moral and aesthetic achievements, understanding each
tradition primarily in terms of its "high culture" accomplishments, following the lead of Matthew Arnold and 20th century critics such as T. S. Eliot,
F. R. Leavis, and more recently E. D. Hirsch. In this respect D'Souza stands
in contrast to those who approach historical tradition by the lower roads of
popular culture mapped by the cultural studies literature discussed at the
end of chapter 2. Authors who take these approaches focus on contemporary
rather than classical texts or alternative canons, but like those who take the
high culture approach to the Western canon as well as to the non-Western traditions emphasized by D'Souza, they assume (and stress to their readers) that
the cultural differences portrayed in literary works such as Alice Walker's *The
Color Purple* or Chinua Achebe's *Things Fall Apart* are authentic expressions of
radically different histories. Here as in D'Souza's pluralism of canons, cultural
literacy is understood to be profoundly historical.[2]

In the professional literature of multicultural education historical conceptions of culture are usually hidden between the lines or, when they do
get explicit mention, appear as part of an informal definition rather than
as an unalloyed formal definition of culture. However, there are exceptions. In a trenchant critique of Hirsch's (1987) well-known conception of
"cultural literacy," Stanley Aronowitz and Henry Giroux (1991) combine
Pierre Bourdieu's (1977) idea of cultural capital with the critical pedagogy
of Paulo Freire (1968), Michael Apple (1986), and others. Aronowitz and
Giroux reject Hirsch's historical conception of culture on the grounds that
it "reproduces rather than critically engages the dominant social order"
(1991, p. 50). In its place they propose an equally historical but otherwise
quite different conception, namely a

❖FD4.2    definition of culture as a set of activities by which different
            groups produce collective memories, knowledge, social rela-

tionships, and values within historically controlled relations of power. (Ibid.)

In other words, Aronowitz and Giroux see culture as an essentially historical process that amounts to an ongoing struggle in which different groups try to canonize their respective collective memories, and to do so in ways that will secure their position in the power structure of society. Culture, they add, is about the production and legitimization of particular ways of life, and one of the most important arenas within which such struggles are carried out is the school, where the usual emphasis is on cultural knowledge and values favorable to the dominant class, gender, and racial groups. All this leads Aronowitz and Giroux to a conclusion that presents their critical-theoretic conception of education, especially multicultural education, as inherently political. This is the conclusion that an adequate conception of culture recognizes

❖ID4.2     that there are different voices, languages, histories, and ways of viewing and experiencing the world, and that the recognition and affirmation of these differences is a necessary and important precondition for extending the possibilities of democratic life. . . . [Different forms of cultural literacy] are to be weighed against the capacity they have for enabling people to locate themselves in their own histories while simultaneously establishing the conditions for them to function as part of a wider democratic culture. (Ibid., p. 51)

Of course Aronowitz and Giroux do not simply equate a group's culture with its history. Their conception of culture is in fact a mixture of definitional approaches—heavily historical but also "critical," using that term in Freire's sense of "critical pedagogy."

Our third example is from Webb and Sherman (1989), who illustrate the point made above that design-for-survival conceptions of culture often locate a group's survival plan in its history. They begin with an open-ended but clearly functionalist formal definition:

❖FD4.3     Cultures solve the common problems of human beings, but they solve them in different ways. (Ibid., p. 49)

In other words cultures are differentiated not by problems but rather by the specific practices that have served over the years as solutions to generic problems or, better, generic *problem areas* such as intragroup communication, power and status, family and reproduction, law and government, the relation to nature, and the symbolic expression of each of these domains

of human life. In Webb and Sherman's account the structure-building sequence of responses that a group makes to these problems constitutes its cultural heritage. Although they offer no arguments or evidence for this claim,
it is continuous with the rest of what they say about the problem-solving
role of culture. A shared practice—be it a linguistic, domestic, political, or
any other sort of shared practice—stabilizes expectations on the part of the
group's members. In the case of specifically *cultural* solutions, the stabilizing
effect is largely a consequence of an internally consistent, well-patterned set
of practices having been passed down from generation to generation. Webb
and Sherman go on to illustrate this point in an informal definition of culture that lists several of its historical and structural contents:

❄ID4.3    Cultures . . . supply a system by which significant lessons of
          the culture (*history*) can be given a physical representation and
          stored and passed on to future generations. The representation
          usually comes in the form of dance, song, poetry, architecture,
          handicrafts, story, design, or painting (*art*). What makes cul-
          tures similar is the problems they solve, not the methods they
          devise to solve them. (Ibid., p. 50)

   In other words, history and art are intertwined parts of larger cultural
systems, providing a momentum thanks to which the social order will continue to solve the "common problems of human beings." A people's history
is important for Webb and Sherman not so much because it is the twilit
zone that never quite belongs to the rest of history as because it contains
the lessons people have learned about solving the common problems of
human beings and the norms that sanction those lessons.
   *Discussion:* It is important not to oversimplify. I know of no culture theorist who believes that a group's culture can be *reduced* to its history, and no
multicultural education agenda that is focused on cultural heritage to the
exclusion of other cultural traits. Here as in the other conceptions of culture
under review, the issue is one of emphasis, not exclusiveness. Raymond
Williams (1961) realized this when he formulated his three-way division
of culture as ideal (universal values), documentary (the historical and literary heritage), and social (institutional and behavior patterns). Within the
group of theorists and educators who stress the second of these features
one finds different educational agendas as well as different pedagogical
methods. There are many ways in which a teacher can promote cultural
literacy—which includes not only appreciation of other people's literary
texts but also knowledge of their political histories. D'Souza looks to a
group's high culture, especially those parts that have shaped public norms
and personal values, and so his central objective is to develop respect for
other cultures by demonstrating their intellectual and moral similarities to

Western high cultures. Aronowitz and Giroux, on the other hand, regard classical historical texts as only one form of cultural literacy and prefer to emphasize the political dimensions of history (Western and non-Western) rather than its literature. As we saw above, their educational agenda is to lead students from all cultural backgrounds to "locate themselves in their own [political] histories" even as they learn to participate in our modern democratic system.

It is probably the case that neither the classical texts approach to history nor the historical power struggle approach is inherently conservative or liberal, but there are undeniable political differences between D'Souza's agenda and that of Aronowitz and Giroux. However, it has been argued by educators[3] from across the political spectrum that the way a teacher approaches the history and literature of other cultures will shape the students' understanding of cultural differences. For instance, data collected by Jordan Meléndez and his colleagues (1997) indicate that teachers who take an objective, "thematic" approach to literature tend to stress the universal messages contained in the cultural heritages represented in the works they teach whereas those who take a more subjective "reader-response" approach are more likely to stress differences between the cultural traditions.

It is harder to locate Webb and Sherman on the political spectrum, but they stand somewhere between the other two positions. They cite Amitai Etzioni's conservative "immodest agenda"' of developing greater concern "with the family, school, neighborhood, nation, and character" (1983, p. xii) but also note that in the United States the "cultural core" is changing rapidly and that educational aims should lay greater stress on norms and values associated with equality and interdependence. In this respect they seem typical of most multiculturalists who view the closely related notions of heritage and history as central features of the concept of "culture." However, not everyone shares that view. For instance, Bullivant (1993, p. 29) explicitly differentiates his own functionalist conception of culture from the history-and-heritage conception—whose roots lie in the American anthropological tradition. Although he clearly "favors" (his word) the relatively ahistorical British approach to culture associated with Radcliffe-Brown, Bullivant does not seem militant on this point. He raises no theoretical or strategic objections to the historically oriented alternative and even-handedly draws an important practical distinction between the types of multicultural pedagogy that each definition serves. Teachers who work with the heritage-and-tradition definition of culture will, he believes, teach about many different cultures, placing emphasis on their historical backgrounds and other sorts of cultural knowledge, for example, familiarity with other literary heritages. In contrast, teachers who work with the shared-survival-plan definition of culture will take as their principal themes the different designs for living found in our pluralist society and, by extension, issues of social justice such as equal opportunity, racism, and homophobia. Bullivant's prediction seems plausible, but what is even more plausible, I think, is that many if not most teachers will consciously or unconsciously mix the two sorts of pedagogy regardless of which definition of culture they favor, just as most literature teachers combine the thematic and reader-response approaches regardless of which one they happen to favor.

One final note: I said just now that Bullivant "does not seem militant" because in this essay, published in 1993 in a handbook designed for an American audience, he softened the strong criticism of the historical approach to culture that he had made a decade earlier as part of the vigorous policy debates in his native Australia over multicultural education (for example, Bullivant, 1981, 1982, 1983; see also Sachs, 1989).[4] As we will see in the next chapter, similar objections to the "cultural heritage" conception of culture were eventually launched in the United States under the banner of Critical Multiculturalism. Bullivant may have lowered his voice as time went on, but as of now the jury is still out on the validity of multicultural agendas centered on historical conceptions of culture.

### 5. Normative Definitions *(Culture is a group's ideals, values, or rules for living.)*

Kroeber and Kluckhohn (1952, p. 98) once distinguished four meanings or "implications" that the word "way" has in anthropological definitions of culture.[5] Two of them correspond to the structural and functionalist approaches discussed in the preceding chapter. The other two senses correspond to the approaches we will now consider, namely the normative approach and, in the subsequent section, the behavioral approach. The present section features three authors whose conceptions of culture are primarily normative but mixed with other definitional modes as follows:

| Authors | Mode of Formal Component | Mode of Informal Component |
|---|---|---|
| Timm (4.4) | Normative | Normative and Functional |
| Ramsey (4.5) | Normative | Normative and Structural |
| Tyler et al. (4.6) | Normative | Normative and Cognitive |

We saw in the last chapter that the sharp distinction which Parsonian sociologists drew between values and norms was important for their homeostatic model of the social system. According to that model personal dispositions and attitudes (values) shape and are shaped by public rules or standards of conduct (norms) that hold the system in equilibrium. However, the distinction between values and norms is not prominent in the multicultural education literature, perhaps because the very idea of social equilibrium seems monocultural, suggesting as it does that cultural diversity is at best a way station on the road to conflict resolution and assimilation and at worst a potentially destructive form of social deviance. For obvious reasons, multiculturalists have tended—consciously or unconsciously—to favor the alternative sociological model of conflict theory, which as we saw in chapter 2 eschews assimilationism (the melting pot image) and instead regards social conflict as inevitable but nonetheless controllable through established norms that call for toleration of differences, respect for diversity, and acceptance of the purposive conflict associated with identity politics and other by-products of cultural pluralism. What the conflict management model does not provide, though, is a firm and explicit distinction between personal values and public norms. Whether this blurring of Parson's distinction is a good thing remains to be seen, but it is important for readers to realize that in the literature of multicultural education the normative order includes much more than personal standards of good character.

Joan Timm's (1996) value-oriented conception of culture illustrates this point. Echoing Kroeber and Kluckhohn as well as Parsons, she first defines the "essence" of culture in unambiguously normative terms, declaring that

❖FD4.4     Cultural values form the essence of any culture. (Ibid., p. 135)

This claim is the basis for Timm's entire educational program, which calls for teachers to introduce their students to the value orientations of other people without subscribing to moral relativism. Then, by way of explaining the meaning and pedagogical importance of FD4.4, she identifies its cultural values as:

❖ID4.4     the reasons why people act the way they do. Without an awareness of these values, we cannot understand the people who hold them. At first, the idea of learning the values of diverse cultures appears to be an almost impossible goal. After all, there are so many different cultures in the world. How can we hope to understand the "essence" of even a fair number of them? (Ibid.)

She answers this last question in terms that reveal a solid layer of Parsonian fuctionalism supporting her understanding of the normative "essence of any culture." Although she understands values as personal dispositions or attitudes (people "hold them") she recognizes that they also operate as public norms. That is, values vary from one society to the next but they always have a problem-solving and integrating function for the society as a whole. Citing the anthropologist Florence Kluckhohn (1956; Kluckhohn & Strodbeck, 1961), whose work on values overlapped with that of her husband and fellow anthropologist Clyde Kluckhohn, Timm explains that the possibility of cross-cultural value inquiry rests on three assumptions: (1) there are a limited number of human problems and these are common to all people; (2) the solutions to these problems are also limited; (3) possible solutions to the basic human problems are present in all cultures. She allows that within a given culture there can be variant value orientations, tolerated by those who identify with the dominant orientation as long as the nondominant values do not threaten the cohesiveness of the society. However, we are left to speculate how these other values fit into the social order. Are they utterly private and hence compatible with any set of public norms? Do they influence the public norms in certain ways, such as creating zones of tolerance for relatively harmless nonstandard values? And most problematic, does a pedagogy that makes no distinction between norms and values risk erasing important differences between cultures by suggesting that at bottom people are all pretty much the same? Such questions remain unanswered by Timm.

Like Timm, Patricia Ramsey adopts Kluckhohn's normative approach to culture and, also like Timm, recognizes that social norms or, as Ramsey prefers to say, "expectations" are more or less explicitly articulated. Thus in the first edition of her much revised but still popular *Teaching and Learning in a Diverse World* (1987, 1998, 2004) Ramsey opens her discussion of young children's responses to cultural differences with a short formal definition that is normative in the narrow, functionalist sense according to which norms are public standards that hold a society together:

❖FD4.5    The terms *culture* and *subculture* can be defined as the overt and covert expectations of particular social groups. (Ramsey, 1987, p. 27)[6]

However, Ramsey says nothing about personal values as such. She elucidates FD4.5 by an informal definition that elaborates her normative definition from a sociological perspective reminiscent of what was said in chapter 2 about Gordon's structuralist analysis of intergroup relations and Barth's idea of boundary maintenance. Then she goes on to tell us—in terms that those authors would vigorously criticize—that cultures and subcultures are identified with the reference groups themselves and that salient differences between cultures are best understood as external social markers rather than internal value orientations:

❖ID4.5    *Culture* refers to one's national group (such as the American culture); *subculture* refers to distinct groups within a society that are delineated by such factors as national origin, gender, religion, occupation, region, generation, and age. (Ibid., pp. 27–28)

As the contrast between her formal definition and informal definition reveals, Ramsey's view of culture is a mixture of anthropological and sociological perspectives: anthropological in that she understands social expectations as Boasian-styled cultural traits, that is, as the content or "stuff" of a culture, and sociological in that she stresses their importance as reference group markers. For instance, her ensuing discussion of the teacher-student relationship is primarily anthropological in that it centers on culture-specific norms, which as she points out are often the source of misunderstanding among people of different cultures (downcast eyes are a sign of respect in some cultures and of evasiveness in others, etc.). However, her discussion of children's relationships to the norms of their own culture is couched in the language of cognitive developmental psychology. Because culture is an abstract concept, she tells us, young children do not use it as an organizing category and for that reason are unable to take an outsider's view on their own behavior or group membership. Nor are they able to appreciate the abstract relationship between culture and subculture, even though they can notice and remember concrete differences between cultures, including not only differences in food, clothing, etc., but also differences in social expectations (concerning behavior patterns, linguistic norms, etc.), and can negotiate them with sometimes surprising empathy.[7] Ramsey's educational program, which is based on a cognitive developmental model of perspective-taking skills, aims to lay the groundwork for more reflective and otherwise complex stages of cross-cultural understanding. It does so by incorporating into the curricula of early childhood education a wide variety of materials and activities that represent diverse cultural expectations, the most important of which are those that lead children to understand and respect alternative cultural norms.

A much different normative conception of culture is found in the educational literature on "cultural discontinuity," a term whose analogues include "cultural conflict," "cultural dissonance," and "cultural misalignment." As defined by Kenneth Tyler and his student co-authors (2008), cultural discontinuity is "a school-based behavioral process where the cultural value-based learning preferences and practices of many ethnic minority students—those typically originating from home or parental socialization activities—are discontinued at school" (ibid., p. 282; see also Sue, 2004). Although the discontinuity in question involves many aspects of culture, the authors focus on norms and values (here again the two terms are used interchangeably) for the obvious reason that these are what nonmainstream schoolchildren find most challenging when they move from their home cultures to the typical American school. There academic contents and social environments (especially the classroom environment) reflect mainstream, Eurocentric values (see also Gay, 2000; Ladson-Billings, 1995a, 1995b; and Nieto, 1999).

With these concerns in mind Tyler and his co-authors offer under a section entitled "Culture in the Study of Psychology and Education" the following brief, unambiguously normative definition of culture, which they draw from a wide variety of sources:[8]

❖FD4.6     Culture has been defined as the values, traditions, and beliefs mediating the behaviors of a particular social group. (Tyler et al., 2008, p. 284)

After a short review of the psychological literature on culture and learning, they amplify their formal definition of culture by reviewing a large number of studies of cultural discontinuity experienced by students from nonmainstream cultures. The upshot of their review is the following informal definition, which was organized as a bulleted list of "salient cultural values":

⬧ID4.6     Culture/Group Salient Cultural Values:

- African American: Communalism, Movement, Verve
- Asian American: Collectivism, Conformity to Norms, Emotional Self-control, Humility, Family Recognition through Achievement, Filial piety, Deference to Authority
- Latin American: Collectivism, Spatiotemporal Fluidity
- Native American: Sharing and Cooperation, Noninterference, Harmony with Nature, Present-time Orientation, Deep Respect for Elders
- U.S./mainstream: Individualism, Competition (Ibid.)

What is most striking in ID4.6 is not the values that are listed but its hard-edged typology. Of course any typology runs the risk of stereotyping, and since the authors call these values "salient" we may assume they are not suggesting that every member of each cultural group takes these values as his or her personal code. Even so, one wonders if many multiculturalists as well as most members of the groups in question will find these thumbnail descriptions unsettling if not simply offensive.

*Discussion:* Kroeber and Kluckhohn's own definition of culture—recycled by Timms in FD4.4—included their belief that the "essential core" of culture consists of "ideas and especially their attached values." This claim, which was also the main premise of Parsons's structural functionalism, continues to surface in sociological discussions of intergroup relations that have in turn influenced multicultural education theory. Few multicultural educators would disagree with these scholarly pronouncements or their curricular corollaries. For instance it hardly needs saying that expanding students' cultural knowledge is an important agenda item in any forum of multicultural education, or that one of the most important content areas of cultural knowledge is that of the norms and values of other cultures—especially when the "otherness" in question is that of mainstream vs. non-mainstream cultures.

However, not all cultural knowledge is well packaged—especially when some of its contents are also central values of other cultural groups. As in other types of cultural knowledge, the extremes of ethnocentrism and simplistic stereotypes such as those listed by Tyler in ID4.6 can be equally corrosive, breeding arrogance or resentment rather than cross-cultural respect. Here as in the interpretive or "hermeneutical" disciplines of classical and biblical studies, factual knowledge needs to be supplemented by other sorts of cognitive skills, such as contextual analysis, cross-cultural communication, and most important of all, perspective-taking skills (see Gay, 1994).

A related but much larger problem is the relation between values and affective dispositions. When Kroeber and Kluckhohn said in 1952 that the essential core of culture was "ideas and especially their attached values," they understood values as clear, distinct, and enumerable cultural traits, associated with specific ideas and differing in notable ways from the values found in other cultures. Unfortunately, there is still no generally accepted answer to the question of whether a culture's values are derived from its central ideas or the ideas are derived from its central values. Most culture theorists continue to assume at least some degree of reciprocity between these two components of culture, as well as some degree of reflective consciousness and articulation on both sides. Moral psychologists and philosophers make similar assumptions (see Wren, 1991).

Throughout this section I have not said much about the difference between values and norms since that distinction is seldom if ever made in the literature of multicultural education. However, the distinction is not unimportant. Values are associated with ideas about how to live and take the shape of ethical principles, moral virtues, judgments of character and personal worth, etc. In contrast, norms are derived from ideas about the nature of a society and its needs, and take the shape of civic engagement, conformity to public standards, loyalty to a monarch or respect for public officials, willingness to sacrifice for the common good, etc. Does this mean that within a specific cultural group, norms and personal values (at least those personal values that are widely shared) constitute some sort of steering mechanism that determines day-to-day practices such as law-abidingness, behavior in public places, acting within established gender roles, or observing discourse conventions? The definitions of culture that we have examined in this section seem to suggest as much, but that suggestion is as debatable as Parsons's own view of the supposedly basic role of norms and values in the maintenance of a social system. What the anthropologist

Ronald Waterbury has said about discussions of values and norms that take place in social studies classes applies to multicultural education in general: it is easy to lose sight of the social conditions under which cultural traits, including norms and values, are learned. His argument is simple but very relevant here. Methodologically, he says, the cart is put before the horse, since although culture influences individual behavior, culture itself is learned. What Waterbury calls the anthropological perspective of values as cultural traits "glosses over the . . . societal conditions within which learning (enculturation) takes place. Thus, it apportions to culture a causal burden that it is unable to bear" (Waterbury, 1993, pp. 64–65). To be a successful multicultural educator, it seems, one must recognize the limitations of the normative conception of culture as well as its variations.

6. Behavioral Definitions *(Culture is shared, learned human behavior, a publicly observable way of life.)*

Multicultural educators who construct behavior-oriented definitions of culture typically understand culture as having an overt dimension consisting of observable actions and a covert dimension consisting of cognitive elements of action such as ideas, beliefs, personal values, and moral principles. Some of their behavioral definitions of culture explicitly invoke this distinction whereas others simply assume it, but in either case they focus on the overt dimension, allowing a little overlap so that action-oriented thoughts and dispositions can be included in the definition. However, as we will see in the definitions featured in this section, the overt-covert distinction is always at least implicit. The behavioral conceptions of culture one finds in the literature of multicultural education are not "behaviorist" in the hard reductionist sense that this term has in the so-called radical behaviorist psychology associated with B. F. Skinner.

The formal components of the definitions we will now examine are unequivocally behavioral in the anthropological sense of that term, whereas the modes of their informal components are mixed, as the following chart shows.

| Authors | Mode of Formal Component | Mode of Informal Component |
|---------|--------------------------|----------------------------|
| King et al. (4.7) | Behavioral | Structural and Functional |
| Locke (4.8) | Behavioral | Behavioral and Symbolic |
| Kendall (4.9) | Behavioral | Behavioral and Cognitive |

Behavior and its patterns are often mentioned in passing in otherwise nonbehavioral definitions of culture.[9] However, some definitions clearly privilege the dimension of behavior or behavioral patterns. A good example is provided by Edith King, Marilyn Chipman, and Marta Cruz-Janzen in their *Educating Young Children in a Diverse Society* (1994). Their opening chapter "The Concept of Culture and Early Childhood Education" begins with a formal definition drawn from an anthropology textbook written by a prominent functionalist anthropologist of the 1960s, Walter Goldschmidt (1963):

❖FD4.7    What does the concept of culture signify? What are the elements of culture? According to Goldschmidt, culture is: *"Learned behavior acquired by each organism in the process of growing up; shared behavior characteristic of a population; based upon customs. Culture is not merely a bag of customs; it is an orientation to life."* (King et al., p. 115; the internal quotation is from Goldschmidt, p. 14.)

Although this definition may suggest to the casual reader that the authors, including Goldschmidt, have simply reduced culture to its behavioral dimension, their view of the behavioral dimension is actually much more complex and interesting. Goldschmidt's remark that culture is more than a bag of customs is particularly revealing. In his own published work he made no secret of his sympathy for the structural-functionalist style of anthropology promoted by Radcliffe-Brown and other social anthropologists, and it is fair to assume that King and her co-authors share his view of the supportive relationship that culture has to society. For early cultural anthropologists such as Boas and his associates it was enough to study the evolutionary pattern of a people's customs. In contrast, social anthropologists held that any given society has the customs that it does simply because those customs (and by extension, its entire set of social institutions) keep the society going. Here as in the Boasian view, customs are treated as causal forces, but with a crucial difference. In social anthropology customs derive their causal efficacy not from their intellectual coherence, emotional appeal, or historical venerability but rather from their character as observable, useful, and well-established patterns of behavior—by which I mean real patterns of real behavior of real human beings who live together in a real society. It is precisely because they are expressed as concrete behaviors that all cultural traits, be they long-standing practices and myths or recently fabricated artifacts and rituals, are causally effective. Even more to the point, though, these patterns are themselves shaped by their function, which is to enable people to live together in a coherent and self-sustaining social system. For those who understand culture in this way—the list includes Goldschmidt and by extension King and her coauthors[10]—it is this functionality, not their historical lineage, that makes customs or "traditional ways of life" the defining feature of the concept of culture.

The metahistorical debate over whether cultures give life meaning (Goldschmidt's "orientation to life") because they articulate our histories or because they meet our present-day social requirements no longer dominates social science, probably because the maxim that cultures are "complex wholes" is no longer the foundational premise for either anthropology or sociology. However, it is clear that the definitional mode of FD4.7 is behavioral in the social anthropological sense just described. This interpretation is borne out by the informal definition that King et al. offer as a gloss on their Goldschmidt citation. In it they emphasize not only the functional role of culture-specific behavior but also its inherently *structural* character (patterned, a configuration, internally consistent, etc.):

◈·ID4.7     Culture is made up of configurations. It is patterned and has an internal consistency. Therefore (sic), the behavior of a group of people reflects the fundamental attitudes and beliefs of their culture. Anthropologists use the classic example of the acquisition of the horse by the Plains Indians to illustrate what is meant by a cultural configuration. The Plains Indians developed their culture around horsemanship. They created mores and folkways related to the use of the horse in their daily lives. Techniques for hunting, for waging war, for exchange and trade, and for estimating economic standards of wealth all revolved around the horse. (Ibid.)

It is clear from this passage that the authors have done serious anthropological homework, but their sources are surprisingly dated for a book published in 1994. The reference to the Plains Indians is drawn from Benedict's *Patterns of Culture* (1934), and they elsewhere cite Tylor (1871), Kroeber and Kluckhohn (1952), White (1959), Mead (1964), Kneller (1965), and Barth (1969) in order to establish the place of symbols, language, and other "covert" features of culture. In the course of laying out concrete recommendations for teaching children about other cultures, the authors employ the structural functionalist notion of culture that was generally accepted in the 1950s and 1960s. For instance, in a later chapter they describe the "Community" unit in a curriculum guide for early childhood education of Native American children and recommend it in terms that could have come straight from Talcott Parsons: "Once children know who they are, what relationship they share with their families and tribe, and something about

their culture, they can enjoy and participate actively in their communities
. . . working together for the common good."[11]

Our second example of a behavioral definition of culture, also written by
a multicultural educator who draws on classical social theory, is from Don
Locke's (2003) discussion of the relation between the behavior patterns of
teachers and their students. He begins his discussion with a ringing call for
educators to have a clear conception of culture. "A common understanding
of the fundamental concept of culture," he declares, "is essential to a shared
understanding of the ideas presented in this chapter." He then serves up
the following formal definition, which he draws from Kroeber and Kluckhohn's famous inventory of definitions of culture:

❖FD4.8     Culture is composed of habitual patterns of behavior that are
           characteristic of a group of people. (Locke, 2003, p. 174)

Although he recognizes that this definition describes only the overt dimension of culture, Locke proceeds to expand it in terms of an intermediate
borderland in the overt-covert distinction, within which cultural symbols
are deemed effective precisely because they are both overt and covert (more
on this distinction in the next chapter). He borrows from the venerable
*Dictionary of Sociology* (Fairchild, 1970) to provide a helpful informal definition that explains how these behavioral patterns take shape:

❖ID4.8     These shared behavioral patterns are transmitted from one gen-
           eration to the next through symbolic communication. [Culture
           is] "all behavioral patterns socially acquired and socially trans-
           mitted by means of symbols, including customs, techniques, be-
           liefs, institutions and material objects." The primary transmitter
           of culture is language, which enables people to learn, experience,
           and share their traditions and customs. (Locke, 2003, p. 174; the
           inner quotation is from Fairchild, 1970, p. 80)

It is evident from his use of Fairchild's identification of symbols as the
vehicle for cultural transmission that Locke understands behavior as having
both subjective and objective dimensions. Unfortunately, at this point the
waters begin to muddy. For some reason—perhaps to fill out his concept of
culture as symbolically transmitted behavior patterns—he offers a sweeping
list of the "components of culture" that includes activity, social relations,
motivation, perception of the world, and perception of self. (This list is
taken from another sociologist of the 1970s, E. C. Stewart [1971].) None of
these components is new or particularly debatable, but together (and with
no further mention of behavioral patterns or symbolic communication)

they provide Locke with a thick conception of culture upon which he attempts to construct a methodology for culturally sensitive education or, as he put it in the title of his chapter, for "Improving the Multicultural Competence of Educators." The multicultural competence he has in mind consists in awareness of diversity and equal respect for all cultures or cultural groups (he uses the latter two terms interchangeably).

Several pages later Locke briefly resurrects his behavioral conception of culture in a one-sentence statement of how a teacher's belief in individualism can mask an ethnocentric "disregard for any culturally specific behaviors that influence student behaviors" (p. 178). However, it remains unclear what the "common understanding of the fundamental concept of culture" that he promised his readers at the beginning of the chapter has contributed to his discussion of multicultural competence.

We see a much more relaxed sort of behavioral definition in the third example, taken from Frances Kendall's introduction to her *Diversity in the Classroom* (1995). There she defines culture ahistorically and in the simplest possible terms:

❖FD4.9    For purposes of this book, *culture* will be defined as a people's way of doing things. . . . (Ibid., p. 18)

In this cryptic definition Kendall uses the little word "way" in a sense that Kroeber and Kluckhohn once identified as one of four meanings the word has in discussions of culture, namely as a pattern of behavior. Here we should note the absence of any attempt to explain *why* a people lives as it does rather than in some other way; no mention is made of either historical traditions or of present-day functionality. As the subtitle of her book suggests,[12] Kendall's focus is on one special sort of "doing," namely early childhood learning. The text that immediately follows FD4.9 provides an informal definition that specifies the range of FD4.9 and tells us a little more about what she means by the open-textured phrase "doing things." Unfortunately, her explanation is not completely consistent.

The problem begins when she supplements her formal definition of culture with a tag line that apparently identifies the aforesaid "people's way of doing things" with a set of rules for what she calls "making meaning of the universe." From this phrase (which was not in her first edition) she goes on to construct an informal definition that cashes out her brief formal definition of culture as a people's way of doing things:

❖ID4.9    Our values and belief systems, ways of thinking, acting, and responding, grow out of this set of rules [for making meaning of the universe] and greatly influence our behavior. (Ibid.)

As is clear from what Kendall says in the pages that follow, ID4.9 also provides the reader with a useful transition from her general conception of culture to the pedagogical applications she wants to discuss. However, her category of meaning-making rules seems to straddle the cognitive and behavioral dimensions of culture (or perhaps belong to neither), since it apparently posits some sort of foundation or deep structure. I use the adjective "deep" to show that this construct is prior to both dimensions. The priority itself can be either causal (the foundational rules are seen to *produce* the cultural patterns of thought and action) or explanatory (the foundational rules describe, reveal, or summarize a people's basic ways of thinking and behaving). It is hard to know which interpretation Kendall would favor, since her formal definition of culture as a people's way of doing things seems to demolish the distinction between overt and covert culture and not simply to blur it. Fortunately, a look at what she is trying to do with this definition suggests a way in which her conception of culture can be rehabilitated and even—as I will try to show—counted as a behavioral definition albeit in a rather wide sense of that term.

Kendall's ensuing discussion of culture-specific learning styles begins with her observation that a teacher's own learning style can be much different than the way many of his or her students learn. She goes on to apply the cognitive developmental theories of psychologists such as Lev Vygotski (1972) and Howard Gardner (1991) to the practical challenges of teaching in a multicultural classroom where students have many different learning styles. What Kendall has to say on this topic is well-informed and compelling (especially in the second edition of her book) but somewhere along the line her conception of learning mutates. At the outset, learning is one of those culture-constituting things that people "do," as explained in FD4.9, which is to say that learning style is itself a cultural trait. But a few pages later the concept of a culture-specific learning style is quietly replaced by the concept of learning style as a personal psychological attribute. Cultural differences give way to individual differences, and although learning behaviors may be influenced by the child's culture they are apparently no longer thought to be a constituent part of it.

However, this is one of those instances where textual interpretation requires what the philosopher Donald Davidson (1984, p. 137) has called the Principle of Charity,[13] according to which Kendall's basic point can be plausibly reconstructed by loosening her formal definition of culture. What she really meant to say, apparently, is that *some* behaviors—including some learning behaviors—are more closely identified with the child's culture than others are, but that no child's behavioral repertoire is completely determined by culture. Individual capacities and situation-specific small-group interactions—especially those that take place in a classroom—also profoundly influence an individual's behaviors, be they cognitive behaviors associated with learning or more overt behaviors such as looking a teacher in the eye when spoken to. She could also agree, without undermining her claim that children have individual cognitive styles, that it would be wrong to think that within a given cultural group there is only one authentic learning style or, to echo her notion of foundational rules, that there is only one way to make meaning of the universe.

*Discussion:* Each of the three definitions of culture examined in this section is developed from a different perspective on cultural behavior, although all are explained with regard to the schoolroom context. King, Chipman, and Cruz-Janzen treat cultural behaviors as system-maintaining customs. Locke understands them as patterns that have been transmitted from one generation to the next by means of culturally established symbols. Kendall focuses on cognitive behaviors, including those involving learning, that are the internal (covert) correlates of external (overt) behaviors. It would be a mistake to ask which of these three conceptual approaches is correct since, as we saw in chapter 1, a theoretical concept can be understood in terms of its use as well as through the theory that produced it. Here the uses are expressly pedagogical. King and her co-authors use the behavioral conception of culture as an entrée into a larger-scaled discussion of how teachers should prepare their students to fit into a diverse but nonetheless relatively stable society, with the concept of diversity having its own diversity, which includes diversities of culture, ethnicity, gender, social class, physical and cognitive abilities—as well as the diversity of learning styles that is the central issue of her book.[14] As they see it, "fitting in" should take place on a two-way street. Students must learn to deal with diversity, but so must society and its institutions (especially the schools). If this is done a new and richer social equilibrium will be achieved, one that seems to combine the best of the sociological paradigms of conflict theory and structural functionalism.

Locke's educational agenda is much broader, but it is difficult to see what his behavioral conception of culture or the emphasis he puts on symbolically transmitted behavior patterns contributes to the goal announced in his title, which we saw was improving the multicultural competence of educators. After an opening section entitled "Defining Culture" he moves on to well-worn images of cultural diversity as a "salad bowl" or a "rainbow coalition" in order to propose to educators a multicultural agenda that features neither behaviors nor symbols, but rather values and norms. "Issues of culturally sensitive education," he eventually concludes, "have been explored from the perspective of a need for educational systems to examine the values being taught and how these values affect the dominant culture and members of culturally different groups" (p. 187). The behavioral and symbolic definitions of culture that he offered early on seem to have slipped below the waves. Although they provide interesting examples of discourse about culture it is not clear how they contribute to the larger goals Locke has set for himself. One is left with the uneasy feeling that, as Wittgenstein put it in a somewhat different context, Don Locke's concept of culture "does no work."

Kendall's behavioral definition of culture has its own problems, as I have already noted, but it is a serious attempt to anchor an educational program of antibias and antiracism education (p. 45).[15] The cognitive informal definition that she offers gives the reader a bridge from her behavioral conception of culture to the culturally responsive pedagogical applications that constitute the agenda of her book. Kendall describes her agenda as an instance of the "Education that is multicultural and social reconstructionist" approach advocated by Sleeter and Grant, but this is only partly correct. Like all arguments for culturally responsive teaching her demand that teachers respect differences in learning styles is a call for a basic change in the way teachers teach, but it is hard to see how it is also an attempt to expose structural injustices, much less to reconstruct our society as a whole. My own view is that none of the agendas discussed in this section is reconstructionist in this strong sense. King and her colleagues, as well as Locke and Kendall, are more concerned with helping students fit into the mainstream without losing their own cultural identities than with exposing the mainstream itself as radically flawed, oppressive, etc. Social conflict issues seem to be gentled by their definitions of culture as established patterns of behavior. If the examples examined here are representative, and I think they are, then behavioral definitions of culture may work well for culturally responsive and antidiscrimination education but not for full-fledged social reconstruction.

## QUESTIONS FOR REFLECTION

Here as at the end of the last chapter many substantive questions remain. For instance, are some of the definitional modes examined in this chapter more appropriate for certain cultural groups than others, such that, say, the dense religious history of a European "ethnoculture" would be more central to its members' cultural identity than the relatively spare history of the gay rights movement would be for the cultural identity of its members? Is it really possible to think of culture in terms of behavior patterns without simultaneously thinking of the values and norms embodied in those behaviors? For instance, marching is a much different behavior on the

Fourth of July than on Mardi Gras or an Occupy Wall Street demonstration, even though the physical actions are similar. Furthermore, is there not a reciprocity between behaviors and norms (marching on Independence Day promotes patriotism even as it expresses it)? And what is the role of cultural symbols in this reciprocity, or the significance of the fact that even the most familiar and heavily value-laden symbols are continually negotiated and renegotiated through interpersonal dialogue?

*Analysis:* It does no harm to repeat the reminder at the end of chapter 3 that the purpose of our content analysis of these sample texts is not to score points on authors of books and articles about multicultural education but rather to show the reader how to "decode" their definitions of culture and look for hints about how they match up with the usual educational agendas. As before, the present chapter concludes with a brief extract from a recent multicultural education textbook that resembles one or more of the definitions discussed above. Use the nine-item template introduced at the beginning of chapter 3 to see if you can discover the "face in the bushes" for this text. To check your understanding of the present chapter, try to answer the reflection questions introduced at the end of chapter 3 (also shown below), keeping in mind the suggestions made there. Don't be afraid to assign more than one definitional mode to either the FD or the ID, but be sure you have clear and distinct reasons for doing so.

1. What is the author's Formal Definition?
2. What is the author's Informal Definition?
3. Can you identify the mode(s) of the Formal Definition?
4. Can you identify the mode(s) of the Informal Definition?
5. Given the importance of coherence between any multicultural education author's *theory* of culture and his or her educational *practice* (curriculum, learning goals, reform program, etc.), what do you think a teacher who shares this author's conception of culture would want his or her K–12 students to know and be able to do?

## DIVERSITY MATTERS

The cumulative effect of our life experiences creates in each of us a lens through which we observe our environment. This cultural lens focuses our attention on particular aspects of what we see. Society defines principles and values for present and future generations through customs, traditions, and rituals that focus the lens through which we view our lives and form our opinions. Throughout history, cultures have passed their family values to future generations by these means. . . . Cultural heritage and background influence our lives in many ways. In fact, all aspects of human life are touched and altered by culture. Our personalities, the way we think, and the ways we solve problems, as well as methods we use to organize ourselves, are all given shape, in large part, by cultural experiences. However, we frequently take the great influence of culture on our lives for granted and fail to identify the significant and sometimes subtle ways culture affects our behavior and thinking. . . .

Culture is defined in various ways. This concept may be broadly described as encompassing a group's common beliefs, including shared traditions, language, styles, values, and agreement about norms for living. Culture, however, always intersects individuals' race, social class, gender, age, ability status, sexual orientation, and family traditions. In this text, the definition of *culture* includes values, beliefs, notions about acceptable and unacceptable behavior, and other socially constructed ideas that members of the culture are taught. As such, culture, in effect, defines and actively guides one's thinking and behavior. If, for you, proper student behavior includes not only making decisions independent of others, speaking up about them, and feeling proud about such an accomplishment, you are not alone among your colleagues in the United States. However, there are many cultural groups, whose values are explored in this text, that embrace interdependence as opposed to independent decision-making, that restrict communication and expression of feelings, and that take pride in group rather than individual accomplishments. . . . It is not uncommon to find references to African American experience or Latino culture or to "the" culture of the Europeans. While those within a culture by definition share much in terms of commonly shared values and behavior, such broad categorization fails to do justice to the wide variation within each cultural group. Thus, a more functional approach for defining culture is one that recognizes intergroup differences in culture as well as the plethora of subcultures that exist.

It is extremely important to note that not all people from one cultural group can be grouped together and assumed to be alike. You can assume that members of a group may share certain cultural characteristics, but you must also recognize subcultural, intracultural, and individual differences. Within a culture, subgroupings around a more specific shared history of experience, social values, and role expectations exist. These subcultures can be formed along racial, ethnic, regional, economic, or social community lines. A subculture provides its members with values and expectations that may not be demonstrated by the larger cultural group or found elsewhere. In addition, these subcultural differences found between groups within a culture may result in the development of communication patterns and barriers, both for members within the same culture and for individuals across many different cultures.

From Lynn K. Spradlin, *Diversity Matters: Understanding Diversity in Schools* (2012, p. 6)

# NOTES

1. The quotation is from O'Brien's 1952 novel *Maria Cross*. The rest of this interesting passage is as follows: "There is for all of us a twilit zone of time, stretching back for a generation or two before we were born, which never quite belongs to the rest of history. Our elders have talked their memories into our memories until we come to possess some sense of continuity exceeding and traversing our own individual being. The degree in which we possess that sense of continuity and the form it takes—national, religious, racial, or social—depend on our own imagination and on the personality, opinions and talkativeness of our elder relatives. Children of small and vocal communities are likely to possess it to a high degree and, if they are imaginative, have the power of incorporating into their own lives a significant span of time before their individual births."

2. Other examples of ethnic-oriented historical definitions of culture are not hard to find but they are not discussed here. Some of the best-known discussions of culture from a historical perspective are Banks's *Teaching Strategies for Ethnic Studies* (2008) and Grant's *Educating for Diversity: An Anthology of Multicultural Voices* (1995), both of which provide historical vignettes for "hyphenated American" children. For concrete examples of ways to include historical and other sorts of intellectual knowledge into teacher education programs see Gollnick and Chinn (2012) and Gay (1994).

3. The list is long. A few that are directly relevant to the points I am making here are Harris, 1993; Ostrowswki, 1997; Meléndez, 1997; Rogers & Soter, 1997; Wren & Mendoza, 2004, 2005; and Botelho & Rudman, 2009.

4. The first round in that debate had taken place yet another decade earlier, when the charismatic politician and author A. J. Grassby (1973) brought multiculturalism and multicultural education into the Australian public consciousness. Grassby argued that the various cultures represented in Australia should be seen in "normative and aesthetic terms," by which he meant in terms of their "historical questions, folk heritages and community groups" (ibid., p. 13). This view was reiterated in Australian educational policy documents during the 1970s but was eventually challenged, quite stridently, by Bullivant and others on the grounds that it not only ignores the adaptive and evolutionary nature of culture (Bullivant, 1985, p. 20), but even worse, papers over social inequalities, preserving the existing power structure and "diverting attention away from cultural examination of the tension and dynamics present within Australian society" (Sachs, 1989, p. 23).

5. "The word 'mode' or 'way' can imply (a) common or shared patterns; (b) sanctions for failure to follow the rules; (c) a manner, a 'how' of behaving; (d) social 'blueprints' for action. One or more of these implications is made perfectly explicit in many . . . definitions" (ibid.).

6. This definition does not appear in later editions of her book, but values and norms continue to be privileged components of Ramsey's conception of culture. For instance in her second edition she tells her readers that to identify their own (implicit) cultures, they should ask questions such as "What values were stressed in my home when I was growing up? How did people in my family and community relate to each other? How did they define success? What were their fears? What

values and priorities underlie the traditions, foods, and festivals that I remember?" (1998, p. 59).

7. For instance, she tells a rather charming anecdote of a four-year-old American boy who regularly adopted a German accent when speaking with a little girl from Germany. Apparently he was not mocking her but simply trying to make himself better understood by speaking in the way he thought she was expected to speak.

8. These sources cited include Baker, 2005; Bohn, 2003; Boykin, 1986; Deyhle, 1995; Gay, 2000; Howard, 1999; Loewen, 2007; Nieto, 1999; Strickland, 2000; Sue, 2004. Of these authors only Strickland is actually a psychologist; the others are education theorists who are familiar in varying degrees with cognitive psychology and its approaches to learning.

9. For instance, Gwendolyn Baker (1994, pp. 5, 20–21) adopts Corrine Brown's much earlier historically oriented conception of culture as including "all the accepted ways of behavior of a given people" (Brown, 1963, p. x).

10. Edith King, who is the first author of the book under discussion, is no naïf regarding the culture-society relationship. As the back cover of her book explains, she is a highly regarded Professor of Education who "specializes in the foundations of education with an emphasis on the sociological and anthropological disciplines."

11. The quotation is from King et al. (1994, p. 124). Their source is L. Harjo and I. Russell's *The Circle Never Ends. A Multicultural Preschool Curriculum Model* (1990). "Working together for the common good" is, of course, often cited as a distinctive cultural trait of Native Americans.

12. The two editions of her book have slightly different subtitles, reflecting the fact that the second edition was extensively revised. The subtitle of the 1994 edition is *A Multicultural Approach to the Education of Young Children*. The subtitle of the 1995 edition is *New Approaches to the Education of Young Children*.

13. "Applied to language, this principle reads: the more sentences we conspire to accept or reject, the better we understand the rest, whether or not we agree." Compare H.-G. Gadamer, 1991, p. 296.

14. "In this book it is our intention to provide information, strategies, techniques, innovative ideas, and most importantly, encouragement for teachers, administrators, educators, and parents in implementing this fresh and essential *diversity perspective* into programs for young children" (King et al., 1994, p. 3).

15. A side note for preservice readers: An important part of early childhood education is the "antibias curriculum" originally developed by Louise Derman-Sparks (1989). Antiracism and antidiscrimination are treated within the generic category of antibias education.

# 5

## Cognitive, Symbolic, and Critical Conceptions of Culture in the Professional Literature of Multicultural Education

Although the books and articles analyzed in this and the previous two chapters are not arranged chronologically, there is a rough temporal order in the nine ways in which multicultural educators have defined culture. The set of approaches we considered in chapter 3 (topical, structural, functional) were first taken by the cultural pluralist educators who wrote in the early days of multicultural education. The next three approaches, considered in chapter 4 (historical, normative, and behavioral), came into their own in the late 1980s although like the first three they have continued to appear over the lifespan of multicultural education. The last three (cognitive, symbolic, and critical) arrived on the scene relatively late, for the most part in or after the mid-1990s. With the critical approach we have arrived at what for many is the cutting edge of multicultural education theory, though in the next chapter I will describe a more thoroughly constructivist approach that I believe is now coming into its own—or at least should be.

However, the older approaches are not extinct. As is the case with most paradigm shifts, many of the elements of the older conceptions of culture—functionality, historical consciousness, normativity, etc.—are carried forward in the new theories but with different degrees of relevance and distinctness. Furthermore, it seems to be a fact of life that old theories fade slowly and die hard. Although the newer conceptions of culture (including those discussed in this chapter) now hold sway in the ivory towers of social theory, they have not yet replaced the old views that play out on the street and in the schoolrooms, that is, in the public consciousness and in auxiliary disciplines such as multicultural education. Those who would contribute to these conversations should respect that fact even as they try to overcome it. I hope you will keep this principle in mind as we resume our analysis of the literature of multicultural education.

7. Cognitive Definitions *(Culture is a complex of ideas and attitudes that inhibit impulses, establish shared meanings and goals, and enable people to live in a social system.)*

We saw in chapter 2 that during the post-Parsonian period of the 1960s and 1970s many psychologists and anthropologists tried to find a middle path between treating culture as an abstract semiotic system and limiting it to overt behaviors and material artifacts. Their strategy was to focus on the way culture conditions psychological processes and vice versa. Although these processes operate "inside the heads" of individual persons, they are considered cultural as well as intrapsychic because of the way they are acquired and sustained. They are shared methods of organizing the world and, taken collectively, constitute a common way of creating order among the various "inputs" from the social and material environment.

As we saw in chapter 2, the cognitive approach to culture first appeared in the social sciences and psychology during the late 1950s and quickly generated a highly technical literature involving psycholinguistics and French structuralism. One or another variation of that approach is now taken by authors of books and articles in which the cognitive dimension of the culture process is related to certain large-scale goals associated with multicultural education. These authors—one might call them cognitive multiculturalists—do not always expressly cite the literatures of cognitive psychology or cognitive social theory as they construct their definitions of culture but the influence of those disciplines is apparent. It is especially obvious when multiculturalist authors apply their notions of culture to some aspect of the broader concept of *culturally responsive teaching,* here understood as including issues of cognitive processing, learning style, cultural frames, beliefs and values, cultural identity, and the whole idea of a worldview. Given this wide range of cognitive themes or issues, it follows that there can be many different cognitive conceptions of culture. However, it is convenient to sort them into two groups: those that focus on *cognitive processes* (including learning styles and cultural frames) and those that focus on *ideational contents* (beliefs, values, and worldviews). As the following chart shows, the first two examples in this section include one definition from each category; the third example is more generic.

| Authors | Mode of Formal Component | Mode of Informal Component |
|---|---|---|
| Robinson (5.1) | Cognitive (process-oriented) | Cognitive |
| García & Guerra (5.2) | Cognitive (content-oriented) | Cognitive |
| Cushner et al. (5.3) | Cognitive and Topical | Cognitive |

The first example of the cognitive approach is a model of clear and distinct definition-making, in which the formal and informal components are each unambiguously cognitive. In her early but still prominent *Crosscultural Understanding* (1988), Gail Robinson draws on the work of George Spindler and other early cognitive anthropologists[1] in order to construct the following formal definition of culture as a process:

❖FD5.1    According to cognitive approaches, culture is not a material phenomenon. "Culture does not consist of things, people, behavior or emotions. It is the forms of things that people have in mind, their models for perceiving, relating, and otherwise interpreting them." The cognitive approach emphasizes the mechanism of organizing inputs. That is, *culture itself is a process* through which experience is mapped out, categorized and interpreted. (Ibid., p. 10, italics added; the internal quotation is from Goodenough, 1964.)

Robinson then uses the metaphors of computer programs and maps to illustrate FD5.1, thereby providing her readers with a short but useful informal definition of culture:

⬩ID5.1     From this perspective, culture is like a computer program. The program differs from culture to culture. The program refers to cognitive maps. Unlike the somewhat fixed notion of world view suggested by Sapir and Whorf, the program is subject to modification. (Ibid.)[2]

In Robinson's account the end of multicultural education is crosscultural understanding (the title of her book) and the means to that end is a version of culturally responsive pedagogy that she has derived from the way aspiring anthropologists are taught the ins and outs of ethnography. The type of ethnography she has in mind is the post-Geertzian methodology of "writing culture" from the perspective of the people who live within the culture under study. As we saw in chapter 2, in this methodology the ethnographer tries to understand and portray to others (especially other anthropologists) the way members of a particular culture typically process the inputs from their encounters with the natural and social world—or as Robinson puts it, the way they "categorize and interpret their experience" (ibid.). However, she is quick to admit that ethnography as it is usually written would be an imperfect template for multicultural education for at least two reasons. First of all, ethnographers do not usually attend to affective and other sorts of nonanalytical inputs, even though these are important features in the day-to-day communication of people who share a culture as well as in their communications with outsiders. Secondly, most ethnography ignores the cognitive processes of the ethnographers themselves (but see the early work of Paul Rabinow and William Sullivan (1979, 1987).[3] In contrast, culturally responsive pedagogy demands that teachers be aware of their own cognitive styles and cultural biases as well as those of their students.[4]

The second example of the cognitive approach straddles the distinction made above between process and product, since it defines culture as the lens though which a comprehensive filtering process takes place, the outcome of which is a mixed set of ideational and behavioral results (products). In an essay entitled "Conceptualizing Culture in Education: Implications for Schooling in a Culturally Diverse Society" (2006), Shernaz García and Patricia Guerra bundle under the generic category *worldview* a variety of ideational contents that range from shared values and beliefs to "assumptions about life."[5]

❖FD5.2    Culture provides the lens through which we view the world; it includes shared values, beliefs, perceptions, ideals, and assumptions about life that guide specific behavior. While this worldview is likely to be modified by our own personalities, experiences, education, and other factors, it is nevertheless the context in which certain values, behaviors, and ideas will be reinforced while others are rejected. (Ibid., p. 105)

Like Robinson and unlike Sapir and Whorf (see ID5.1), García and Guerra recognize that each person's worldview is to some extent shaped by him- or herself, which implies that worldviews are in our heads and that each person's worldview is different in spite of its cultural commonalities. However (and now unlike Robinson), García and Guerra do not treat these individual differences as the result of differences in *cognitive processing,* with that term understood in the sense it had for Goodenough and the other cognitive anthropologists discussed in chapter 2. For those authors each person's worldview is the *product,* not the source, of ideational contents that are themselves generated according to culture-specific transformative rules, whereas for García and Guerra our shared beliefs and values are what is left after our array of worldly experiences is somehow "filtered" through a worldview that already exists as a common instrument or device which individuals learn to use. As García and Guerra explain,

◈ID5.2    A distinguishing characteristic of cultural values is that they are shared by members of the group, rather than reflecting individual beliefs. While not all members of a culture [subscribe] to these values, these beliefs represent group tendencies or "ecological correlations." (Ibid.)

Our final example of the cognitive approach is another definition that is more concerned with ideational contents (attitudes, values, and other "intangible aspects of culture") than with the cognitive processes that generate them, although the difference here is one of emphasis rather than opposition. It is also less clear cut than the previous two definitions and in that respect more typical of the cognitive approaches to culture that show up in the literature of multicultural education. The example comes from the seventh edition of Kenneth Cushner, Averil McClelland, and Philip Safford's *Human Diversity in Education* (2011), and reveals the authors' implicit commitment to a strong cognitive view of culture.

First of all, we should note that in the chapter containing their definition of culture, Cushner and his colleagues have assembled a wide collection of issues, concepts, and practices. As its title, "Culture and the Culture-Learning Process," promises, the chapter opens with an analysis of culture and concludes with a discussion of the controversial issue of learning styles. The rest of their book is about learning and related topics such as language and cognitive development, but what is interesting here is the way in which the authors' underlying conception of culture as a cognitive style becomes increasingly evident as the chapter moves from the general topic of culture to the specific topics of learning and learning styles.[6] They tell us that culture is learned (that is, not innate), and that it is shared and nurtured (that is, socially and historically transmitted), all of which is true but does not constitute a definition of culture even in the widest sense of either "culture" or "definition." However, the authors' gears eventually engage, and drawing on Triandis they provide the following bimodal (that is, both topical and cognitive), ingredient-oriented formal definition of culture. Culture, they tell us, has

❖FD5.3    two components: objective elements and subjective elements (Triandis, 1972). The objective components of culture consist of the visible, tangible elements of a group; that is, the endless array of physical artifacts the people produce, the language they speak, the clothes they wear, the food they eat, and the unending stream of decorative and ritual objects they create. . . . [I]t is the objective components of culture that are most commonly thought of when cultural differences are considered. Subjective components of culture are the invisible, less tangible aspects of culture, such as the attitudes people hold, the values they defend, their norms of behavior, the manner in which they learn, and the hierarchy of social roles—in short, the *meaning* that the more objective components of culture have for individuals and groups. (Ibid., pp. 74–75)

The "objective components" mentioned in this definition are artifacts, not actions, but there is no reason to think behaviors and behavior patterns have been deliberately omitted. On the contrary, it seems clear that the authors simply see no need for a comprehensive list of either set of components. However, their list of "subjective components" is incomplete in a somewhat more important way. It fails to distinguish the two important and importantly distinct categories mentioned above, namely ideational contents (attitudes, values, norms) and cognitive processes (learning styles and social roles). Cushner and his colleagues may very well be aware of these omissions and imprecisions but they are obviously not interested in dwelling on them. Nor are they interested in engaging in any debate over whether the primary sense of the term "culture" is the overt/objective component or covert/subjective component. The wording of FD5.3 is neutral as to which of the two kinds of elements is more basic or more important, but the authors themselves are not at all neutral. The passage continues with a familiar metaphor that serves as an informal definition of their predominantly cognitive orientation toward the topic of culture:

⁂ID5.3     In this respect, culture can be likened to an iceberg: only 10% of the whole is seen above the surface of the water. It is the 90% of the iceberg that is hidden beneath the surface of the water that most concerns the ship's captain who must navigate the water. Like an iceberg, the most meaningful (and potentially dangerous) part of culture is the invisible or subjective part that is continually operating at the unconscious level and shapes people's perceptions and their responses to those perceptions. It is this aspect of culture that leads to most intercultural misunderstandings, and that requires the most emphasis in good multicultural or intercultural education. (Ibid., p. 75)

The rest of their book (this is only the third of eleven chapters) is devoted to the underwater portion of the iceberg. For instance we are told a few pages later that culture is learned when, thanks to socializing agents, "we acquire the specific knowledge, attitudes, skills, and values that form our cultural identity" (ibid., p. 70). Behavior patterns, artifacts, and other elements of overt culture are no longer part of the discussion. The authors have taken their readers into an extended analysis of the relationship of culture and the learning process, which in turn takes them into learning styles, perspective-taking skills (empathy), and other manifestly cognitive sorts of cultural traits. The fact that objective features like "behavior," "behavioral patterns," "artifacts," and "material objects" are not even mentioned in the book's index is further evidence that Cushner, McClelland,

and Safford's de facto conception of culture is overwhelmingly cognitive despite their pro forma reference to Triandis's division of culture into objective and subjective components.

*Discussion:* Each of the pedagogical issues and agendas discussed in this section revolves around a set of cultural traits thought to have great importance for teachers as well as for their students, and each issue and agenda is the subject of extensive research and controversy. This is especially true in the case of learning styles, which are a problematic subset of cognitive styles (see Timm, 1996). I say "problematic" because there is no consensus among educators regarding the connection between culture and modes of learning. What the comparative education scholar Ted Ward wrote in 1973 remains true: "Our comprehension of the meaning and implications of cultural differences among learners is at a stage roughly equivalent to the awareness of individual differences in the early 1950s: we are surely coming to accept the phenomenon, but we have little knowledge of what we might do to relate educational resources to the needs of those who are different" (p. 10).[7]

One reason, if not *the* reason, that the whole idea of culture-specific learning styles is still controversial is the confusion surrounding the notions of culture that show up in that literature. For instance, Craig Frisby (1993a; 1993b), no friend of Afrocentric education in general, regards the existence of Black Cultural Learning Styles (BCLS) as a myth based on "pseudoscientific theories that promise a perception of African-Americans as having a mysterious culture which can be 'truly' understood only by a handful of 'experts'" (1993b, p. 569). In contrast, Afrocentric educator Janice Hale (1994, p. 559; see also Hale, 1982) insists that African and African-American culture has a deep structure of which one of the most important surface manifestations is the existence of BCLS.[8] Over the last two decades research on learning styles in general as well as culture-specific learning styles has continued, but this is not the place to review that literature (but see Wren & Wren, 2003).

Even so, some mention of the closely related concept of "cognitive frames" is in order here, since educators familiar with cognitive processing theories have distilled its general ideas into what Spring and other multiculturalists have called cultural frame theory and cognitive psychologist and anthropologists call "schemas," "scenarios," "frames," "scenes," "scripts," or "models" (Mandler, 1984; Shore, 1996; Strauss & Quinn, 1994). Suffice it to say that multicultural educators who base their pedagogy and curriculum on a cognitive conception of culture will find in this context an unusually close link between theory and practice. For them, the phrase "culturally responsive teaching" will be almost redundant: a teacher who fails to accommodate the cultural frames and competencies of his or her students will not be much of a teacher.

Finally, we must remember that the agenda of what I have called cognitive multiculturalism is not limited to developing the cultural knowledge and sensibilities of students. Teachers must expand their own repertoires of cultural knowledge and skills, and in doing so they are likely to change not only the atmosphere of their individual classrooms but the ethos of their schools and other institutions. Indeed, if the cognitive view of culture is correct in assuming that the way we live and think shapes our culture at the same time that it is shaped by our culture, then it logically follows that the long-term effects of this kind of teaching are literally unimaginable at the present moment.

### 8. Symbolic Definitions *(Culture is a set of shared, socially constructed representations and meanings.)*

In chapter 2 we saw that in the aftermath of Parson's grand synthesis, anthropologists such as Geertz developed an abstract conception of culture as a public semiotic system in which symbols operate as interpretative keys for discourse within and across cultures. From his premise that culture is "an ordered system of meaning and symbols" that individuals use to construct and define their worlds, Geertz concluded that culture is a "text" in need of interpretation, not a group of people or a set of traits and behaviors to be observed and catalogued. Over the next decades other anthropologists and culture theorists followed this approach as they tried to rehabilitate Max Weber's thesis that ideas have a causal role in human affairs, a role that ideas supposedly play at the group level as well as between and within individuals. Considering the enthusiasm with which scholars and the general public greeted Geertz's *Interpretation of Cultures* in the mid-1970s, one might have expected that it would shape the multiculturalist discourse emerging in educational circles at roughly the same time. Surprisingly, this did not happen. True, the semiotic character of culture is often acknowledged in the literature of multicultural education, but for some reason—perhaps it seems too abstract to be a useful point of departure for understanding practical problems of cultural diversity—few multiculturalists have explicitly adopted the interpretative approach associated with it or stressed its discursive character. However, there are important exceptions, including the three approaches shown on the following chart.

| Authors | Mode of Formal Component | Mode of Informal Component |
|---------|--------------------------|----------------------------|
| Banks (5.4) | Cognitive and Symbolic | Symbolic and Cognitive |
| Page (5.5) | Symbolic | Symbolic |
| Yon (5.6) | Symbolic | Symbolic |

The best known of these authors is of course James Banks. In his introduction to an influential collection of essays by himself and other multicultural educators (Banks & Banks, 2010), he offers a hybrid definition of culture as a mix of cognitive and symbolic categories that jointly make up "the meaning of culture." This overarching meaning is itself a collection of more specific meanings, so that culture itself is defined as the

❖FD5.4 knowledge, concepts, and values shared by group members through systems of communication. Culture also consists of the shared beliefs, symbols, and interpretations within a human group. (Ibid., p. 8)

The first part of FD5.4 may seem similar to the cognitive definitions considered in the previous section, but it is importantly different in that Banks identifies these cognitive contents as parts of "systems of communication."[9] The second part reinforces the dialogical theme by its reference to the shared character of these contents. However, it is in the informal definition ID5.4 that Geertz's influence on Banks comes through most clearly. After citing what he now considers the prevailing social science view of culture "as consisting primarily of the symbolic, ideational, and intangible aspects of human societies," Banks rounds out his discussion of culture with an informal definition that leaves no doubt as to his own current commitment to the interpretative approach:

❖ID5.4 The *essence* of a culture is not its artifacts, tools, or other tangible cultural elements but how the members of the group interpret, use, and perceive them. It is the values, symbols, interpretations, and perspectives that distinguish one people from another in modernized societies; it is not material objects and other tangible aspects of human societies. People within a culture usually interpret the meanings of symbols, artifacts, and behaviors in the same or in similar ways. (Ibid., italics added)

Echoing the literature of interpretive anthropology, he describes society as having an inner core or "essence" of more or less abstract philosophical ideas, expressed in more or less aesthetic symbols, and enacted in more or less explicitly religious rituals, all of which give meaning to a people's shared world in the same way that a story or written text gives meaning to a set of otherwise incomprehensible events. In short, Banks believes culture is the text expressed in a group's symbols and rituals, which may but need not have explicitly economic and political dimensions.

A similar use of the symbolic conception shows up in Reba Neukom Page's (1991, pp. 13–15) account of where culture fits into the school curriculum. After repeating Geertz's oft-cited definition of culture as the "webs of significance [in which] man is suspended [and which] he himself has spun" (Geertz, 1973, p. 5) and then recalling George Spindler's general definition of cultural knowledge as what people know that makes what they do sensible (Spindler, 1982), Page condenses their ideas into a four-word formal definition according to which culture is

❖FD5.5     a symbolic, social process. (Page, p. 14)

Page has chosen her words carefully. Culture is *symbolic* because it is a web of meanings, not a set of facts. It is *social* because it is dialogical, not monological, and it is a *process* because it is not an object or thing that has been produced. Expanding her rather compact definition, she then declares:

❖ID5.5     People make or "spin" signs, which constitute, and are constituted by, a culture's particular order or "webs." Moreover, people live suspended within the webs, so that culture is neither a subjective abstraction in someone's head nor an objective structure that dictates behavior. . . . Thus, like language, culture simultaneously differentiates and integrates. It is a process of carving the inchoate world into distinctive domains while also integrating the domains in a system of relationships. (Ibid.)

From there she goes on to compare culture to language, both of which order the "inchoate world" in an ongoing double process of differentiating it into specific domains and integrating them into a more or less unified system of relationships. Through this comparison she shows how the idea of culture as a meaning-making system can explain the ambivalence regarding individualism and community that she believes pervades American politics in general and educational policy in particular.

Although the explicit endorsements and uses of the symbol-oriented conception of culture by Banks and Page are unusual in the literature of multicultural education,[10] its echoes can be heard in various definitions of culture cited in the previous chapters, such as Bullivant's reference to religious beliefs in ID3.7, and the importance that Hoopes and Pusch gave in ID3.8 to values, beliefs, aesthetic standards, linguistic expression, patterns of thinking, behavioral norms, and styles of communication. Similar sensibilities to the semiotic function of culture can be found in the normative and culture-as-heritage definitions. It would therefore be a mistake to think that because few educational multiculturalists dwell on the nature or importance of the images, beliefs, myths, rituals, or other semiotic features of culture so important to Geertz and his fellow interpretative anthropologists, they are oblivious to the meaning-making function of culture.

The final example of a symbolic definition of culture is much different than the two we have just considered. It comes from Daniel Yon's curiously titled book *Elusive Culture* (2000), in which a discourse model of contemporary culture theory is used to analyze data collected in a yearlong ethnographic study of an inner-city Toronto high school. In the course of delineating the theoretical frame within which he examines the students' and teachers' discourse about culture, race, and identity, Yon sketches three stages in the history of cultural anthropology, according to which culture was first understood empirically as a collection of observable "attributes" (the period from Tylor to Parsons), then hermeneutically as "webs of meaning" (Geertz and his followers), and finally poststructurally (here he is influenced by Stuart Hall) as "elusive culture" (ibid., p. 9). His definition of this third stage retains Geertz's interpretive approach to "representations and the complex relationships that individuals take up in relation to them," but he analyzes more carefully than Geertz ever did the nature of the social relationships that constitute discourse situations. In his formal definition of culture Yon agrees with Geertz and others who share Geertz's hermeneutical, semiotic conception of culture according to which

❖FD5.6    culture [is] an open-ended text. Thinking about culture as text allows for multiple meanings and, as Geertz put it, insists upon the refinement of debates rather than the closure of consensus. (Ibid., pp. 8–9)

What Yon does with this symbolic definition of culture goes beyond Geertz in many ways,[11] but it can be generally characterized as relocating the interpretive activity of ethnographers—and by extension that of teachers engaged in multicultural education—from the storyteller's bench to the fora of discourse.[12] Monologues are only special moments within dialogues, and ethnography is transformed from third person descriptions to first and second person scripts. Yon explains his refinement of the Geertzian conception of culture a few lines later, where he not only summarizes anthropology's historical shift from holistic explanations to situation-specific "partial truths" but also intimates that the interpretive conception of culture is itself an interpretation, keyed to the ambivalence and internal contradictions of our everyday lives:

ID5.6    The monologic voice of the ethnographer gave way to an engagement with multiple voices that are competing and contradictory. Far from being a stable and knowable set of attributes, culture has now become *a matter of debate about representations* and the complex relationships that individuals take up in relation to them. (Ibid., p. 9; italics added)

In the next chapter I will pick up on these themes, which in my view constitute the most adequate way of understanding culture in general and the best way to bring the concept into the classroom without falling into the extremes of either essentializing it (culture as a thing or set of things one has) or trivializing it (culture as food fairs, etc.). For now, suffice it to say that what Yon calls "elusive culture" is not so much a repudiation of earlier theories of culture as a new, heavily situational and dialogical incorporation of those earlier theories.

In other words, when people—including the high school students whom Yon interviewed—talk to each other about culture and cultural identity they are not writing books for anonymous and timeless audiences, but rather trying to make themselves understood to other concrete individuals for reasons that can vary from one day, place, or interlocutor to the next. When someone speaks passionately about his or her cultural heritage at a zoning commission hearing the meaning of culture will be different than when the same person talks about cultural identity to a buddy, lover, or bully, to a therapist, lawyer, or fellow devotee of some musical genre. On St. Patrick's Day I may be full of intense "recreational ethnicity," to use Kenneth Appiah's delicious phrase, whereas at a union meeting I make common cause with my fellow workers without a thought of our different cultural heritages. And so on.

I said a moment ago that Yon's elusive culture was a "dialogical incorporation" of prevailing anthropological views. To that I would now add that the setting within which the dialogues take place need not be academic. Indeed, academic debates about culture are only a small part of a larger phenomenon of people talking about culture. As in other discourse situations, participants in dialogues about culture shape their comments and responses to what (they think) is in the minds of their interlocutors, as symbolic interactionist sociology has shown. What makes culture "elusive" is the simple fact that every interlocutor and therefore every discourse situation is different. From these differences it follows that in ordinary discourse the use (and hence the meaning) of the word "culture" and its symbolic forms will vary from one dialogue to the next, often in profoundly different ways. To say as Yon does that culture is elusive is, to put it mildly, not at all the same thing as saying it is meaningless.

*Discussion:* Not surprisingly, multicultural authors who work with a symbolic conception of culture seem inclined to favor pedagogical agendas that fall under the general category of cultural competence. In this respect they resemble the authors discussed in the previous section, who favored cognitive definitions of culture. However, although both groups focus on the "invisible" portion of the culture iceberg, an important difference in their theories of culture is reflected in their pedagogies. The difference is in the emphasis each approach places on intersubjective dialogue, which as we saw is much greater in the case of those authors discussed in the present section. Assuming as I do that Banks, Page, and Yon are representative of the semiotic approach, it seems fair to tie that approach to a broader view of cultural responsiveness, in which not only is the teacher attuned to the cultural backgrounds of his or her students but also the students are culturally competent discourse partners with each other.

Banks does not emphasize the ambiguities of cultural symbols, probably because he understands the social discourse about them as relatively straightforward and not particularly conflictual (his is definitely not a conflict model of society), whereas Page and Yon see symbols as forming loose "webs" rather than internally coherent structures. This implies a need for what personality theorists call "tolerance of ambiguity" on the parts of the students and teachers. How these different views of the symbolic interaction affect one's views of cultural identity and self-esteem is an open question, but it seems reasonable to expect that multicultural educators who take a semiotic approach to culture will have at the center of their notion of cultural competence a fairly robust conception of cultural identity.

Another central part of cultural competence, more emphasized by Page and Yon (and of course Geertz) than by Banks, is the ability to live "suspended" within the webs of meaning that are neither purely subjective soliloquies nor rigidly objective structures or codes of behavior. In other words, culture is made by people interacting with each other, sometimes as individuals and sometimes as members of groups, but always negotiating practical priorities, personal and group identities, and understandings of how to balance the conflicting meanings carried by symbols of, say, an individual's right to pursue his or her own conception of the good life on the one hand and symbols of loyalty and commitment to the common good on the other. The most important and yet most problematic of these ambiguities is probably the political significance of cultural symbols. Should the discourse and symbols of justice issues that are associated with multicultural education center on specifically *cultural* differences (and tolerance of those differences) or on *political* and *economic* inequalities such as access to quality education, equal pay, and participation in the political process?

In the present context, the basic question seems to be whether educators must choose between the political and cultural agendas associated with multicultural education. Here Geertz's metaphor of being suspended within webs of meaning is especially appropriate. For those who hold wholly or even in part a symbolic conception of culture, the "sub-agenda" underlying their other educational agendas is that of preserving and promoting open, shared inquiry. Cultural symbols are the vehicles by which people construct their social worlds and their personal identities. In this respect culture consists in the same sort of discourse as that of political interaction: a negotiation of differences that is always full of surprises.

## 9. Critical Definitions *(Culture consists in those symbols and symbol-making activities that typically reflect and promote a society's current power relationships.)*

The three symbolic definitions of culture discussed in the previous section rest on the notion of cultures as networks of symbols that when interpreted as a kind of literary text reveal worldviews rich in metaphysical, social, normative, and other sorts of Weberian "meaning of life" implications. In that interpretative process the symbols themselves—rituals, legends, honorific titles, etc.—are seen as directing people's lives largely because of their long-standing historical cachet, even though members of the culture often differ among themselves as to just how the symbols should be interpreted. The present section exhibits a very different semiotics of culture, in which the symbols under discussion have little to do with metaphysics and the meaning of life and everything to do with power and social control. This is the approach taken in the educational literature that calls itself "critical multiculturalism."

Unfortunately, the concept of culture is seldom spelled out in this literature, which is more concerned with exposing the political uses of culture than with distinguishing it from related categories such as society, ethnicity, race, gender, or social class. Its contributors do not draw their inspiration directly from anthropology or sociology but rather from the interdisciplinary cultural studies movement discussed at the end of chapter 2 as well as from the predominantly European literatures of postmodernism, poststructuralism, and critical theory. As we will see here and in the next chapter, their multicultural education representatives—most of whom are as American as apple pie—have adopted a continental writing style that is often dauntingly ornate but nonetheless rich in implications, irony, and arresting metaphors or turns of phrase. Of the few critical multiculturalist texts that do present distinct definitions of culture I will review three, taken from Carl Grant and Judyth Sachs (1995), Antonia Darder (1995), and Carmen Montecinos (1995). Their definitional modes are not always obvious, especially in the authors' respective formal definitions, but the following chart shows how I have parsed the statements showcased in this section:

| Authors | Mode of Formal Component | Mode of Informal Component |
|---|---|---|
| Grant & Sachs (5.7) | Critical and Symbolic | Critical |
| Darder (5.8) | Symbolic and Critical | Critical |
| Montecinos (5.9) | Critical and Symbolic | Critical |

That multicultural education has an irreducible political dimension is hardly news. The basic idea of cultural hegemony surfaced regularly in the early literature of cultural pluralism and was thematized by Sleeter and Grant as the most comprehensive of their classic five approaches to multicultural education, namely "Education that is Multicultural and Social Reconstructionist." What *was* new, though, was the merger of multicultural education and the critical pedagogy movement originally associated with the "pedagogy of the oppressed" advocated by Latin American liberation theorists, most famously Paulo Freire (1968). That merger, which Sleeter and McLaren (1995, p. 8) have called a "precipitous theoretical and political convergence," moved the social reconstructionist agenda further to the political left as well as squarely within the methodological and rhetorical style of postmodernism and poststructuralism.[13] As Freire once explained, whereas the dialogue of traditional pedagogy "confirms the dominant mass culture and the inherited, official shape of knowledge," the liberatory dialogue characteristic of his own pedagogy "disconfirms domination and illuminates while affirming the freedom of the participants to remake their culture" (Shor & Freire, 1987, p. 99).

It was perhaps inevitable that the merger of multiculturalism and critical pedagogy would incorporate the insights and discursive styles of the emerging cultural studies literature, which as we saw at the end of chapter 2 was the intellectual heir of the symbol-centered theories of sociologists and humanities scholars such as Blumer in the United States and Williams in Great Britain. The early critical multiculturalists quickly appropriated this array of ideas and agendas, as did a few anthropologists such as Roger Keesing, who in 1989 chided his colleagues of the American Anthropological Association for not being more concerned with the "hegemonic force" of culturally established meanings.[14] A few years later two critical multiculturalist educators, Carl Grant and Judyth Sachs (1995), imbedded Keesing's definition of culture as the symbolic production of meanings in their programmatic essay about how postmodernism provides a "useful lens for educators of multicultural education":

❖FD5.7     Keesing makes a useful suggestion about how we might proceed by advocating a critical conception of culture. Such a conception would take the production and reproduction of cultural forms as problematic: that is, "it would examine the way culture as symbolic production is linked to power and interest (in terms of class, hierarchy, gender, etc.). . . . [A] critical conception of the cultural would begin with the assumption that in any 'community' or 'society' there will be multiple, subdominant and partially submerged cultural traditions (again, in relation to power, rank, class, gender, age, etc.), as well as the

dominant tradition." (Ibid., p. 100–102; the internal quotation
is from Keesing, 1989, p. 57)

Their explanatory comments focus on Keesing's idea that educators
should take cultural forms as problematic because doing so would show
the link between social critique and the personal and moral growth of the
students themselves:

❧ID5.7    By focusing on the everyday and how this is experienced by
          various sectorial interests, the multicultural education we
          envisage, informed by postmodern perspectives on concepts
          such as discourse and culture, provides powerful ways for
          students to rethink their own personal and group experiences
          and strategies for dealing with these. One outcome may well
          be that ideas such as equity and social justice become the stuff
          of education, not just abstract peripheral rhetoric favored by
          bureaucrats and politicians. (Ibid., p. 101)

Grant and Sach's use of Keesing's conception of culture as "symbolic
production" is a welcome exception to the triple generalization that in the
literature of critical multiculturalism the concept of culture is usually invisible, that when it does appear the authors offer no distinctive conception of
culture as such, and that the formal definitions they occasionally supply do
little or no work.[15] In short, for most critical multiculturalists the importance
of their approach usually lies in what they go on to say about exposing the
largely invisible but nonetheless oppressive *abuses* associated with some indeterminate conception of culture. However, FD5.7 is not the only exception to
this general neglect of the culture concept by critical multiculturalists.
    In the same year that Grant and Sach's essay appeared, Antonia Darder
(1995) provided a fairly straightforward definition and explanation of
culture in her introduction to *Culture and Difference* (1995), a collection of
critical multiculturalist essays about bicultural identity. (Of the volume's
fourteen essays only Darder's introduction identifies an underlying conception of culture.) Her account of culture is derived in large part from the
work of critical theorist Iris Marion Young, for whom group meanings are
encased in symbols or "cultural forms" that the members know are theirs,
either because they were shaped by them or forced upon them, or both.[16]
However, this merger of symbols, group meanings, and personal identities
is not a fixed, once-and-for all relationship, as Darder explains in her formal definition of what she appropriately calls "a foundational understanding of culture." Culture, she tells us, is

❖FD5.8    an epistemological process that is shaped by a complex dia-
          lectical relationship of social systems of beliefs and practices

which constantly moves members between the dynamic tension of cultural preservation and cultural change. (Ibid., p. 6)

In spite of its reference to social systems, FD5.8 might seem at first sight
better located under the general category of a "symbolic definition of
culture" discussed in the previous section. However, Darder's underlying
critical-theoretic orientation shows up in the very next sentence (ID5.8),
in which she explains the "dialectical relationship" featured in her formal
definition. This explanation lays the groundwork for Darder's subsequent
critique of the usually unexamined assumption that in any society, especially ours, the mainstream culture is an "absolute entity" in terms of which
nonmainstream cultures should be understood. Her argument is poststruc-
tural and symbolic interactionist in its concepts and its scholarly references
though not in its prose style, which is mercifully straightforward:

⁂ID5.8    This is to say that no culture (particularly within the Western
          postmodern context of advanced capitalism) exists as a fixed,
          static, or absolute entity, since culture, and hence cultural iden-
          tity, is a relationally constituted phenomenon, activated and
          produced through constant social negotiation between others
          and one's own integration in the daily life and history of the
          community." (Ibid.)

Darder begins with Hall's view of culture as inherently "subject to the
play of history and the play of difference" (from Hall, 1990, p. 150). Writing from this general symbolic interactionist perspective she proceeds to
draw sharp political conclusions concerning such issues as the politics
of identity, resistance, self-determination, and cultural nationalism in
the United States and across the world. For instance, she claims that
biculturalism—which is the main subject of the volume which her comments introduce—should be understood in terms of the realities that shape
the struggle for survival by nondominant persons and groups who have
been stigmatized as unfit to enter the mainstream.

A third critical conception of culture was offered by Carmen Montecinos
(1995), relating the postmodernist cultural anthropology of Ronaldo
Rosaldo (1989) to Sleeter and Grant's social reconstructionist stage of
multicultural education. Appropriating Rosaldo's conception of culture in
the same way that Grant and Sachs used Keesing's conception, Montecinos
writes that the idea of culture as a holistic structure is obsolete:

❖FD5.9    Culture in multicultural societies cannot, therefore, be un-
          derstood as a self-contained whole. Instead, it must be un-
          derstood as a "porous array of intersections where distinct
          processes criss-cross from within and beyond its borders."

> (Montecinos, 1995, pp. 294–95; the internal quotation is
> from Rosaldo, 1989, p. 20)

These "distinct processes" include both large scale institutional (that is, socioeconomic and political) exchanges and small scale interpersonal symbolic interactions. Expanding on Rosaldo's statement, Montecinos clarifies the importance of FD5.9 as follows:

❖ID5.9    This definition of culture shifts the focus of multicultural
           knowledge away from knowing about within-group patterns
           towards knowing about the patterns of social relations *between*
           groups. (Ibid., italics added)

Montecinos's view of culture is "open-textured." I say this not because it is vague or indeterminate in the fashion of, say, the topical definitions discussed in chapter 3, but because it reflects her belief that the details of any culture are determined by the *social relations* within which its members live their lives and understand them. She goes on to argue that this emphasis on the strongly relational character of culture produces a much more adequate conception of culture even though it poses new problems for the multicultural educators who adopt it. They must find ways to represent a plurality of cultural groups nonhierarchically and from the inside. That is, they must as far as possible represent to their students each cultural group as it is understood by its own members, at the same time making it clear that cultural groups overlap in various ways and that many of their members live in cultural "borderlands." It is precisely this challenge that makes Montecinos's view of culture an excellent illustration of *critical* multiculturalism. Her stress on the symbolic self-representations of "minority" groups entails a dethroning of the "majority" group, using these two terms to denote a difference in political power, not a simple numerical difference. Individuals may vary in the degree to which they identify with established cultural groups, but in all cases the maxim holds that cultural identities are defined in terms of personal and group relationships and maintained by social institutions.

*Discussion:* Even when they do take time to define the concept of culture, critical multiculturalists are mainly interested in going beyond it, focusing their critique on basically flawed socioeconomic and political orders and, correlatively, on the support that cultural symbols give to these flawed orders. In a word, culture itself is not interesting to them, except insofar as it can be deconstructed and inspected for collusion with unjust power structures. Their own educational agenda is based on the primary premise that cultural identities are relationally defined and institutionally maintained, as well as on the secondary premise that the intergroup relations and socioeconomic institutions in question really can be transformed, and that cultural traits need not be forms of oppression by or complicity with "the powers that be."

This is not to say that critical multiculturalists reject the other agendas and goals usually associated with multicultural education, such as developing cultural knowledge and related sorts of competence on the part of students, promoting culturally competent pedagogy and respect for diversity on the part of teachers, antibias education, and so on. However, critical multiculturalists tend to view the pursuit of such goals with some suspicion, on the grounds that they often divert attention from the deeper problems in our society. They are especially wary of any pedagogical treatment of cultural identities, symbols, or social interactions that essentialize cultures, not only because of their postmodern/poststructuralist aversion to any suggestion of "primordial" cultural traits but also because they find the subtle but powerful forms of oppression associated with cultural essentialism morally repugnant.

## SUMMARY

The late Donald Campbell, a prominent psychologist whom I was privileged to know, once complained to me that *Time* magazine had "overclarified" an important address he had given as president of the American Psychological Association. I hope that I have not committed the same offense, and that my attempts to identify and chart the many ways in which multicultural educators have understood culture have not overclarified either their work or the concept itself. Even if I did, though, the textual analysis provided in this and the preceding chapters will have succeeded if it shows its readers how to go about looking for the faces in the bushes, that is, how to recognize the implicit conceptions of culture that are in play in the important but often unkempt professional literature of multicultural education.

## QUESTIONS FOR REFLECTION

As always, many questions remain, some broad and others narrow. For instance, to what extent are multicultural educators' goals shaped by their conceptions of culture? Is it possible that things are really the other way around, that is, that their conceptions of culture are shaped by their goals, or even that they shape each other? Furthermore, are the answers to these and similar questions different when the "multicultural educator" is a classroom teacher, an administrator, or the author of a textbook or scholarly article?

As in the two previous chapters, our analysis of multicultural texts has proceeded in fairly abstract terms, using categories and metaphors found ready-made in the literature itself. But are the terms really clear? What would be some concrete examples of a "cognitive style," a "worldview," a "symbolic interaction," the "historically constituted relation of power," or "the politics of identity"? These are important questions, but the most important ones have to do with the intellectual adequacy of the views of culture and their consistency with the educational agendas of their authors. Although I have not attempted to answer those questions in the preceding pages, by now my own views may be showing through—and will be still more obvious in the coming chapter. Even so, what I have just called "the most important questions" must ultimately be answered by the person reading these pages.

*Analysis:* Although the following long and sometimes grammatically flawed passage presents several conceptions of culture, only one of them is actually accepted and used by its authors. Find that conception and then, using the same five questions found at the end of the two previous chapters (repeated below), identify its formal definition and informal definition and try to specify their dominant modes. (Hint: Expect both its FD and ID to be richly multimodal.) Finally, ask yourself why the authors decided not to use any of the several other definitions they mention. Also ask why they even bothered to cite those definitions if they did not intend to use them. (Another hint: Check the title of their book. Are the unused definitions less relevant to their educational agenda? If so, why so? If not, why not?)

1. What is the authors' Formal Definition?
2. What is the authors' Informal Definition?
3. Can you identify the mode(s) of the Formal Definition?
4. Can you identify the mode(s) of the Informal Definition?
5. Given the importance of coherence between any multicultural education author's *theory* of culture and his or her educational *practice* (curriculum, learning goals, reform program, etc.), what do you think a teacher who shares these authors' conception of culture would want his or her K–12 students to know and be able to do?

### CULTURE, THE MAGIC WEB OF LIFE

The concept of culture has been a focus of discussions among social scientists, educators, philosophers, and people in general for generations. Many learned and famous people have searched hard and debated long trying to define the meaning of culture. No one seems to be able to agree on one definition. However, everybody acknowledges that we all have a culture.

#### The Need for Guideposts: What Culture Does for Human Beings

Imagine a world with no rules. Think about how it would be if there were no directions to guide our existence, no principles to tell us what is right or wrong, no frames of reference to give us clues as we confront things never encountered before. Those are the problems we would face if there were no culture.

Culture provides a framework for our lives. It is the paradigm humans use to guide their behavior, find meaning in events, interpret the past, and set aspirations. From very early in life, we learn to follow and apply the recognized guidelines of our society, sometimes without even being consciously aware of them. For a child, cultural guidelines are discovered through daily interactions with others, observing, and modeling some of the behaviors learned from families and adults. Psychologist Jerome Bruner says that when the child enters into a group, the child does so as a participant of a public process where meanings are shared. This participant status entitles the child to learn the ways of the group. Learning makes the child a member of a group. These "ways of the group" are what we call culture. As social human beings, we all belong to a group, and all groups have culture.

#### We All Have a Culture

Social scientists—sociologists, anthropologists, and psychologists—believe that culture demarcates all manners people use to interact in the context of society. Culture is needed by humans to survive in a social group. Bruner affirms that "the divide in human evolution was crossed when culture became the major factor in giving form to the minds of those living under its sway." Clearly, as humans strive for survival, the need for an organizing pattern becomes a necessity. This is what makes culture a thing shared by all social groups.

There are many ways to describe and define culture. For Freire, culture encompasses all that is done by people. Hernandez says that culture refers to "the complex processes of human social interaction and symbolic communication." Arvizu, Snyder, and Espinosa describe culture as an instrument people use as they struggle to survive in a social group. The definition used throughout this book identifies culture as the ways and manners people use to see, perceive, represent, interpret, and assign meaning to the reality they live or experience. Culture is a glass prism through which we look at life. Like a prism, culture has many facets. Early childhood educators need to be cognizant and aware of these various angles that help explain the behavior, reactions, and manners of children in the classroom.

*(continued)*

## CULTURE, THE MAGIC WEB OF LIFE (*continued*)

Some of the key aspects of culture that contribute to understanding and responsively planning experiences for young children and their families are the following:

*Culture defines the accepted behaviors, roles, interpretations, and expectations of a social group.* Every social group has norms; principles reflect agreed meanings.

*Culture is present in visible, tangible ways.* Culture also exists in abstract ways that are not physically perceived by the eye.

*Culture offers stable patterns to guide human behavior.* Although stable, culture is also dynamic as it constantly responds to the various influences in the surroundings, affecting changes whenever necessary.

*Culture is acquired through interactions with the environment.* The major settings where this occurs are the family and the school. One of the most evident aspects of culture acquisition is how, through interactions with parents and family members, children learn the language of their group.

*We begin learning the patterns and shared meanings of the group we belong to at birth.* This knowledge increases and changes as we grow and develop, both individually and as a member of society.

*Culture influences different aspects of life.* Nothing escapes the power of culture.

*Cultural differences also exist among people of the same culture.* Within a same group, differing lifestyles and values are not uncommon. Experiences, including personal and historical circumstances, shape people's views.

*Culture gives people identity.* Sharing ideas, values, and practices gives humans a sense of being part of an entity.

### Cultural Dimensions

The influence of culture is so powerful that it covers every aspect of behavior. As Hall says, "[t]here is not one aspect of life that is *not touched and altered* by culture" (emphasis added). This includes personality, how people dress themselves (including shows of emotions), the way they think, how they move, how problems are solved, how their cities are planned and laid out, how transportation systems function, and how economic and government systems are put together and function.

Hall's ideas remind us that culture can be exhibited in visible ways (that is, with our body movements, our gestures, and the physical distribution of our cities) and invisible ways (such as how we think and how we solve problems). This premise suggests another relevant feature of culture: the twofold way in which we exhibit its influences and effects. Visible to the eye are dress codes, eating patterns, and even the games played by children. Other things remain invisible to the eye, but are perceived through actions.

Whether visible or not, culture provides patterns to interpret life.

From W. Robles de Meléndez and V. Beck, *Teaching Young Children in Multicultural Classrooms: Issues, Concepts, and Strategies* (2010, pp. 44–48, passim)

## NOTES

1. She cites Goodenough (1964), Triandis (1972), and Spindler (1974, 1979, 1980, 1982).

2. The reference here is to E. Sapir and B. Whorf's alleged claim that language determines all thought. (Note: Less famous, weaker versions of this claim have survived but the strong version that worries Robinson is no longer taken seriously and was probably never held by Sapir or his student Whorf [see Kay & Kempton, 1984; see also Sapir, 1929]).

3. See also the self-referential approach to ethnography taken by interpretive anthropologists such as James Clifford, George Marcus, and Michael Fischer (Marcus & Fisher, 1986; Clifford & Marcus, 1986).

4. Robinson develops this point more extensively later in her book, in the context of selective perception and information processing.

5. They are either unfamiliar or unconcerned with the "somewhat fixed" use of the term "worldview" that Robinson dismissed in ID5.1. Her reference is to E. Sapir and B. Whorf's famous claim that language determines all thought. (Note: Less famous, weaker versions of this claim have survived but the strong version that worries Robinson is no longer taken seriously [see Kay & Kempton, 1984]).

6. Their opening move is to divide the question of how to define culture into what they call "Three Views of Culture," corresponding to the three traditional disciplines of anthropology, sociology, and psychology. Unfortunately this heading is misleading since only the first of these three views turns out to be a view of culture as such: the other two views concern the construction of social groups and of frameworks for cross-cultural research. This infelicity, unimportant in itself, is a signal to the reader to be prepared to do a certain amount of charitable reconstruction of the authors' exposition. Throughout this undeniably important chapter there is considerable meandering and other sorts of indirection. Even the authors' discussion of the first, anthropological view uses several pages of seemingly disconnected information to prepare readers for the formal definition of culture that is to come.

7. The idea that children have not only different levels of intelligence (whatever that means) but also different cognitive styles and hence different learning needs goes back to Piaget, but he saw these differences as stages of a hierarchical process of cognitive development that is itself universal. In the 1950s and 1960s educational psychologists such as H. A. Witkin (1962, 1967) broke away from the hierarchical developmental model and posited that cognitive style is basically a matter of individual differences that have little or nothing to do with developmental stages. The conversation about cognitive style changed in the next decade, when educators attuned to the new themes of cultural pluralism began to shift their attention from individual differences among children to supposed cognitive differences among cultural groups. Unlike cognitive developmentalists for whom the child is an active participant in small-scale interactions that push him or her to increasingly higher cognitive levels, the early cultural-difference theorists not only emphasized the role of culture in a child's cognitive formation but also used basically the same model of reciprocal influence that others would invoke in the 1990s. Anticipating Robinson's comparison of culture to a computer program, Ward declared in an article on African cognitive styles that thanks to language, culture is virtually a program of the mind such that "the

individual as a learner is both bounded and shaped according to the world-and-life view and the mental-process styles of his culture" (Ward, 1973, p. 2).

8. Many other authors have weighed in on this delicate issue. Some like Hale have invoked a structural conception of culture drawn from Boas and post-Boasians such as Melvin Herskovits ([1941] 1958); others such as Thomas Kochman (1981, p. 14) have acknowledged the rather different, more sociological point (also made by Herskovits ([1941] 1958, p. xxvi) that distinctively "black" cultural styles tend to be more prevalent among African-Americans at a lower socioeconomic level, at least in the United States.

9. Recall the discussion in chapter 2 of Geertz's strident objection to cognitive anthropologists such as Goodenough, precisely because they located culture "in the head" rather than in the inherently public realm of interpersonal discourse.

10. But see the work of Hervé Varenne, especially his *Symbolizing America* (1986).

11. "It is impossible to adequately survey the range of positions that mark this phase of critique except to note that among the influences are neo-Marxism, structuralism and poststructuralism, psychoanalytic theory, discourse theory, postmodernism, feminist theory, and postcolonial theory" (ibid., p. 9).

12. In his foreword to Yon's book Stuart Hall (2000, p. xi) observes that the high school Yon studied appears "less as an institutional site with structural properties and more as a 'discursive space'."

13. Since these two terms are often used interchangeably in discussions of multicultural education, it would be misleading to draw a hard and fast distinction between them here. Suffice it to say that the dominant theme of postmodernism is its rejection of the master narratives characteristic of "modern" intellectuals (that is, Western thinkers from Descartes onwards), whereas poststructuralism is dominated by its rejection of the capitalist model of social structure in which culture simply replaces religion as the opiate of the people.

14. In the revised version of this address Keesing declares "that these alternative approaches to cultural theory being developed in 'cultural studies' have much to teach anthropology. They are squarely concerned with precisely what anthropology's 'culture' as coral reef hides: the historical situatedness, production, and hegemonic force of cultural meanings in terms of the internal structures and cleavages of 'society'" (Keesing, 1994, p. 309).

15. For instance, Alicia Gaspar de Alba's discussion of "Chicano/a popular culture" includes the Webster Dictionary's formal definition of culture as "the customary beliefs, social forms, and material traits of a racial, religious, or social group" (cited in Gaspar de Alba, 1995, p. 106). However, this definition has nothing to do with her poststructuralist thesis that "cultural production" consists in a multitude of voices and conflicting meanings of individual signs. The Webster definition seems to be pure window dressing, irrelevant to the genuinely interesting ideas she has to offer in a book whose subtitle begins with the words "Critical Perspectives."

16. "Group meanings partially constitute people's identities in terms of the cultural forms, social situations, and history that group members know as theirs. . . . Groups are real not as substances, but as forms of social relations. . . . A person's sense of history, affinity, and separateness, even the person's mode of reasoning, evaluation, and expressing feelings, are constituted partly by her or his group affinities" (Young, 1990, pp. 44–45).

# 6

# Beyond the Critical Turn

In 1999 a short article appeared in the *Anthropology and Education Quarterly* entitled "What Will We Do When Culture Does Not Exist Anymore?" Its author, educational anthropologist Norma González,[1] acknowledged that in the 19th century the emergence of culture as a theoretical concept was a welcome shift from long-standing notions of immutable racial differences. However, she explained, it has become an embarrassment to contemporary anthropologists because of its assumption that cultural traits are fixed things and cultures are essences. In the decade following Geertz's *Interpretation of Culture* anthropologists began to "write against culture" but, González complained, their critiques of the concept of culture have had surprisingly little effect on the theory and practice of multicultural education. "While anthropologists may bemoan the essentialization and reification of bounded and shared cultural traits," she wrote, "the reality is that academic critical discourses have been slow to penetrate curricular practices in schools" (1999, p. 431).

Setting aside for the moment her point about curricular practices (which I think is still valid), we should ask just who are the "we" in her title? González correctly observes that the decline of the culture concept "is hardly news to anthropologists," who as we saw in chapter 2 have been writing against culture since the 1980s. However, as an educational anthropologist she wears two hats. Wearing her anthropology hat she laments that although "we [anthropologists] preach to each other and the already converted, schools continue to operate on texts that emphasize the norms and customs that shape individual behavior and learning" (ibid.). Later, wearing her other hat, she asks "How can we [educators] abandon a tool that helped us to theoretically conceptualize diversity?"

(p. 432), and eventually concludes—correctly, I believe—that before scrapping the concept of culture as we know it, we must have in hand an equally powerful organizing concept. We must not, she cautions us, throw the baby out with the bathwater.

What are we to make of this and similar laments?[2] Has culture really lost its value as an organizing concept, or has it simply morphed to accommodate new social realities? In other words, should we think of culture as a Cheshire Cat fading away until nothing is left but its grin, or as a phoenix rising from its own ashes? This is the question addressed in the present chapter.

My own response to González's title query is first to update her description of the way theorists think about culture, and then to consider how the concepts of culture and multicultural education are likely to change over the next decade or so. Although she was right about the deep misgivings that many anthropologists and other social theorists have about culture, there are still many careful thinkers who use the term, usually in some sense that emphasizes its symbolic and dialogical character. My own reading of the recent literature, much which was published after her article appeared, is that today the dominant view of culture in the social sciences, cultural studies, and philosophical anthropology is that culture is essentially *discourse* on a grand scale. In the 1980s unruly post-Geertzian anthropologists such as such as Clifford, Rosaldo, and Turner represented culture as a kaleidoscopic gallery of symbols, constantly changing and often at odds with establishment interests. In doing so they built on the plainspoken symbolic interactionism of Blumer and other sociologists of the 1960s and 1970s, which was subsequently "postmodernized" in the prolix cultural studies literature whose authors, fired with British neo-Marxism, German critical theory, and French deconstructionism, sought to expose the generally unremarked symbol systems that keep ruling classes in power. Thanks to this confluence of intellectual currents, these symbol-oriented accounts of culture were subsequently politicized and otherwise transformed by a wide variety of postmodern educational theorists whose views are, as we saw at the end of last chapter, usually lumped together under the generic label of Critical Multiculturalist Education.

In addition to viewing culture as discourse, there are other similarities between the ways scholars in various disciplines have progressively thematized and re-thematized culture. For instance, anthropology, sociology, and multicultural education theory have each undergone relatively abrupt shifts in focus away from the symbols and other "cultural traits" of a culturally marked group such that much of this literature now focuses on socioeconomic structures, including globalized versions of those structures. Yet another change running through the literature of these three disciplines is what might be called the interiorization of cultural pluralism, such that instead of thinking of a culture as something shared by many individual persons, today's anthropologists, sociologists, and multicultural educators tend to think of individual persons as containing many cultures. In other words, the multiculturalists' original dream of a culturally pluralist society in which different cultural groups flourish intact but side by side is now giving way to the dream of an enlightened ongoing conversation among culturally complex individuals. Their new ideal society is not a salad bowl but a chat room, where culturally competent participants are Whitmanesque figures who each "contain multitudes." For these reasons, I would rephrase González's question as "What will we do when Culture *as the last generation of scholars and educators knew it* does not exist anymore?"

The answer to this question involves three large issues that frame the problem. The first and second have to do with important frontiers or border areas of culture theory in general and multicultural education in particular. In the first case the concept of culture is changing as a result of multicultural education's critical turn, and so I will discuss this frontier under the heading of "Culture in Post-Critical Multicultural Education." The second frontier is that of post-national multicultural education, so I will label it as "Culture in a Globalized World." In each case I will ask "Where are we now?" and then answer with a snapshot of recent developments in the literature of multicultural education and culture theory, all in hopes of providing a few very tentative clues as to how we might eventually address the much harder question, "Where are we going?"

The third issue is basically retrospective, since it deals with the equally important question, "How did we get to where we are now?" The answer to this question is found in the social construction processes within which the theoretical concepts of culture and cultural identity have been generated (and regenerated) over the last two centuries. Although social construction theory is a staple of contemporary social science, how it actually works in the context of culture paradigm-building and cultural identity formation is seldom spelled out. My hope is that by taking a close look at this process you will be able to see what lies behind the complaints of critical multiculturalists that mainstream multicultural education literature has tended to reify or essentialize the concept of culture.

Each of these three issues, culture in post-critical multicultural education, culture in a globalized world, and the social construction of the very concept of culture, has been examined at length by other authors and in other contexts, but are seldom addressed in terms of the foundational literature of multicultural education. In the following pages I will take this approach in order to provide a few more tools for sorting out hidden assumptions and implications in the way multicultural education authors use the term "culture."

## The First Issue: Culture in Post-Critical Multicultural Education

We saw at the end of the last chapter (FD 5.7) that in the late 1980s early critical multicultural education scholars such as Grant and Sachs were influenced by the anthropologist Roger Keesing's claim that postmodernism provides educators with a "lens" for examining the way symbolic production is linked to various forms of status and power. From this point of departure many important social, political, and educational ideas have been developed under the label of critical multiculturalism, even though those ideas seldom added any new content to the concept of culture itself. The earliest and probably most important contribution of postmodern theory to the practice of multicultural education was the criticism that pedagogies promoting liberal values such as mutual respect, equal rights, and reparation for past wrongs were not enough, since the social order must be reconstructed, not simply reformed. By the beginning of the new millennium the fast growing literature of critical multiculturalism had become almost entirely devoted to social issues such as *hegemony* (the exploitative power of symbols promulgated as part of a society's so-called mass culture), *signifying practices* (group labels that organize persons according to existing inequities of privilege and power), and *critical pedagogy* (rearrangement of the power relationships between students, teachers, and the school system). Since then still more themes have come to the fore, such as the use of post-colonial consciousness as a model of cultural hybridity or the repudiation of master narratives (universal human rights, democracy, etc.).

However, in spite of its postmodern, politically radical and often Marxist character, the literature of critical multiculturalist education almost never proposes new definitions of the concept of culture itself. Instead it takes over the same symbol-oriented or semiotic conception of culture that politically moderate thinkers such as Blumer and Geertz had introduced in the 1960s and 1970s. In other words, although not every multicultural educator who has a semiotic conception of culture is a critical theorist, all or virtually all critical multiculturalist education scholars have built their theories on a semiotic foundation. They routinely disassociate themselves from earlier definitions of culture as a stable, more or less well-integrated set of specific cultural traits or objects such as tools and folk tales, all of which were thought to constitute a group's cultural heritage. Instead, their accounts of culture are future oriented, marked by clearly reform-ist—or better, reconstructionist—agendas directed at the symbol systems of contemporary social structures, especially structures that oppress specific social groups. These groups were once called by the relatively neutral term "subcultures" but are now identified as "subalterns," "minorities," or "disadvantaged persons" to denote their relative lack of power rather than their distinctive cultural heritages or the relative size of their memberships.[3]

As we saw at the end of the last chapter, it is precisely because of its systematic exposure of unacknowledged and unjust power relations that this phase of multicultural education is called "critical." It is important to keep in mind that this word has many meanings that have little to do with education or social theory.[4] In the present context it has the general sense of "uncovering" or "explicating" that are associated with literary criticism. The difference here is that what are uncovered and explicated in the critiques launched by critical multiculturalists are not literary texts but rather the unwritten subtexts of social or political institutions, or better, the terms and symbols taken for granted in the public discourses that supposedly justify such institutions.

One consequence of this almost exclusive focus on social critique is that multicultural education is now moving away from what Stuart Hall has called "the traditional 'culture of origin' that provides an anchor and point of reference in this fluid world" (2000, p. xi). Although critical multiculturalists do not discuss them on their own terms or in any detail, these so-called cultures of origin (the "origin" usually being the homeland of one's immigrant ancestors) constitute the conceptual background of their commentaries on the "border cultures" that are so prominent in inner-city neighborhoods and their schools.[5] These border cultures are not the holistic structures or internally coherent symbol systems of 20th century classical anthropology (though Hall's "traditional cultures of origin" probably are) but rather jumbles of symbols, hierarchies, and normative codes.

## Varieties of Critical Multiculturalism

"Critical multiculturalism" is an umbrella term that covers a broad range of socioeconomic critiques drawn from or inspired by postmodern and poststructuralist social theories. For our purposes they can be gathered under two main headings, each with variants and subheadings that are not relevant here, namely *Critical multiculturalism as social reconstruction* and *Post-critical multiculturalism*. Although the authors in the first group have had little to say about the concept of culture as such, they have set the stage for those in the second group, who do indeed examine and reconstruct the concept of culture. However, the relevance of all this to multicultural education needs to be explained more fully.

1. *Critical multiculturalism as social reconstruction.* This form of critical multiculturalism has a minimalist view of culture, according to which it is merely a register of more basic socioeconomic forces, and the function of culture is the preservation of existing patterns of political and economic power. The sites of power typically discussed by critical multiculturalist *educators* are school settings, whereas the critical multiculturalists who work

outside of educational contexts have broader targets: they analyze national and multinational power structures, colonial and postcolonial narratives, systematic inequities in the areas of race, ethnicity, gender, class, sexual orientation, disabilities, and so on.

Even so, the most cursory glance at this extensive literature shows that there are no sharp lines between the ways critical multiculturalists approach these sites of power, since regardless of social context (that is, regardless of whether they are talking about schools or other sorts of power structures) there is wide variation in the ways power differences operate and are sustained. More generally: critical multiculturalism was founded on the joint premise that in pluralist societies disadvantaged groups are boxed up and labeled with distinctive identities so that everyone, including those in the disadvantaged groups, literally comes to "know his or her place" in the social order and to behave accordingly. Cultural identities are seen by critical multiculturalists as problematic not because they are imposed or because they preserve a status quo but because the status quo is a system of intrinsic inequity.

To correct these systemic inequities critical multiculturalists have usually promoted social goals involving equal opportunity and the direct or indirect redistribution of wealth. However some, influenced by poststructuralist arguments against "grand narratives" framed by poststructuralists such as Homi Bhabha (1994) and Lawrence Grossberg (1997), go on to expose what they consider an even more basic problem, namely the blithe willingness of the general public—especially school children and members of low status groups—to embrace the very cultural identities and symbol systems that keep individuals safely corralled within their respective group boundaries. As educators they reject not only the very idea of a closed, internally integrated symbol system but also any educational approach in which holistic conceptions of cultural identity and generic labels are imposed indiscriminately and nonconsensually on all members of a cultural group. In their view culture and cultural identity are on a par with other theoretical schematics or grand narratives of modernity, such as the Enlightenment, Hegelian and Marxist dialectics, the march of progress, declarations of universal human rights, democratization, or salvation history: they are all forms of false consciousness whose very coherence makes them all the more oppressive.

However, except for their conflicting views about grand narratives, critical multiculturalist educators have a common educational agenda as far as culture and cultural identity are concerned, namely that schoolchildren learn to build for themselves what Hall (1988) has called "new ethnicities." To this end teachers are expected to show their students how to construct new narratives, new symbol systems, new norms, and hence (in some still undefined sense) new cultures. Accordingly, the specific agenda of critical multiculturalist educators is to equip their students with what the Australian poststructuralist educator Fazal Rizvi has called the "critical skills that enable them to imagine alternative moral configurations" (1993, p. 137). In doing so they—that is, the students themselves—supposedly undermine the authority of existing collective identities and in the process help create a more just social order.

2. *Post-critical multiculturalism.* A few of the many multicultural education authors whose thinking is grounded in critical theory have proposed a rather different approach to the challenge of constructing one's own labels or (in the longer run) one's own cultural identity. I call this challenge *post-critical* multiculturalism[6] since its authors—for example, McDonough, McCarthy, Yon, Hall, and others not discussed here—draw deeply from the insights, reconstructionist agendas, and expressive styles found in the literature of critical multiculturalism. However, for them the new agenda of post-critical multicultural education goes beyond the exposure of structural injustices, though it includes that too. As I see it, the center of their educational agenda is the development of interpretive and communicative skills that students need in order not only to imagine social alternatives within their own heads (Rizvi's view) but also to *converse effectively with others* who share their various fields of action. Furthermore, students are to learn how to do this even when they do not fully share their interlocutors' cultural symbols or their views about where they stand or should stand in the social order. Although these conversations usually take place against a backdrop of more or less classical culture systems, they do not constitute what the cultural pluralists of the 1970s would have promoted as "culturally authentic" discourse. Instead the conversations are like cultures themselves—full of little and not so little contradictions, inconsistencies, and ambiguities, in constant yet typically productive conflict. In this discourse individual students jockey for position in much the same self-interested way that interest groups do in identity politics, but in the course of doing so they learn and appropriate new symbols, values, social perspectives, and large-scale meanings from their interlocutors. These symbols, values, perspectives, and meanings often come not from anyone's culture of origin but from the conversation itself. The end result is a new kind of hybridity: not the biculturalism of Irish-Germans or Mexican-Americans but a new combination that is neither "bi-" nor "cultural" in the classical sense.

At this point an anthropologist might feel a bit of *déjà vu*, recalling the late 19th century debates (see chapter 2) about whether cultural changes in primitive societies were the result of internal evolution or of the external "diffusion" typically produced by encounters between nomadic tribes. In such cases new symbols or practices—a novel way of farming or worshipping, say—were incorporated into the group's existing web of symbols and practices, which is simply a long way of saying that the *group's culture* changed. However, the point here is really quite different. In the case of diffusion and elsewhere in classical anthropology, culture was understood as a property of the *group*, not of individuals.[7] Its members draw their symbols, values, and practices from a cultural matrix that for the most part is "already there" for them. Of course as they do so the matrix itself gradually changes, so that in later generations the members will interact with each other within somewhat different cultural contexts. This is only the first part of the story, though. As our conception of culture itself evolves so do our symbols and discourse. Until now individuals have been understood largely though never completely through markers designating groups, especially if they are ethnic markers. ("So of course he likes opera. He's Italian.") However, in the currently emerging era of biculturality and other forms of cultural hybridity (note that the Latin *hybrida* means "mongrel") *culture* is no longer understood as the defining property of a specific group. Consider the cultural intersections reported in Yon's ethnographic study of teenagers in a large, extremely diverse Toronto high school:

> Jack [a black Canadian student] sat wearing a pair of jeans twice his size, a huge jacket and a bright red bandana around his head, obvious signifiers of his passion for rap music and the hip-hop culture associated with it. With respect to how he wished to be identified, Jack was emphatic about being Canadian. His mother emigrated from Jamaica but [he stressed] he was born in Toronto. He described how his mother's emigration to Canada was helped by a Chinese Jamaican woman who had earlier come to Canada. His mother was brought up by this woman back in Jamaica, which explains why she now "listens to reggae music while she is cooking Chinese food and is surrounded by Chinese things in the house." Consequently, how Jack, the well-known hip-hop student around the school, imagines "Canadian" and "Jamaican" and his place within these categories is not so easily reducible to simple notions of race or culture. (2000, pp. 50–51)

The net result, if all goes well, is a negotiated hybridity, both on the sociocultural level and on the level of individual self-awareness, by which I mean the sort of personal identity that is the product of this new social dynamic, which Yon has called "elusive culture." This dynamic is only one dimension of a more extensive and multilayered hybridization process that is analogous to the much-discussed colonial and postcolonial hybridization or "disalienation" that often takes place when colonized people absorb and adapt certain practices of their current or former colonial masters.[8] The conversations that generate this hybridity are not about the simple reconciliation of differences but rather an attempt to repackage old oppositions (master and servant, colonizer and colonized, mainstream and minority) in novel ways that, though always awkward and sometimes demeaning, enable the participants to "transfigure" their own perspectives and develop new and productive understandings of their differences. The paradigm of this sort of dialogue is the discourse that takes place in the aftermath of colonial oppression, which Cameron McCarthy (echoing Fanon) describes as "interactive, developmental bricolage of postcolonial knowledge production that produces discontinuity and disquiet for the colonizer" (McCarthy, 1998, p. 149).

The analogy between postcolonial hybridization and what I am calling post-critical multiculturalism works best when one recalls the root meaning of Claude Lévi-Strauss's favorite term "bricolage," which is the creativity shown by a bricoleur (handyman) in improvising or "making do" with whatever materials were at hand. The absence of general formulas and technical expertise, which in France was considered a virtue rather than a defect, is characteristic of the negotiations between interlocutors from different cultures of origin, be they schoolmates in a comprehensive high school such as the one studied by Yon or between former colonial masters and subalterns: in either case the participants work without blueprints or clear and distinct criteria of success. They also work without a guarantee that they are really understanding each other. For instance, one party can easily mistake another's silence or lack of opposition for agreement, middle class White students talking with African-American peers might inadvertently patronize their interlocutors by assuming "that all non-Whites must idealize their identities to mirror White identities" (Jackson, 1999, pp. 46–47), and so on. More generally, it is precisely because of its bricolage character that the transformational discourse can easily deteriorate into what Aaron Gresson (1995, 2004) has called "recovery rhetoric," in which the motivation for some or all of the discourse is the recovery of group identity, solidarity, and power. These are only a few of the ways that transfigurative discourse can misfire, but my own view is that it would be a serious mistake to write this approach off as hopelessly utopian.[9]

*Summary:* Critical multiculturalism began with a mainly negative and "thin" theory of culture, roughly akin to the Marxist notion of ideology or (at the other end of the political spectrum) Parsons's notion of a normative system: in either version culture is treated as a network of meretricious symbols that together make existing socioeconomic structures seem normal and desirable. Eventually this thin view of culture as ideology thickened. Post-critical multiculturalists have begun to develop positive conceptions of culture as a morally valid symbol system generated in discourse among equals rather than an evil ideology imposed from above. Negative critiques of existing symbol systems are now fleshed out by theoretical accounts of how new symbols and identity markers are constructed.

The critical multiculturalists' educational agenda is also evolving. We see post-critical multiculturalists such as those cited above replacing or at least supplementing critical exposés of false consciousness. The jargon is still there, but these theorists are beginning to offer multicultural educators concrete strategies and objectives for developing the communicative skills needed for engaging in the "transfigurative discourse" described above. With these skills they can establish new and authentic "subject positions" in richly diverse albeit culturally scrambled learning environments as well as in the equally scrambled world outside the schoolroom. Perhaps— though it is still just perhaps—the post-critical multiculturalists' model of culture as a forum for transfigurative discourse will provide the "powerful organizing concept" that Norma González called for in the article cited at the beginning of this chapter.

## The Second Issue: Culture in a Globalized World

Something quite different from the transition from critical to post-critical versions of multiculturalism seems to be at issue in recent discussions of globalization, where the fate of culture is still undecided. Here there are several tensions. One is the apparent opposition between the general conception of culture as *heritage* (linkage to the past) and as *values* (guidelines for shaping the future). The relative weighting of past memories to future hopes varies from person to person, group to group, time to time, and context to context, but it seems safe to say that however culture is conceived, it will have the Janus character of looking to the past and the future simultaneously. A better figure, though, is the image of culture looking at the past in terms of the future and vice versa. Of course this is more easily said than done. Today's forces of globalization, which are essentially future-oriented, seem to threaten cultural heritages in many disturbing ways. National traditions are undermined by transnational economic forces such as the technologies, procedures, production methods, and commodities that streamline and economize our everyday lives at the expense of cherished customs and symbols. Simply put, culture, however conceived, seems in danger of being extinguished, devalued, or co-opted by global economic forces. On the other hand, many globalization theorists feel threatened by the power and ubiquity of culture. As Arjun Appadurai (2008, p. 30) has observed, "it is hardly a surprise that nine out of ten treatises on development treat culture as a worry or a drag on the forward momentum of planned economic change."

Of course for some vanished or vanishing traditions we say "good riddance"—foot binding in China, castrating boy sopranos in Italy, slavery in the United States, female circumcision in Africa, child marriages everywhere, and so on. But what of the Confucian virtue of filial piety that until recently rendered retirement homes unthinkable for East Asian families (Ikels, 2004), or the decline of American civic virtue lamented by Robert Putnam (2000)? Taken one at a time, these changes in everyday cultural practices are not earth shattering, but it is not hard to find intelligent, active, and otherwise secure people in all parts of the world who feel seriously threatened by the disappearance of such traditions. How should we, as multicultural educators, regard such trade-offs between culture and development, which is to say the competition between the venerable and feasible?

In other words, is there some way of understanding culture that fits with and contributes to our understanding of the new—yet of course not completely new—movement of goods and persons and symbols across borders? Recall Yon's description in the previous chapter (ID5.6) of the shift from monological ethnography to multiple and contradictory voices, such that culture has now become "a matter of debate about representations and the complex relationships that individuals take up in relation to them." In the mid-1990s the anthropologist Joel Kahn made a similar claim in connection with recent struggles over which person or national group owns cultural traits such as Maori art or Koranic texts (1995, pp. 124 ff.). More bluntly: Nowadays culture is hot and multiculturalism even hotter. Indonesians covet Levis and Californians love batik. The consumers have spoken. Read the sales figures.

The current fascination with foreign cultures and their symbols is hardly new, and certainly not without its dark side, as Edward Said (1978) showed a generation ago in his critique of "orientalism."[10] However, the relation between culture and globalization is a two-way street. On one side, commercial forces of globalization tend to erase cultural differences in everyday patterns of consumption as well as in less tangible aspects of Western and non-Western cultures such as worldviews, gender roles, sacred symbols, and interpersonal relations. On the other side, though, cultures act as vehicles for globalization. Culture-specific symbols from abroad (especially from exotic places) are commodities in what seems to be a new orientalism, though its postcolonial elements are less oppressive or at least less evident.

From this reciprocity between culture and globalization the possibility emerges that globalization may itself be a kind of culture. If we imagine cultures (now using that term to designate national or regional cultures) as having the iceberg character described in chapter 5, with an invisible and relatively stable dimension consisting of a shared worldview, historical heritage, linguistic structure, etc. and a visible dimension of more malleable behavior patterns, status symbols, tastes, etc., then the question arises: Are large-scale cultural patterns the result or the cause of a people's (spoken or unspoken) attitudes and beliefs? Or are the two domains largely independent of each other, such that a long-standing religious culture such as Christianity has an invisible past that has remained basically the same regardless of changes over the centuries in its visible practices, doctrines, and symbols?

There are still other ways to reconcile the demands of culture and globalization. One is simply to accept the idea of an overarching *global culture*.

Behind this idea, more popular in the 1990s but still accepted by many cultural theorists, globalization is understood as interconnection not homogenization, a distinction that applies to both culture and economics. What is really new is simply that cultural differences are now more evident than they used to be. This is the view of the English culture theorist Mike Featherstone, who declared nearly two decades ago that

> the sense of spatial distances which separated and insulated people from the need to take into account all the other people which make up what has become known as humanity has become eroded. In effect, we are all in each other's backyard. (Featherstone, 1993, pp. 169–70; see also Featherstone, 2006)

Featherstone's idea of a global culture made up of smaller, loosely connected but basically intact cultures is not much different from Boas's view of cultures as geographically adjacent but internally unified structures, since even he allowed for a certain amount of cross-cultural "borrowing" of myths, artifacts, and so on. However, important questions remain open. One is: How have the new economic "border crossings" associated with globalization affected the way members of non-Western societies think of themselves and their cultures? Another is: How—and to what extent—have our own (Western) perceptions of non-Western societies and their cultures changed as a result of the social and economic changes wrought by globalization? A Pashtun student of mine recently told me there are many very different types of rap in her part of the world (her favorite is Kurdish rap). How does this astonishing news (astonishing to me, at least) affect one's understanding of the Middle East? Of American rap? Of the concept of culture? And probably more relevant to the present issue: What is really different between the Kurds' appropriation of rap in our time and the Parisians' reception of American jazz in the 1920s or, well before that, the White Americans' appropriation of African musical styles?

What, one might go on to ask, are the implications of a global culture for multicultural educators? As we saw in the previous section, the emerging post-critical agenda of multicultural education is to prepare students to know their home cultures but not to be afraid to modify them by importing symbols and normative codes from the cultures of classmates and others with whom they interact. Presumably this means that as time goes on each of us develops his or her own personal culture, built out of a treasure horde of symbols and values drawn from our parents and grandparents, schools, workplaces, friendships, and of course the ever-present media. Each of us will have his or her own hybrid self, unique but continually open to new ways of understanding ourselves and our lifeworlds. What we may not have, though, is the comfort and reassurance that comes with a strong sense of membership in a richly historical "ethnoculture" (Goldberg, 1993). Indeed, it would seem logical to expect that after a few generations the idea of a family or an ethnic-based cultural heritage may be replaced by or almost completely absorbed into other sorts of symbol systems, such as economic or professional brackets, religious or political affiliations, geographical regions, or personal interests and hobbies.

This new sort of hybridity (critics might prefer to call it deracination) is now an increasingly prominent theme in the political forum as well as in our schools and other social institutions. Over the last decade or so political philosophers such as Nancy Fraser (2000, 2005) and Seyla Benhabib (2002) have made it clear that the emerging "claims of culture" no longer require us to be true to a single culture but rather call us to be open to the new demands and opportunities created by our ever more globalized political economy. McDonough's (2008) statement of this idea is especially apt though some might find it unsettling. Living in a world with others who have different cultural vocabularies, he declares, "necessitates that each participant engage in a process of normative inquiry and *experimentation, invention, and discovery*" (p. 342, italics added). Citing Dhillon and Halstead (2003, p. 160), he cheerily concludes that the task at hand for 21st century multicultural educators is to forge "robust new cultural identities . . . not tied to reductive identifications" (McDonough, p. 342). Not everyone is likely to regard this as good news, but it seems clear that the strange career of culture will continue to be full of surprises. One of those surprises, I expect, will be either a virtual fusion of the concepts of culture and identity or a complete disconnection between them. Exactly how this fusion or disjunction will come about and what its end product will be like are questions that cannot be answered at the present stage of cultural and educational theory.

For all this, it seems clear that today there is indeed something quite new on the international cultural scene, and that its novelty is in large part a function of the extraordinarily rapid economic changes that go under the title of globalization. Kahn has suggested that part of what is new—which is to say one reason that culture theorists are now talking about a globalized culture or cultural net—is the apparent decline of American hegemony in the global system (1995, pp. 127–28). He may be correct. However, there are surely also other reasons for the novelty, some of which have to do with wider, more global issues. For our purposes the most important feature of what might be called globalized multiculturalism is its epistemological status, not its size or age. Kahn would probably concur, since he also notes that "notions like culture, other cultures, cultural difference and so on, are cognitive structures with a significance which is more or less independent of the world they seek to represent. Put most simply, I assume that 'culture' is a cultural construction" (p. 128). Here I agree with Kahn entirely, except that I prefer the more common label "social construction." The rest of the present chapter is devoted to this important issue.

*Summary:* The second major frontier in culture theory and multicultural education is the place of culture in our increasingly globalized world. More specifically, what is at issue is the *global* and not merely international character of culture as well as adjacent problems such as whether in our globalized world "culture" is best thought of (and taught) as a national heritage or as a transnational guidance system, whether the idea of a "global culture" is really all that new or just a variant on the old idea of cultures as interconnected but not homogeneous, and of course whether economic changes drive cultural changes or the other way around—or both.

Whether the old nostalgic notion of culture as national heritage will survive or perhaps mutate into some future-oriented kind of symbol system centered on economic or political issues remains to be seen, but the global dimension of culture is now an increasingly important educational theme. What used to be squeezed into the curriculum under the heading of Geography or International Studies is now seen, or will soon be seen, as a natural extension of the agenda of multicultural education. Of course not every school's curriculum uses the tag "multicultural education," but every student should have the chance to participate in identity-shaping discourses about culture and its place in the context of globalized political economy.

## The Third Issue: The Social Construction of Culture

The final issue of this chapter has to do with the social constructionist approach now generally accepted in the social sciences (though not in the natural or "basic" sciences). Its basic premise is that the theoretical concepts of our social world, one of which is the concept of culture, are themselves best understood as products of that world. If it is true that as our social world changes, the paradigms and categories we use to understand it also change, then it is only to be expected that the theoretical concept of culture will evolve in tandem with other deep changes in the social order.

At the end of the last section I cited Kahn's view that ideas like culture "are cognitive structures with a significance which is more or less independent of the world they seek to represent." In this section we will see how this and similar construction projects actually work, as well as why it is important that we see this. That is, we need to understand why any theory or practice (but especially the theory and practice of multicultural education) that uses the concept of culture should rest on a clear understanding of how social construction works, in general but especially in the case of culture. As in the first chapter of this book, the ideas presented in this section are drawn from academic philosophy as well as social science, but they are relatively jargon-free (especially if they are compared to the postmodernist ideas discussed above). They are offered here as an answer to the questions posed by the anthropologist Michael Taussig (1993, p. xvi) about the idea that culture is constructed: "What do we do with this old insight?" and "How come culture appears so natural?"

Social construction theory is hardly new—it can be traced back to Protagoras' famous dictum that man is the measure of all things—but it is generally agreed that its present instantiation began with Peter Berger and Thomas Luckmann's *Social Construction of Reality* (1966). Over the last few decades other social theorists and philosophers[11] have refined and sharpened the insights of these foundational thinkers, but unfortunately a multitude of less careful authors (including, alas, some multicultural educators) have used the expression "socially constructed" with such reckless abandon that it is hard to know what the term means anymore. The problem is especially acute when it is used in connection with the equally open-ended term "culture."

Matters are not helped by the grammatical ambiguity of phrases like "the social construction of X," which is ambiguous as to whether X is the source or object of a specific constructing activity, as well as whether the term "construction" is used to refer to the process or to the outcome of some sort of doing or making.[12] Philosophers such as Ian Hacking and Rom Harré have tried to disentangle these meanings as well as the variety of objects that can be socially constructed. Anything that a group of people agree to can be considered a construction, be it a Bill of Rights or a rule of etiquette, but as those examples make clear the point in time at which the object is constructed need not be sharp: the Bill of Rights was ratified on December 15, 1791, but exactly when were men no longer expected to remove their hats when a woman entered an elevator?

As for the social construction of culture, a good place to start is the question of exactly *what* is constructed. One way to address this "what question" is to draw a formal contrast between cultures understood as idealized *objects* and the *methods* we use to represent them. However, in actual practice these two ways of understanding culture are not all that distinct, since how we proceed to represent culture determines what we get, just as what we want to get determines how we proceed. Indeed, we seem to have here what philosophers like to call a distinction without a real difference.

A better way to represent *what* is constructed in the social construction of culture is, I suggest, to distinguish three different levels of "whats." As we saw in chapter 2, in classical anthropology (roughly, up to the end of the 1960s) what was constructed at the ground level were descriptions of phenomena such as the beliefs, norms, values, symbols, way of life or set of meanings that, say, the ancient Greeks, Hopi Indians, or inner-city teenagers have fashioned for themselves. In more recent decades the "what" has usually been understood primarily in terms of symbols and discourse (other cultural traits, especially as beliefs and norms, are not forgotten but they usually remain in the background). At a second, "meta" level, what is constructed includes the various definitions of culture, ethnographic conventions, and technical nomenclatures (for example, the terms *taboo, ritual, kinship system*) that anthropologists and other social theorists have cooked up to represent those ground-level phenomena. Finally, add to these two levels a third, comprising what Hacking (1995; 1999) has called the "looping effects" of social constructions. At this level theoretical conceptualizations of the ground-level practice become part of the repertoire or mind-set of the very people whose interactions make their culture the kind of culture that it is. Then, having sorted out these three levels, we will have succeeded in answering, very abstractly to be sure, the important question "Just what is constructed in the social construction of culture?"

## The Matrix Metaphor

One more important question remains: "Just *how* is the construction carried out?" A good answer is provided by Hacking's metaphor of a "matrix" within which any social construction takes place (1999, pp. 10–14). To set the stage for this very important concept, consider a widely quoted conversation that Ruth Benedict had with her Digger Indian informant Ramon, whose hands trembled and voice broke with excitement as he told her of shamans who had transformed themselves in the old bear dances. "It was," she later declared, "an incomparable thing, the power his people had had in the old days" (Benedict, 1934, p. 33).

In his description of "the old days" Ramon laid another small brick in the ongoing construction of meanings that he shared with his tribal consociates as well as with Benedict and the millions of other people who subsequently read the account of their conversation in her best-selling *Patterns of Culture*. His reminiscences were a small part of the large matrix within which his tribal culture was originally shaped by his people and continues to be shaped by those of us who read and cite Benedict's account. Every culture or indeed any social reality or idea thereof is constructed within a womb-like environment (Hacking notes that the root of the word "matrix" is "mother") within which various social and personal forces come into play. Today the term "matrix" has a variety of rather technical meanings, including an array of numbers arranged in rows and columns, a set of perpendicular lines, the intercellular substance of a tissue, the setting in which fossils are embedded, a die or mold used to shape something, or most generally, a framework on which something is built. A recent and I think especially suggestive meaning of the word, given its etymology, is its use in computer technology to refer to the Internet and other networks that flow into it—a mother network of networks, as it were. Unfortunately, the living "matrix" within which the concept of culture has been formed is not nearly as well structured as the matrices one encounters in mathematics and the other technological contexts just mentioned. Without pretending to be exhaustive or particularly systematic, I suggest that the culture matrix which we have today includes the following components:

1. Obvious and largely objective features of the group's physical and socioeconomic-political environment. (*Examples:* climate, living conditions, commercial and political systems, civic institutions, and intellectual resources such as schools, libraries, the media, and other sorts of informational mechanisms.)
2. Obvious but relatively subjective features such as the way a group understands its physical environment. (*Examples:* relationships that the group has developed with other groups, religious, scientific, and other sorts of generally accepted beliefs about the world and norms that follow from these beliefs, and of course the linguistic categories that enable group members to talk to each other about all these features.)
3. Reflexive concepts that people apply to themselves. (*Examples:* sisterhood, diaspora, master narratives of progress or eternal return, and— of greatest importance here—the concept of culture itself.)

Of these three components of the culture matrix the third is most central to the social construction process. Reflexive concepts are "interactive," which is another term I have borrowed from Hacking, who uses it to identify categories or ideas that interact with their referents or members. In the usual case these terms refer to persons or groups of persons, and the "interaction" is the effect that the use of such categories has on people when they learn that others have applied the category to them. Hacking is right to say that the noninteractive idea of *quark* has no effect on quarks (1999, p. 32), but the interactive idea of *stupid* can devastate people who learn that others apply that category to them. Other interactive ideas may have less drastic effects on their recipients (*artist, compatriot, Chicano, lesbian, Lutheran, parent, published author, refugee, teenager, undocumented, working class* . . . the list seems endless), but the essential point remains the same. Our self-understandings are shaped by the interactive discourse that takes place within social matrices. Notice the use of the plural here: just as in mathematics a matrix can be embedded (usually only partly) in other matrices, so also with arenas of discourse, which include the network of one's peers, one's professional world, the political system, and of course one's culture (however understood). Keeping in mind all these distinctions and qualifications, let us now reflect on the "strange career of culture" that has been charted in the previous chapters as well as in the massive anthropological, sociological, educational, and general literature that traces how the term has been used over the last two centuries.

## Cashing Out the Matrix Metaphor

The metaphor of a matrix, if not the name itself, is hardly new in the culture literature. Contemporary anthropologists seem especially disposed to reflect on the history of their discipline and in doing so they reveal much of the matrix within which various stages of their central category, culture, have been constructed. What they do not tell us is also revealing. For instance chapter 2 began with the observation that "culture" as a social category first appeared toward the end of the 18th century in the Counter-Enlightenment literature of German writers such as J. G. Herder and J. G. Hamann. What was not explained, though, is why before that time scholars and literary figures felt no need even to use the word "culture," much less to turn it into an object of systematic inquiry. Europeans were, of course, quite aware of the existence of non-European peoples, but they felt no need to "anthropologize" them. Temperamental stereotypes were noted but one searches in vain for culturally aware passages in, say, Shakespeare's *Othello* or Locke's comments on American Indians in his *Second Treatise of Civil Government*. Why is this? Why did medieval, renaissance, and enlightenment Europeans not feel a need to construct a special category "culture" to house the considerable information they had about what we today would call the cultural differences between themselves and the non-Europeans of the old East and the new West (not to mention the many differences among the Europeans themselves)? The answer to this question may have something to do with Christianity's long-standing religious hegemony according to which all "real Europeans" were Christians, all non-Europeans were not, and Jews were just "other." It may also have to do with commonalities such as the Europeans' relatively light skin color and the fact that only a few daring explorers, merchants, adventurers, and desperate early colonists ever traveled outside their own geographical regions. For these reasons and notwithstanding the risk of grossly oversimplifying the matter, it would seem that before the rise of the Counter-Enlightenment, Europeans were simply not interested in cultural differences and hence felt no need to construct a methodology or set of categories to explain them.

It is much easier to speculate on the social conditions that gave rise to the culture talk of the late 18th and 19th centuries. Empires flourished, as did travel abroad and the Industrial Revolution at home, as well as—perhaps most important of all—the natural and social sciences. Tylor and Darwin were accomplished travelers and paradigm breakers. Comte and Marx were theoretical as well as social revolutionaries. Arnold and Huxley epitomized their century's two most powerful alternatives to Christianity, and so on. By the time Tylor sat down to write his *Primitive Culture*, a clear and viable market had been created for the concept of culture—and so the concept was constructed accordingly. Over the next century and a half the culture market and its conceptual product changed but did not diminish—at least not until recently.[13]

So what were some of the social matrix requirements that the concept of culture met, for the general public but especially for the culture theorists who came after Tylor? The most obvious and perhaps the most urgent demand was the scientific imperative. By the end of the 19th century classical anthropologists and, in varying degrees, most other social theorists felt obliged to ensure the scientific character of their discipline, which meant observing and recording data in a recognized format: hence the increasing importance of ethnography as well as physical artifacts that, when properly described and exhibited, supplemented the ethnographic accounts. The criteria for a good ethnography changed over the years, as did the criteria for any scientific report. Tylor was content with inferences from travelers' testimonies, Boas and his followers focused on founding myths and the narratives that distinguished people's patterns of values and beliefs as well as their overarching worldviews, Radcliffe-Brown served up accounts of the patterns according to which people, not beliefs and values, were arranged, and so on. In the United States most of the job of sorting out people patterns was left to sociologists, communication theorists, and sometimes economists, but embedded within objective surveys of socioeconomic status, opinion polls, and other sorts of empirical data were references to systems of beliefs and values that either produced or were produced by the social order.

Throughout all this inquiry, a single overarching demand controlled the research design and the publications that justified the existence of the social sciences (called by John Stuart Mill "the moral sciences"), namely the demand for scientifically established explanations of how things really are. Thus Radcliffe-Brown (1940, p. xi) explained that the aim of his comparative studies of cultural groups was basically the same as the aim of any natural science inquiry, namely "to discover the universal, essential, characters which belong to all human societies, past, present, and future." Commenting on this passage as well as on a similar remark by Benedict,[14] Michael Carrithers (1992) has observed that anthropology's embrace of the language of science reveals another trait characteristic of classical cultural theory, namely an "orientation away from history and towards timelessness" (p. 19). In other words, a major part of the social matrix within which the concept of culture was constructed and maintained during the 19th and 20th centuries was the prevailing authority of the scientific method, which led anthropologists and others who considered themselves social scientists to think they must establish their legitimacy as a precondition for debates with natural scientists on the importance of their findings. Accordingly, they tried to achieve this legitimacy though systematic fieldwork and ethnographic accounts that claimed to produce universal truths about social life.

Of course the culture matrix included more than the demands of scientific discourse. The age of imperialism, the Industrial Revolution, new political economies, devastating wars, large-scale immigration and emigration patterns, new religious voices, the civil rights movement—these were all part of the mix. Since this is not the place to catalogue their impact on the concept of culture, suffice it to say that as the 19th century faded and the 20th century progressed the culture matrix continued to change, and in the wake of those changes came new social constructions of culture as well as of related concepts such as race, gender, poverty, personality, health, and even—as we saw in the previous chapters—multicultural education. After Parsons's grand edifice of structural functionalism collapsed in the 1960s, one of the two most important changes was that the inherently *historical* nature of human collectives became part of the subject matter studied under the heading of "culture." Anthropologists and other culture theorists began to recognize that even relatively primitive groups change much more rapidly than was previously thought, and that nearly everyone except the theorists themselves was well aware of that fact.[15] The rate of change within the American and European societies also picked up, so that the time was ripe for new conceptions of culture that were more historical, more sensitive to changes in the social, economic, and political spheres, and even more closely modeled on the "interpretive disciplines" than on the natural sciences.

I said above that the recognition of the historical nature of human collectives was one of the two most important changes in the culture matrix. The other was the raised consciousness of the American people in general and the education establishment in particular, in response to calls by minority groups for a more fair social arrangement, that is, for a society in which the old ideal of cultural assimilation would be displaced by *cultural pluralism*. This response was double-edged: as educators and social activists drew on the existing anthropological and sociological literature of culture in order to design the new order, they pushed the authors of that literature to new and highly critical reflections on the ever-changing career of culture. It is probably no coincidence that while multicultural educators were finding their voices, established anthropologists were publishing books and articles with titles like "What Is Culture? Does It Matter?," "Writing Against Culture," "Beyond 'Culture'," "The Culture Concept as Ideology," and "The Predicament of Culture."[16]

With these changes came greater differentiation within the increasingly fuzzy boundaries of cultures, so that cultural pluralism itself began to assume the character of a life form, that is, a de facto culture in its own right. People who shared the same physical or virtual spaces but not the same history or worldview or cultural identity somehow found it not only possible but even relatively easy to communicate with each other, and with this discovery the mid-20th century model of culture as a self-contained symbol system began to wither away, as did other grand narratives. To be sure, there is still a market for the culture concept (with a standing offer of free updates as they become available) and there are still channels and textures in the social matrix that continue to require us to think of our shared lifeworld as a more or less unified symbol system. Earlier in this chapter, at the end of the discussion of transfigurative multiculturalism, I said that we seem to be moving to a lifeworld in which everyone has his or her own mix of symbols and hence is a unique sort of hybrid. Perhaps this has always been the case, in spite of the stories we construct about our shared lives and our theoretical models of symbolic interaction. If so, then the concept of culture may continue to have its uses, even if it is reduced to the Nietzschean category of a vital lie.

## CONCLUSION: BUILDING THE FUTURE INTO THE PRESENT

I have tried to provide an intellectual compass to help educators and their students find their way through the poorly charted terrain of multicultural education. The compass consists in a philosophical framework, a social theory knowledge base, and a content analysis of existing pedagogical materials of multicultural education as well as, in this final chapter, a few suggestions about where the current literature of critical multiculturalist education seems to be taking us. Much of what I have said was arranged chronologically, but this should not mislead the reader into thinking that just because a conception of culture or educational agenda is old it must be of antiquarian interest only. Nothing could be further from the truth. Our review of the way multicultural education texts (and the teachers who use them) define culture and the practical implications of those definitions makes it clear that none of the nine approaches to culture that we considered is really extinct. The field of multicultural education is like an English garden that has fallen on hard times: old and new concepts of culture grow and even flourish alongside each other, some of which are grand and venerable and others modest, boring, trivial, and occasionally noxious. I leave it to the readers and workers in the field to decide which are which, though my comments on these definitions in chapters 3–5 are hardly value free.

I will close with two final observations, both of which concern the relationship of the multicultural educator to the rest of the scholarly world. The first observation is this: Although educators did not invent the concept of culture, the uses they have made of it over the last three decades have provided important feedback into the more "pure" domains of social theory. For instance, it is now generally agreed that the culture tours approach used in the early days of cultural pluralism education did not produce genuinely cross-cultural competence, and this failure has told social psychologists much about what to avoid—and why—in the theory and practice of intercultural communication. Similarly, the relatively unsuccessful attempt to understand cultural differences in terms of learning styles (or vice versa) has provided cognitive psychologists with important data on the hardwiring involved in different modes of learning. Finally, the more recent dialogical approach described by Hall and McDonough and implemented by Yon draws from the rich wells of symbolic interactionist and poststructuralist theory but it also pours important ideas back into those wells, providing researchers with a promising cultural interaction paradigm that does not presuppose a holistic model of culture or an essentialist notion of the self. From these examples I suggest that although their contributions differ, multicultural educators can and do work as equal partners with anthropologists, sociologists, culture and communications theorists, and yes, philosophers, in the grand task of explaining the complex but undeniable fact of human diversity.

My second observation concerns a possible implication of the foregoing discussion of the social matrix within which the concepts of culture and cultural identity have been constructed—and reconstructed—over the last two centuries. It may be that culture is indeed at the end of its career, and that "transfigurative" concepts like *hybridity* will evolve into some totally new theoretical construct for making sense of human diversity along with new educational practices for enabling students to take their places in the global or post-global future.

Or perhaps not. It is too early to tell. Certainly reports of the death of culture have been greatly exaggerated or, to borrow a line from Don Marquis's irrepressible alley cat Mehitabel, there's a dance in the old dame yet. We must keep in mind that the transformative discourse that takes place between students in a large, diverse, metropolitan high school is quite different from discourse between students in smaller or less culturally diverse schools. We must also recognize that there is a natural inertia in the discursive practices of teachers, families, and communities, which will keep the concept of culture alive for a good while regardless of its diminishing utility for theorists. For these and other reasons we should expect any radical revision or dismantling of current multicultural education practices concerning culture to proceed very slowly. Regardless of whether the concept of culture has a future, though, the present generation of teachers cannot and should not ever forget—or let their students forget—that what we now call cultures are not primordial essences, "things always already there." Culture, like history itself, is an idea that can be abused as well as used.

## NOTES

1. Professor González is an educational anthropologist in the College of Education at the University of Arizona, and former president of the Council of Anthropology and Education.

2. See, for instance, Yengoyan (1986), Rosaldo (1989), Abu-Lughod (1991), Gupta & Ferguson (1992), Keesing (1994), Bhabha (1994), and Fox (1995).

3. Gayatri Spivak (1988) has argued that not all oppressed groups are subalterns because that term, derived from the postcolonialist literature of the last generation, applies to those who are not only oppressed but also voiceless, completely unrepresented in the society's symbol system and without access to any instruments of political power. However, not all critical multiculturalists follow Spivak in this matter: some use the term in the more general sense employed by Gramsci (1973), in which it is roughly the same as the concept of "proletariat."

4. For instance, the word means "urgent" or "extreme" when we say a patient's condition is critical, "disapproving" or "faultfinding" when we speak of someone who is critical or hypercritical of another's behavior, and "crucial" or "decisive" when we speak of a critical moment.

5. McLaren and others use this term differently, to refer to "cultures in which a repetition of certain normative structures and codes often 'collide' with other codes and structures whose referential status is often unknown or only partially known." For instance a student in an inner-city high school may be in daily contact with many different cultural groups that "border" on each other and require students from different groups to constantly negotiate with each other. The net result is "a space where one can find an overlay of codes, a multiplicity of culturally inscribed subject positions, at this placement of normative reference codes, and a polyvalent assemblage of new cultural meanings" (McLaren, 1995, p. 57).

6. What I am calling "post-critical" multiculturalism is similar to what McDonough (2008) has called "transfigurative" multiculturalism in order to signal its aim of "transforming existing articulations of right and wrong" (p. 336).

7. There is, of course, an extended notion of group properties such that if you are recognized as belonging to a cultural, ethnic, or other sort of social group it is assumed that you have appropriated (that is, taken ownership of) most of its symbols, values, practices, etc. Thus we say that Sven is a typical Swede. However it would still be odd to say that Sven *is* his culture. In the case of gender groups the difference between individual and group properties is conveniently more precise: only individual women are "female," whereas styles, symbols, and even the ethos of their various subgroups are (or could be) "feminine."

8. The "hybridization" under discussion here is an analogue of Franz Fanon's postcolonial concept of "disalienation." Fanon is often represented as an angry, violent enemy of colonial powers, but his ultimate goal was the freedom of both colonizer and colonized: "Both must turn their backs," he wrote, "on the inhuman voices of their respective ancestors in order that authentic communication be possible" (Fanon, 1967, p. 224).

9. For a promising account of this approach, see Yon (2000), especially his concluding chapter.

10. Said's *Orientalism* is generally regarded as a "foundational text [for] postcolonial thought" (Kahn, 1995, p. 5). The term "orientalism" was used in the early decades of the 20th century to refer to the implicitly racist fascination that Europeans had with the exotic and erotic cultures of Africa and what is now known as the Mideast.

11. A few of my favorites: Burr (2003); Gergen (1999, 2001), Goodman (1978), Harré, (1993), and Hacking (1999).

12. "Most words ending in 'tion' are ambiguous between process and product, between the way one gets there, and the result. The termination of the contract: that can mean the process of terminating the contract. It can also mean the upshot, the product, the end of the contract. The pattern is not identical for each 'tion' word, because each word nuances the ambiguity in its own way. 'Production' itself can mean the process of producing, or, in other circumstances, the result of producing. Is the production of a play process or product? What about movies?" (Hacking, 1999, p. 36.)

13. Consider the discussion of González's article at the beginning of this chapter as well as my own remarks at the very end.

14. In her *Patterns of Culture*, Benedict wrote that "societies historically as little related as possible to our own" are "the only laboratory of social forms that we have or shall have" (1934, p. 17).

15. Reflecting on his famous study of the pygmies in the Ituri Forest of what was once the Belgian Congo, Colin Turnbull wrote: "I was first among the Mbuti pygmies . . . in 1951. I went back for something over a year in 1954. Even in the short space of time things had changed, and initial impressions had to be corrected. When I returned again in 1957–9 I had quite a hard time reconciling some of my earlier findings with what I found then. And on returning to the same part of the same forest yet again in 1970–2, it seemed as though I had to contradict myself all over again" (Turnbull, 1983, p. 5). See also Carrithers (1992, p. 22–23), who is careful to explain in this connection that the ethnographer's first task is translation, that is, to "describe what is going on." *How* what is going on changes over the years is a separate question.

16. "What Is Culture? Does It Matter?" is by M. Steedly (1996); "Writing Against Culture" is by L. Abu-Lughod (1991); "Beyond 'Culture'" is by A. Gupta and J. Ferguson (1992); "The Culture Concept as Ideology" is by J. Moore (1974); and "The Predicament of Culture" is by J. Clifford (1988).

# References

Abu-Lughod, L. (1991). Writing against culture. In R. G. Fox (Ed.), *Recapturing anthropology: Working in the present*, (pp. 137–162). Santa Fe, NM: School of American Research Press.

Abu-Lughod, L. (1999a). The interpretation of culture(s) after television. In S. B. Ortner (Ed.), *The fate of culture: Geertz and beyond* (pp. 101–135). Los Angeles: University of California Press.

Abu-Lughod, L. (1999b). *Veiled sentiments: Honor and poetry in a Bedouin society* (2nd ed.). Berkeley: University of California Press.

Adler, P. S. (2007). Beyond cultural identity: Reflections on multiculturalism. In M. Bennett (Ed.), *Basic concepts of intercultural communication: Selected readings* (pp. 225–245). Boston: Intercultural Press.

Appadurai, A. (1997). *Modernity at large: Cultural dimensions of globalization*. Minneapolis: University of Minnesota Press.

Appadurai, A. (2008). The capacity to aspire: Culture and the terms of recognition. In D. Held & H. Moore (Eds.), *Cultural politics in a global age: Uncertainty, solidarity, and innovation* (pp. 29–35). Oxford: Oneworld Publications.

Apple, M. W. (1986). *Teachers and texts: A political economy of class and gender relations in education*. London: Routledge and Keegan Paul.

Aronowitz, S., & Giroux, H. A. (1991). *Postmodern education: Politics, culture, and social criticism*. Minneapolis: University of Minnesota Press.

Baker, G. C. (1994). *Planning and organizing for multicultural instruction* (2nd ed.). Menlo Park, CA: Addison-Wesley Publishing Co.

Baker, P. B. (2005). The impact of cultural biases on African American students' education: A review of research literature regarding race-based schooling. *Education and Urban Society, 37,* 243–256.

Banks, J. A. (1974). "Multicultural education: In search of definitions and goals." *Association for Supervision and Curriculum Development Institute on Cultural Pluralism,* Chicago, IL. (Also available from ERIC database [EDI00792]).

Banks, J. A. (1979a). Shaping the future of multicultural education. *Journal of Negro Education, 48* (Summer), 237–252.

Banks, J. A. (1979b). *Multiethnic/Multicultural teacher education: Conceptual, historical, and ideological issues.* Rosslyn, VA: National Clearinghouse for Bilingual Education. [ED175278]

Banks, J. A. (2008). *Teaching strategies for ethnic studies* (8th ed.). Boston: Allyn and Bacon.

Banks, J. A., & Banks, C. A. (1993). *Multicultural education: Issues and perspectives* (2nd ed.). Boston: Allyn and Bacon.

Banks, J. A., & Banks, C. A. (2010). *Multicultural education: Issues and perspectives* (7th ed.). Boston: Allyn and Bacon.

Baptiste, H. P., & Baptiste, M. (1980). Competencies toward multiculturalism. In H. P. Baptiste, M. Baptiste, & D. Gollnick (Eds.), *Multicultural teacher education. Preparing educators to provide educational equity* (Vol. 1, pp. 44–72). Washington, DC: American Association of Colleges of Teacher Education.

Barth, F. (1969). Introduction. In F. Barth (Ed.), *Ethnic groups and boundaries: The social organization of culture difference* (pp. 9–38). Boston: Little, Brown & Company.

Barth, F. (1994). Ethnicity, nationalism, and state-making. In H. Vermeulen & C. Grovers (Eds.), *The anthropology of ethnicity: Beyond "Ethnic Groups and Boundaries"* (pp. 11-31). Amsterdam: Het Spinhuis.

Bellamy, R. (2008). *Citizenship: A very short introduction.* Oxford: Oxford University Press.

Benedict, R. (1934). *Patterns of culture.* New York: Houghton Mifflin Company.

Benhabib, S. (2002). *The claims of culture: Equality and diversity in the global era.* Princeton, NJ: Princeton University Press.

Bennett, C. I. (2010). *Comprehensive multicultural education: Theory and practice* (7th ed.). Boston: Allyn & Bacon.

Berger, P., & Luckmann, T. (1966). *Social construction of reality: A treatise in the sociology of knowledge.* New York: Doubleday.

Bhabha, H. (1994). *The location of culture.* New York: Routledge.

Bigelow, D. N. (1971). *The liberal arts and teacher education: A confrontation.* Lincoln: University of Nebraska Press.

Blumer, H. (1969). *Symbolic interactionism: Perspective and method.* Englewood Cliffs, NJ: Prentice-Hall.

Blumer, H. (1981). Untitled review. *The American Journal of Sociology, 86*(4), 902–904.

Boas, F. (1898). *The mythology of the Bella Coola Indians.* New York: American Museum of Natural History.

Boas, F. (1904). The history of anthropology. Science, 20, 513–524. Reprinted in F. Boas, *The shaping of American anthropology, 1893–1911. A Franz Boas reader,* ed. by G. Stocking. New York: Basic Books, 1974, pp. 23–36.

Boas, F. (1911). *The mind of primitive man.* New York: The Macmillan Company.

Boas, F. (1930). Anthropology. In E. R. A. Seligman (Ed.), *Encyclopedia of the social sciences* (vol. 2, pp. 73–110). New York: Macmillan.

Bodley, J. H. (1994). *Cultural anthropology: Tribes, states, and the global system.* Mountain View, CA: Mayfield Publishing Company.

Bohn, A. P. (2003). Familiar voices: Using Ebonics communication techniques in the primary classroom. *Urban Education, 38,* 688–707.

Borofsky, R. (1994). *Assessing cultural anthropology.* New York: McGraw-Hill.

Botelho, M., & Rudman, M. (2009). *Critical multicultural analysis of children's literature: Mirrors, windows, and doors.* New York: Routledge.

Bourdieu, P. (1977). *Outline of a theory of practice.* Cambridge: Cambridge University Press.

Boykin, A. W. (1986). The triple quandary and the schooling of Afro-American children. In U. Neisser (Ed.), *The school achievement of minority children* (pp. 57–92). Hillsdale, NJ: Lawrence Erlbaum.

Brown, C. (1963). *Understanding other cultures.* Englewood Cliffs, NJ: Prentice Hall.

Bullivant, B. M. (1981). *The pluralist dilemma in education: Six case studies.* Boston: Allen & Unwin.

Bullivant, B. M. (1982). Pluralist debate and educational policy—Australian style. *Journal of Multilingual and Multicultural Development, 3*(2), 129–147.

Bullivant, B. M. (1983). Australia's pluralist dilemma: An age-old problem in a new guise. *Australian Quarterly, 55*(2), 136–148.

Bullivant, B. M. (1984). *Pluralism, cultural maintenance, and evolution.* Clevedon, Avon, UK: Multilingual Matters.

Bullivant, B. M. (1985). Educating the pluralist person: Images of society and educational responses in Australia. In M. E. Poole, C. de Lacy & B. Randwa (Eds.), *Australia in transition: Culture and life possibilities* (pp. 8–22). Sidney: Harcourt Brace Jovanovich.

Bullivant, B. M. (1993). Culture: Its nature and meaning for educators. In J. A. Banks & C. A. M. Banks (Eds.), *Multicultural education: Issues and perspectives* (2nd ed., pp. 29–47). Boston: Allyn and Bacon.

Burr, V. (2003). *Social constructionism* (2nd ed.). London: Routledge.

Carrithers, M. (1992). Why humans have cultures: Explaining anthropology and social diversity. Oxford: Oxford University Press.

Cartledge, G., & Feng, H. (1996). The relationship between culture and social behavior. In G. Cartledge (Ed.), *Multicultural diversity and social skills instruction* (2nd ed., pp. 13–44). Champaign, IL: Research Press.

Clifford, J. (1988). *The predicament of culture: Twentieth-century ethnography, literature, and art.* Cambridge. MA: Harvard University Press.

Clifford, J., & Marcus, G. E. (Eds.) (1986). *Writing culture: The poetics and politics of ethnography.* Berkeley, CA: University of California Press.

Collins, R. (Ed.) (1994). *Four sociological traditions: Selected readings.* New York: Oxford University Press.

Cook, J. W. (1999). Boas's criticisms of cultural evolution. In *Morality and cultural differences* (pp. 56–61). Oxford: Oxford University Press.

Cushner, K., McClelland, A., & Safford, P. L. (2011). *Human diversity in education.* (7th ed.). New York: McGraw-Hill.

D'Andrade, R. G. (1995). *The development of cognitive anthropology.* Cambridge: Cambridge University Press.

Darder, A. (1995). Introduction: The politics of biculturalism. In A. Darder (Ed.), *Culture and difference: Critical perspectives on the bicultural experience in the United States* (pp. 1–20). Westport, CT: Bergin & Garvey.

Davidman, L., & Davidman, P. (2001). *Teaching with a multicultural perspective* (3rd ed.). New York: Longman.

Davidson, D. (1984). *Inquiries into truth and interpretation.* Oxford: Clarendon Press.

Dawkins, R. (1976). *The selfish gene.* New York: Oxford University Press.

Derman-Sparks, L. (1989). *Anti-bias curriculum: Tools for empowering young children.* Washington, DC: National Association for the Education of Young Children.

Dewey, J. (1925). *Experience and nature.* Chicago, London: Open Court Publishing Company.

Deyhle, D. (1995). Navajo youth and Anglo racism: Cultural integrity and resistance. *Harvard Educational Review, 65,* 403–444.

Dhillon, P., & Halstead, J. M. (2003). Multicultural education. In N. Blake, P. Smeyers, R. Smith, & P. Standish (Eds.), *The Blackwell guide to the philosophy of education* (pp. 160). Oxford: Blackwell.

Dickey, G. (1984). *The art circle.* New York: Haven Publications.

Dilworth, P. (2007). Multicultural education: Some implications for teachers. In M. Gordon & T. O'Brien (Eds.), *Bridging theory and practice in teacher education* (pp. 107–118). Rotterdam: Sense Publishers.

D'Souza, D. (1991a). Multiculturalism 101: Great books of the non-western world. *Policy Review, 56* (Spring), 22–30.

D'Souza, D. (1991b). *Illiberal education: The politics of race and sex on campus.* New York: Vintage Books.

Durkheim, E. (1915/1964). What is a social fact? In E. Durkheim, *The rules of sociological method* (pp. 1–13). New York: Free Press.

Durkheim, E. (1965). *The elementary forms of the religious life.* New York: Free Press.

Eliot, T. S. (1948). *Notes towards the definition of culture.* London: Faber and Faber.

Etzioni, A. (1983). *An immodest agenda: Rebuilding America before the 21st century.* New York: McGraw-Hill.

Fairchild, H. P. (1970). *Dictionary of sociology.* Westport, CT: Greenwood Press.

Fanon, F. (1967). *Black skin, white masks.* New York: Grove Press, 1967.

Featherstone, M. (1993). Global change and local cultures. In J. Bird, B. Curtis, T. Putnam, G. Robertson, & L. Tickner (Eds.), *Mapping the futures: Local cultures, global change* (pp. 169–187). London: Routledge.

Featherstone, M. (2006). Genealogies of the global. *Theory, Culture & Society, 23,* 387–392.

Feng, H., & Cartledge, G. (1996). Social skill assessment of inner city Asian, African, and European American students. *School Psychology Review, 25,* 227–238.

Fox, R. (1995). Editorial: The breakdown of culture. *Current Anthropology, 36*(1), i–ii.

Fraser, N. (2000). Rethinking recognition. *New Left Review,* 3(May–June), 107–120.

Fraser, N. (2005). Reframing justice in a globalizing world. *New Left Review,* 36(Nov–Dec): 69–88.

Freire, P. (1968/1970). *Pedagogy of the oppressed.* New York: Herder and Herder.

Frisby, C. (1993a). One giant step backward: Myths of black cultural learning styles. *School Psychology Review, 22*(3), 535–557.

Frisby, C. (1993b). "Afrocentric" explanations for school failure: Symptoms of denial, frustration, and despair. *School Psychology Review, 22*(3), 568–577.

Gadamer, H.-G. (1991). *Truth and method.* New York: Crossroads.

Gans, H. (1988). *Middle American individualism: The future of liberal democracy.* New York: Free Press.

Gans, H. J. (1974). *Popular culture and high culture: An analysis and evaluation of taste.* New York: Basic Books.

García, S. B., & Guerra, P. L. (2006). Conceptualizing culture in education: Implications for schooling in a culturally diverse society. In J. Baldwin, S. Faulkner, M. Hecht, & S. Lindsley (Eds.), *Redefining culture: Perspectives across the disciplines* (pp. 103–115). Mahwah, NJ: Erlbaum.

Gardner, H. (1991). *The unschooled mind: How children think and how schools should teach.* New York: Basic Books.

Garfinkel, H. (1967). *Studies in ethnomethodology.* Englewood Cliffs, NJ: Prentice-Hall.

Gaspar de Alba, A. (1995). The alternative grain: Theorizing Chicano/a popular culture. In A. Darder (Ed.), *Culture and difference: Critical perspectives on the bicultural experience in the United States* (pp. 103–122). Westport, CT: Bergin & Garvey.

Gay, G. (1994). *A synthesis of scholarship in multicultural education.* Washington, DC and Oak Brook, IL: U.S. Dept. of Education, Office of Educational Research and Improvement, and North Central Regional Educational Laboratory Urban Education Monograph Series.

Gay, G. (2000). *Culturally responsive teaching.* New York: Teachers College Press.

Geertz, C. (1973). *The interpretation of cultures.* New York: Basic Books.

Gergen, K. (1999). *An invitation to social construction.* London: Sage.

Gergen, K. (2001). *Social construction in context.* London: Sage.

Gibson, M. A. (1976). Approaches to multicultural education in the United States: Some concepts and assumptions. *Anthropology & Education Quarterly, 7*(4), 7–18.

Gibson, M. A. (1984). Approaches to multicultural education in the United States: Some concepts and assumptions. (Revised version). *Anthropology & Education Quarterly, 15*(1), 94–119.

Glazer, N., & Moynihan, D. P. (1963). *Beyond the melting pot: The Negroes, Puerto Ricans, Jews, Italians, and Irish of New York City.* Cambridge, MA: MIT Press.

Glazer, N., & Moynihan, D. P. (1970). *Beyond the melting pot: The Negroes, Puerto Ricans, Jews, Italians, and Irish of New York City* (2nd ed.). Cambridge, MA: MIT Press.

Goffman, E. (1959, 1958). *The presentation of self in everyday life.* Garden City, NY: Doubleday.

Goldberg, D. T. (1993). *Racist culture: Philosophy and the politics of meaning.* Oxford: Basil Blackwell.

Goldschmidt, W. R. (1963). *Exploring the ways of mankind.* New York: Holt, Rinehart, and Winston.

Gollnick, D. M., & Chinn, P. C. (1983). *Multicultural education in a pluralistic society* (1st ed.). St. Louis: Mosby.

Gollnick, D. M., & Chinn, P. C. (1994). *Multicultural education in a pluralistic society* (4th ed.). New York, NY: Macmillan.

Gollnick, D. M., & Chinn, P. C. (2012). *Multicultural education in a pluralistic society* (9th ed.). Upper Saddle River, NJ: Pearson Merrill.

González, N. (1999). What will we do when culture does not exist anymore? *Anthropology and Education Quarterly, 30*(4), 431–435.

Goodenough, W. H. (1957). *Cultural anthropology and linguistics*. Washington, DC: Georgetown University Monograph Series on Language and Linguistics.

Goodenough, W. H. (1964). *Explorations in cultural anthropology*. New York: Mc-Graw-Hill.

Goodenough, W. H. (1994). Toward a working theory of culture. In R. Borotsky (Ed.), *Assessing cultural anthropology* (pp. 262–273), New York, McGraw-Hill.

Goodman, N. (1978). *Ways of worldmaking*. Indianapolis, IN: Hackett.

Gordon, M. M. (1964). *Assimilation in American life: The role of race, religion, and national origins*. New York: Oxford University Press.

Govers, C., & Vermeulen, H. (1997). *The politics of ethnic consciousness*. New York: St. Martin's Press.

Gramsci, A. (1973). In Q. Hoare & G. Nowell-Smith (Eds.), *Selections from the prison notebooks*. New York: International Publishers.

Grant, C. A. (1977). *Multicultural education: Commitments, issues, and applications*. Washington, DC: Association for Supervision and Curriculum Development.

Grant, C. A. (1995). *Educating for diversity: An anthology of multicultural voices*. Needam Heights, MA: Allyn and Bacon.

Grant, C. A., & Sachs, J. (1995). Multicultural education and post-modernism: Toward a dialogue. In B. Kanpol, & P. McLaren (Eds.), *Critical multiculturalism: Uncommon voices in a common struggle* (89–106). Westport, CT: Bergin Garvey.

Grassby, A. J. (1973). *A multicultural society for the future*. Canberra: AGPS Press.

Gresson, A. (1995, 2004). *America's atonement: Racial pain, recovery rhetoric, and the pedagogy of healing*. New York: Peter Lang.

Grossberg, L. (1997). *Bringing it all back home: Essays on cultural studies*. Durham, NC: Duke University Press.

Gupta, A., & Ferguson, J. (1992). Beyond 'culture': Space, identity, and the politics of difference. *Cultural Anthropology, 7*(1), 6–23.

Habermas, J. (1984, 1987). *The theory of communicative action*. Boston: Beacon Press.

Hacking, I. (1995). The looping effect of human kinds. In D. Sperber, D. Premack, & A. J. Premack (Eds.), *Causal cognition: An interdisciplinary approach* (pp. 351–383). Oxford: Oxford University Press.

Hacking, I. (1999). *The social construction of what?* Cambridge, MA: Harvard University Press.

Hale, J. E. (1982). *Black children: Their roots, culture, and learning styles*. Provo, UT: Brigham Young University Press.

Hale, J. E. (1994). *Unbank the fire: Visions for the education of African American children*. Baltimore: Johns Hopkins University Press.

Hall, E. T. (1989). Unstated features of the cultural context of learning. *Educational Forum, 54*, 21–34.

Hall, S. (1988). New ethnicities. In K. Mercer (Ed.), *Black film, British cinema* (pp. 27–31). London: Institute of Contemporary Arts.

Hall, S. (1990). Ethnicity: Identity and difference. *Radical America, 13*(4,), 9–20.

Hall, S. (2000). Foreword to Daniel Yon's *Elusive culture*. In D. Yon, *Elusive culture: Schooling, race, and identity in global times* (pp. ix–xii). Albany, NY: SUNY Press.

Hall, S., & Held, D. (1989). Citizens and citizenship. In S. Hall & M. Jacques (Eds.), *New times: The changing face of politics in the 1990s*. London: Lawrence & Wisehart.

Handler, R. (1990). Ruth Benedict and the modernist sensibility. In M. Manganaro (Ed.), *Modernist anthropology: From fieldwork to text* (pp. 163–180). Princeton, NJ: Princeton University Press.

Harjo, L., & Russell, I. (1990). *The circle never ends. A multicultural preschool curriculum model.* Denver, CO: Circle of Learning Denver Indian Center and the Bernard Van Leer Foundation.

Harré, R. (1993). *Social being* (2nd ed.). Oxford: Blackwell Publishers.

Harris, V. J. (Ed.). (1993). *Teaching multicultural literature in grades K–8.* Norwood, MA: Christopher-Gordon Publishers.

Herskovits, M. J. (1941). *The myth of the Negro past.* NY: Harper & Brothers.

Herskovits, M. J. (1948). *Man and his works: The science of cultural anthropology* (1st ed.). NY: A. A. Knopf.

Herskovits, M. J. (1958). *The myth of the Negro past.* Boston: Beacon Press.

Hirsch, Jr., E. D. (1987). *Cultural literacy: What every American needs to know.* Boston: Houghton Mifflin.

Hirschfeld, L. (1998). *Race in the making: Cognition, culture, and the child's construction of human kinds.* Cambridge, MA: MIT Press.

Hong, Y., Morris, M., Chiu, C., & Benet-Martinez, V. (2000). Multicultural minds: A dynamic constructivist approach to culture and cognition. *American Psychologist, 55*(7) 709–720.

Hoopes, D., & Pusch, M. (1979). Definition of terms. In M. Pusch (Ed.), *Multicultural education: A cross-cultural training approach* (pp. 2–9). Yarmouth, ME: Intercultural Press.

Howard, G. R. (1999). *We can't teach what we don't know: White teachers, multiracial schools.* New York: Teachers College Press.

Hutnik, N. (1991). *Ethnic minority identity: A social psychological perspective.* Oxford; New York: Clarendon Press; Oxford University Press.

Ikels, C. (Ed.). (2004). *Filial piety: Practice and discourse in contemporary East Asia.* Stanford, CA: Stanford University Press.

Jackson, R. (1999). White space, white privilege: Mapping discursive inquiry into the self. *Quarterly Journal of Speech, 85,* 38–54.

Kahn, J. (1995). *Culture, multiculture, postculture.* New York: Sage.

Kay, P., & Kempton, W. (1984). What is the Sapir–Whorf hypothesis? *American Anthropologist, 86*(1), 65–79.

Keesing, R. M. (1989, November). Theories of culture revisited. Paper presented at the meeting of the American Anthropological Association, November 1989, Washington, DC. Revised version in R. Borofsky (Ed.), *Assessing cultural anthropology* (pp. 301–310). New York: McGraw-Hill, 1994.

Kendall, F. E. (1983). *Diversity in the classroom: A multicultural approach to the education of young children.* New York: Teachers College Press.

Kendall, F. E. (1995). *Diversity in the classroom: New approaches to the education of young children* (2nd ed.). New York: Teachers College Press.

Kim, U. (2001). Culture, science, and indigenous psychologies: An integrated analysis. In D. Matsumoto (Ed.), *Handbook of culture and psychology* (pp. 51–76). New York: Oxford University Press.

Kincheloe, J. L., & Steinberg, S. R. (1997). *Changing multiculturalism.* Buckingham, England; Philadelphia: Open University Press.

King, E. W., Chipman, M., & Cruz-Janzen, M. (1994). *Educating young children in a diverse society.* Boston: Allyn and Bacon.

Kluckhohn. F. R. (1956). Dominant and variant value orientations. In C. Kluckhohn (Ed.), *Personality in nature, society, and culture* (pp. 342–357). New York: Knopf and Co.

Kluckhohn, F. R., & Strodtbeck, F. L. (1961). *Variations in value orientations.* Evanston, IL: Row, Peterson.

Kneller, G. F. (1965). *Educational anthropology: An introduction.* New York: Wiley.

Kochman, T. (1981). *Black and white styles in conflict.* Chicago: University of Chicago Press.

Kroeber, A. L., & Kluckhohn, C. (1952). *Culture: A critical review of concepts and definitions.* New York: Vintage Books.

Kroeber, A. L., & Parsons, T. (1958). The concepts of culture and of social system. *The American Sociological Review, 23,* 582–583.

Kuhn, T. S. (1962). *The structure of scientific revolutions.* Chicago: University of Chicago Press.

Kuper, A. (1999). *Culture: The anthropologists' account.* Cambridge, MA: Harvard University Press.

Ladson-Billings, G. (1995a). But that's just good teaching: The case for culturally relevant pedagogy. *Theory into Practice, 34,* 159–165.

Ladson-Billings, G. (1995b). Toward a theory of culturally relevant pedagogy. *American Education Research Journal, 35,* 465–491.

Lasswell, H. (1948). The structure and function of communication in society. In L. Bryson (Ed.), *The communication of ideas* (pp. 37–51). New York: Institute for Religious and Social Studies/Harper.

Leggett, G. H., Mead, C. D., & Charvat, W. (1965). *Prentice-Hall handbook for writers* (4th ed.). Englewood Cliffs, N.J.: Prentice-Hall.

LeVine, R. A. (1991). Discussion. In P. M. Greenfield & R. Cocking (Chairs), *Continuities and discontinuities in the cognitive socialization of minority children.* Proceedings from a workshop, Department of Health and Human Services, Public Health Service, Alcohol, Drug Abuse, and Mental Health Administration, Washington, DC.

Levinson, B., Foley, D., & and Holland, D. (1996). The cultural production of the educated person: An introduction. *The cultural production of the educated person: Critical ethnographies of schooling and local practice* (1–56) Albany, NY: SUNY Press.

Lewontin, R. C. (1992; 1991). *Biology as ideology : The doctrine of DNA* (1st ed.). New York: HarperPerennial.

Lieblich, A., Tuval-Mashiach, R., & Zilber, T. (1998). *Narrative research: Reading, analysis and interpretation.* Thousand Oaks, CA: Sage Publications.

Locke, D. (2003). Improving the multicultural competence of educators. In P. Pedersen. & J. C. Carey (Eds.), *Multicultural counseling in schools: A practical handbook* (pp. 171–190), Boston: Allyn and Bacon.

Locke, D. C., Myers, J. E., & Herr, E. L. (Eds.). (2001). *The handbook of counseling.* Thousand Oaks, CA: Sage Publishing.

Loewen, J. (2007). *Lies my teacher told me: Everything your American history textbook got wrong.* New York: Simon & Schuster.

Lumsden, C. J., & Wilson, E. O. (1981). *Genes, mind, and culture: The coevolutionary process.* Cambridge, MA: Harvard University Press.

Lyotard, J. (1984). *The postmodern condition: A report on knowledge.* Manchester: Manchester University Press.

Maehr, M. L. (1974). *Sociocultural origins of achievement.* Monterey, CA: Brooks/Cole Pub. Co.

Malinowski, B. (1922). *Argonauts of the Western Pacific.* London: Routledge and Kegan Paul.

Malinowski, B. (1929). *The sexual life of savages in northwestern Melanesia. An ethnographic account of courtship, marriage and family life among the natives of the Trobriand Islands, British New Guinea.* London: G. Routledge and Sons.

Malinowski, B. (1941). Man's culture and man's behavior, Part I. *Sigma Xi Quarterly, 29*(3-4), 170–196.

Mandler, G. (1984). *Mind and body: Psychology of emotion and stress.* New York: W.W. Norton.

Marcus, G. (1999). The uses of complicity in the changing mise-en-scène of anthropological fieldwork. In S. Ortner (Ed.), *The fate of "culture": Geertz and beyond* (pp. 86–109). Berkeley: University of California Press.

Marcus, G. E., & Fischer, M. (1986). *Anthropology as cultural critique: An experimental moment in the human sciences.* Chicago: University of Chicago Press.

Marshall, B. (2009). Models of multi-culturalism in an international context. In M. Sengstock (Ed.), *Voices of diversity: Multi-culturalism in America* (pp. 239–274). New York: Springer.

McCarthy, C. (1998). *The uses of culture: Education and the limits of ethnic affiliation.* New York: Routledge.

McCarthy, C., & Crichlow, W. (1993). *Race, identity, and representation in education.* New York: Routledge.

McDonough, T. (2008). The course of "culture" in multiculturalism. *Educational Theory, 58*(3), 321–342.

McLaren, P. (1995), White terror and oppositional agency (pp. 33-70). In C. E. Sleeter & P. McLaren (Eds.), *Multicultural education, critical pedagogy, and the politics of difference.* Albany: State University of New York Press.

Mead, G. H., & Morris, C. W. (1934). *Mind, self and society from the standpoint of a social behaviorist.* Chicago, Ill.: The University of Chicago Press.

Mead, M. (1964). *Continuities in cultural evolution.* New Haven: Yale University Press.

Meléndez, J. (1997). A theoretical and practical conclusion. In G. Cruz, S. Jordan, J. Meléndez, S. Ostrowski, & A. Purves (Eds.), *Beyond the culture tours: Studies in teaching and learning with culturally diverse texts* (pp. 69–98). Mahwah, NJ: Lawrence Erlbaum Associates, Inc.

Miller, J. G. (1997). Theoretical issues in cultural psychology. In J.W. Berry, Y. Poortinga, & J. Pandey (Eds.), *Handbook of cross-cultural psychology. Vol. 1: Theoretical and methodological perspectives* (revised ed., pp. 85–128). Boston: Allyn and Bacon.

Mitchell, B. M., & Salsbury, R. E. (1999). *Encyclopedia of multicultural education.* Westport, CT: Greenwood Press.

Montecinos, C. (1995). Culture as an ongoing dialogue. In C. Sleeter & P. McLaren (Eds.), *Multicultural education, critical pedagogy, and the politics of difference* (pp. 291–305). Albany, NY: SUNY Press.

Moody-Adams, M. M. (1997). *Fieldwork in familiar places: Morality, culture, and philosophy.* Cambridge, MA: Harvard University Press.

Moore, J. (1974). The culture concept as ideology. *American Ethnologist, 1*(3), 537–549.

Morey, A., Ed. (1983). *Excellence in professional education.* Long Beach, CA: Office of the Chancellor, California State University System.

Mullen, C., Greenlee, B., & Bruner, D. (2005). Exploring the theory-practice relationship in educational leadership curriculum through metaphor. *International Journal of Teaching and Learning in Higher Education, 17*(1), 1–14.

Neuendorf, K. A. (2002). *The content analysis guidebook.* Thousand Oaks, CA: Sage Publications.

Nieto, S. (1992). *Affirming diversity: The sociopolitical context of multicultural education.* New York: Longman.

Nieto, S. (1999). *The light in their eyes: Creating multicultural learning communities.* New York: Teachers College Press

Nieto, S. (2004). *Affirming diversity: The sociopolitical context of multicultural education* (4th ed.). Boston, MA: Allyn and Bacon.

Nieto, S. (2010). *The light in their eyes: Creating multicultural learning communities* (10th anniversary edition). New York: Teachers College Press.

Oakland, T. (2005). "What Is Multicultural School Psychology?" In C. Frisby & C. Reynolds (Eds.), *Comprehensive handbook of multicultural school psychology* (pp. 3–13). New York: Wiley and Sons.

O'Brien, C. C. (1952). *Maria Cross.* Oxford, England: Oxford University Press.

O'Byrne, D. (2003). *The dimensions of global citizenship: Political identity beyond the nation-state.* Portland, OR: Frank Cass.

Ortner, S. B. (1999). *The fate of "culture": Geertz and beyond.* Berkeley: University of California Press.

Ostrowski, S. (1997). Teaching multicultural literature. In G. Cruz, S. Jordan, J. Melendez, S. Ostrowski, & A. Purves (Eds.), *Beyond the culture tours: Studies in teaching and learning with culturally diverse texts* (pp. 47–68). Mahwah, NJ.: Lawrence Erlbaum.

Page, R. N. (1991). *Lower-track classrooms: A curricular and cultural perspective.* New York: Teachers College Press.

Park, R. E., & Burgess, E. W. (1924). *Introduction to the science of sociology.* Chicago: The University of Chicago Press.

Parsons, T. (1937). *The structure of social action: A study in social theory with special reference to a group of recent European writers.* New York: McGraw-Hill Book Company.

Parsons, T. (1951). *The social system.* Glencoe, IL: Free Press.

Parsons, T., & Shils, E. (1951). *Toward a general theory of action.* Cambridge, MA: Harvard University Press.

Peoples, J. G., & Bailey, G. A. (1991). *Humanity: An introduction to cultural anthropology* (2nd ed.). St. Paul: West Publishing Co.

Putnam, H. (1975). *Mind, language, and reality.* New York: Cambridge University Press.

Putnam, R. (2000). *Bowling alone: The collapse and revival of American community.* New York: Simon and Schuster.

Rabinow, P., & Sullivan, W. (1979). *Interpretive social science: A reader.* Berkeley: University of California Press.

Rabinow, P., & Sullivan, W. (1987). *Interpretative social science: A second look.* Berkeley: University of California Press.

Radcliffe-Brown, A. R. (1930). *Applied anthropology.* Report of the Australian and New Zealand Association for the Advancement of Science, pp. 1–12.

Radcliffe-Brown, A. R. (1935). On the concept of function in social science. *American Anthropologist, 37*(3), 394–402.

Radcliffe-Brown, A. R. (1940). On social structure. *The Journal of the Royal Anthropological Institute of Great Britain and Ireland, 70*(1), 1–12.

Radcliffe-Brown, A. R. (1940). Preface. In M. Fortes & E. E. Evans-Prichard (Eds.), *African political systems* (pp. xi–xxiii). London: Oxford University Press.

Radcliffe-Brown, A. R. (Ed.). (1952). *Structure and function in primitive society.* New York: Free Press.

Ramsey, P. G. (1987). *Teaching and learning in a diverse world: Multicultural education for young children.* New York: Teachers College, Columbia University.

Ramsey, P. G. (1998). *Teaching and learning in a diverse world: Multicultural education for young children* (2nd ed.). New York: Teachers College Press.

Ramsey, P. G. (2004). *Teaching and learning in a diverse world: Multicultural education for young children* (3rd ed.). New York: Teachers College Press.

*Random House Webster's College Dictionary* (1991). New York: Random House.

Rivlin, H. N., & Fraser, D. M. (1973). Cultural pluralism in education. In M. D. Stent, W. R. Hazard, & H. N. Rivlin (Eds.), *Cultural pluralism in education: A mandate for change* (pp. 4–7). New York: Appleton-Century-Crofts.

Rizvi, F. (1993). Children and the grammar of popular racism. In C. McCarthy & W. Crichlow (Eds.), *Race, identity and representation in education* (pp. 126–139). New York: Routledge.

Robinson, G. L. (1988). *Crosscultural understanding.* Englewood Cliffs, NJ: Prentice-Hall International.

Robles de Meléndez, W., & Beck, V. (2010). *Teaching young children in multicultural classrooms: Issues, concepts, and strategies* (3rd ed.). Belmont, CA: Wadsworth.

Rogers, P., & Soter, A. (1997). *Reading across cultures: Teaching literature in a diverse society.* New York: Teachers College Press.

Rosaldo, R. (1989). *Culture and truth: The remaking of social analysis.* Boston: Beacon Press.

Sachs, J. (1989). Match or mismatch: Teachers' conceptions of culture and multicultural education policy. *Australian Journal of Education, 33*(1), 19–33.

Said, E. (1978). *Orientalism.* New York: Pantheon.

Sapir, E. (1929). The status of linguistics as a science. *Language* 5:207–214.

Schneider, L., & Bonjean, C. M. (1973). *The idea of culture in the social sciences.* Cambridge: Cambridge University Press.

Shade, B. J., Kelly, C. A., & Oberg, M. (1997). *Creating culturally responsive classrooms.* Washington, DC: American Psychological Association.

Shade, B. J., & New, C. A. (1993). Cultural influences on learning: Teaching implications. In J. A. Banks & C. A. M. Banks (Eds.), *Multicultural education: Issues and perspectives* (3rd ed.), (pp. 317–331). Boston: Allyn and Bacon.

Shapiro, J. P., Sewell, T. E., & DuCette, J. P. (1995). *Reframing diversity in education.* Lancaster, PA: Technomic Publishing.

Shohat, E., & Stam, R. (1994). *Unthinking Eurocentrism: Multiculturalism and the Media.* London: Routledge.

Shor, I., & Freire, P. (1987). *A pedagogy for liberation: Dialogues on transforming education*. Westport, CT: Bergin & Garvey.

Shore, B. (1996). *Culture in mind*. New York: Oxford University Press.

Singer, M. (1971). Culture: A perceptual approach. In D. Hoopes (Ed.), *Readings in intercultural communication* (pp. 6–20). Pittsburgh, PA: Regional Council for International Education.

Sleeter, C. E., & Grant, C. A. (1988). *Making choices for multicultural education: Five approaches to race, class, and gender* (1st ed.). Columbus, OH: Merrill Publishing.

Sleeter, C. E., & Grant, C. A. (2006). *Making choices for multicutural education: Five approaches to race, class, and gender* (5th ed.). Hoboken, N.J.: John Wiley & Sons.

Sleeter, C. E., & McLaren, P. (1995). *Multicultural education, critical pedagogy, and the politics of difference*. Albany, NY: SUNY Press.

Solis, J., & Jackson, S. (1995). *Beyond comfort zones in multiculturalism: Confronting the politics of privilege*. Westport, CT: Greenwood Publishing Group.

Spindler, G. D. (1974). *Education and cultural process: Toward an anthropology of education*. New York: Holt, Rinehart and Winston.

Spindler, G. D. (1979). *Cultural transmission*. Unpublished manuscript. Cited in G. L. Robinson, *Crosscultural understanding*. Englewood Cliffs, NJ: Prentice-Hall International, 1988.

Spindler, G. D. (1980). *The making of psychological anthropology*. Berkeley: University of California Press.

Spindler, G. D. (1982). *Doing the ethnography of schooling: Educational anthropology in action*. New York: Holt, Rinehart, and Winston.

Spindler, G. D., & Spindler, L. S. (2000). *Fifty years of anthropology and education, 1950–2000: A Spindler anthology*. Mahwah, NJ: L. Erlbaum Associates.

Spivak, G. C. (1988). Can the subaltern speak? In C. Nelson & L. Grossberg (Eds.), *Marxism and the interpretation of culture* (pp. 271–313). Urbana: University of Illinois Press.

Spradlin, L. K. (2012). *Diversity matters: Understanding diversity in schools* (2nd ed.). Belmont, CA: Wadsworth.

Spring, J. (1995). *The Intersection of cultures: Multicultural education in the United States* (1st Ed.). New York: McGraw-Hill, 1995.

Spring, J. (2008). *The Intersection of cultures: Multicultural education in the United States and the global economy* (4th Ed.). New York: Lawrence Erlbaum Associates.

Steedly, M. (1996). What is culture? Does it matter? In M. Garber, P. Franklin, & R. Walkowitz (Eds.), *Field work: Sites in literary and cultural studies* (pp. 18–25). New York: Routledge.

Stent, M. D., Hazard, W. R., & Rivlin, H. N. (1973). *Cultural pluralism in education: A mandate for change*. New York: Appleton-Century-Crofts.

Stewart, E. C. (1971). *American cultural patterns: A cross-cultural perspective*. Pittsburgh, PA: Regional Council for International Education.

Stewart, E. C., & Bennett, M. J. (1991). *American cultural patterns: A cross-cultural perspective* (Rev. ed.). Yarmouth, ME: Intercultural Press.

Stocking, G. (1966). Franz Boas and the culture concept in historical perspective. *American Anthropologist, 68*, 867–882.

Strauss, C., & Quinn, N. (1994). A cognitive cultural anthropology. In R. Borofsky (Ed.), *Assessing cultural anthropology* (pp. 284–297). New York: McGraw Hill.

Strickland, B. R. (2000). Misassumptions, misadventures, and the misuse of psychology. *American Psychologist, 55*, 331–339.

Subhabrata, B. B., & Linstead, S. (2001). Globalization, multiculturalism, and other fictions: Colonialism for the new millennium? *Organization, 8*, 683–722.

Sue, D. W. (2003). *Overcoming our racism: The journey to liberation.* San Francisco: Jossey-Bass.

Sue, D. W. (2004). Whiteness and ethnocentric monoculturalism: Making the "invisible" visible. *American Psychologist, 59*, 761–769.

Taussig, M. (1993). *Mimesis and alterity: A particular history of the senses.* New York and London: Routledge.

Timm, J. T. (1996). *Four perspectives in multicultural education.* Belmont, CA: Wadsworth Pub. Co.

Triandis, H. C. (1972). *The analysis of subjective culture.* New York: Wiley-Interscience.

Turnbull, C. (1983). *The Mbuti pigmies: Change and adaptation.* New York: Holt, Rinehart and Winston.

Turner, J. H. (1985). *Sociology: The science of human organization* (2nd ed.). Chicago: Nelson-Hall.

Turner, T. (1993). Anthropology and multiculturalism: What is anthropology that multiculturalists should be mindful of it? *Cultural Anthropology, 8(4)*, 411–429.

Tyler, K. M., Uqdah, A. L., Dillihunt, M. L., Beatty-Hazelbaker, R., Conner, T., Gadson, N., et al. (2008). Cultural discontinuity: Toward a quantitative investigation of a major hypothesis in education. *Educational Researcher, 37*, 280–297.

Tylor, E. B. (1871). *Primitive culture: Researches into the development of mythology, philosophy, religion, art, and custom.* London: J. Murray

Tylor, E. B. (1873/1958). *Primitive culture.* New York: Harper.

Ulin, R. C. (1991). Critical anthropology twenty years later: Modernism and postmodernism in anthropology. *Critique of Anthropology, 11*, 63–89.

van Haaften, A. W., Korthals, M., & Wren, T. E. (1997). *Philosophy of development: Reconstructing the foundations of human development and education.* Dordrecht ; Boston: Kluwer Academic Publishers.

Varenne, H. (1983). *American school language: Culturally patterned conflicts in a suburban high school.* New York: Irvington Publishers.

Varenne, H. (1986). *Symbolizing America.* Lincoln: University of Nebraska Press.

Vygotsky, L. (1972). *Thought and language.* Cambridge, MA: MIT Press.

Ward, T. (1973). Cognitive processes and learning: Reflections on a comparative study of "cognitive style" (Witkin) in fourteen African societies. *Comparative Education Review, 17(1)*, 1–10.

Waterbury, R. (1993). Culture, society, and the interdisciplinary teaching of world studies: An anthropological perspective. *Social Studies, 82(2)*, 63–66.

Webb, R. B., & Sherman, R. R. (1989). *Schooling and society* (2nd ed.). New York and London: Macmillan.

Weber, Max. (1946). Class, status, party. In H. H. Girth & C. Wright Mills (Eds.), *From Max Weber: Essays in sociology* (pp. 180–195). New York: Oxford University Press.

*Webster's new collegiate dictionary* (1980). Springfield, MA: G. & C. Merriam Co.

Weitz, M. (1956). The role of theory in aesthetics. *The Journal of Aesthetics and Art Criticism. 15(1)*: 27–35.

White, L. A. (1959). *The evolution of culture: The development of civilization to the fall of Rome.* New York: McGraw-Hill.

White, L. A. (2007). *The evolution of culture: The development of civilization to the fall of Rome.* Walnut Creek, CA: Left Coast Press.

Williams, R. (1961). *The long revolution.* London: Chatto & Windus.

Wilson, J. (1969). *Moral education and the curriculum. A guide for teachers and research workers* (1st ed.). Oxford; New York: Pergamon Press.

Witkin, H. A. (1962). *Psychological differentiation: Studies of development.* New York: Wiley.

Witkin, H. A. (1967). *A cognitive-style approach to cross-cultural research.* Albany, NY: SUNY Press.

Wittgenstein, L. (1967). *Philosophical investigations.* Oxford: Blackwell.

Wren, C., & Wren, T. (2003). The capacity to learn. In R. Curren (Ed.), *A companion to the philosophy of education* (pp. 246–260). Oxford: Blackwell Publishing.

Wren, T. E. (1991). *Caring about morality: Philosophical perspectives in moral psychology.* Cambridge, MA: MIT Press.

Wren, T., & Mendoza, C. (2004.). Cultural identity and personal identity: Philosophical reflections on the identity discourse of social psychology. In D. Lapsley & D. Narvaez (Eds.), *Moral development, self, and identity* (pp. 239–266). Mahwah, NJ: Lawrence Erlbaum Associates.

Wren, T., & Mendoza, C. (2005). Striving to be one: Personal and cultural identity as a moral issue. In W. van Haaften, T. Wren, & A. Tellings (Eds.), *Moral sensibilities and education. Vol. 2: The adolescent.* (pp. 33–52). Bemmel, London, Paris: Concorde Publishing.

Wuthnow, R. (1992). *Vocabularies of public life: Empirical essays in symbolic structure.* London; New York: Routledge.

Yengoyan, A. (1986). Theory in anthropology: On the demise of the concept of culture. *Comparative Studies in Society and History, 24*(2), 368–374.

Yon, D. (2000). *Elusive culture: Schooling, race, and identity in global times.* Albany, NY: SUNY Press.

Young, I. M. (1990). *Justice and the politics of difference.* Princeton: Princeton University Press.

# Index

*Index*

# About the Author

Thomas E. Wren (Ph.D., Northwestern) is professor of philosophy at Loyola University Chicago and director of its graduate program in social philosophy. He holds master's degrees in education and English as well as philosophy, and teaches graduate and undergraduate courses in ethics, social philosophy, and educational theory. He has published widely in ethical theory and related areas such as moral development and civic virtue, and has served as a board member for several journals and professional associations having to do with philosophy and moral education. He began his career as an educator with nine years of teaching at the secondary level.

CPSIA information can be obtained at www.ICGtesting.com
Printed in the USA
BVOW042001160712

295374BV00002B/5/P